T0300251

ROUTLEDGE LIBRARY EDITIONS:
SMALL BUSINESS

Volume 16

THE SMALL FIRM

THE SMALL FIRM

An International Survey

Edited by
DAVID J. STOREY

Routledge
Taylor & Francis Group

LONDON AND NEW YORK

First published in 1983 by Croom Helm Ltd

This edition first published in 2016
by Routledge
2 Park Square, Milton Park, Abingdon, Oxon OX14 4RN

and by Routledge
711 Third Avenue, New York, NY 10017

Routledge is an imprint of the Taylor & Francis Group, an informa business

British Library Cataloguing in Publication Data
A catalogue record for this book is available from the British Library

ISBN: 978-1-138-67308-3 (Set)
ISBN: 978-1-315-54266-9 (Set) (ebk)
ISBN: 978-1-138-68346-4 (Volume 16) (hbk)
ISBN: 978-1-315-54447-2 (Volume 16) (ebk)

Publisher's Note
The publisher has gone to great lengths to ensure the quality of this reprint but points out that some imperfections in the original copies may be apparent.

Disclaimer
The publisher has made every effort to trace copyright holders and would welcome correspondence from those they have been unable to trace.

THE SMALL FIRM
AN INTERNATIONAL SURVEY

Edited by David J. Storey

CROOM HELM
London & Canberra

© 1983 David J. Storey
Croom Helm Ltd, Provident House, Burrell Row,
Beckenham, Kent BR3 1AT
Croom Helm Australia, PO Box 391,
Manuka, ACT 2603, Australia

British Library Cataloguing in Publication Data

The Small firm
   1. Small business
   I. Storey, David J.
   338.6   HD2341

   ISBN 0-7099-2351-1

Library of Congress Card Catalog Number: 83-40075

ISBN 0-312-72980-4

CONTENTS

CONTENTS

PART ONE

PART TWO

TABLES

Tables

CONTRIBUTORS

Douglas Anthony — Joint Lecturer, Centre of Japanese Studies, Division of Economic Studies, University of Sheffield, Sheffield S10 2TN, England.

Michael Cross — Senior Research Fellow, The Technical Change Centre, 114 Cromwell Road, London SW7 4ES, England.

Chris Hull — Research Fellow, International Institute of Management, Platz der Luftbrücke 1–3, D-1000 Berlin 42, Germany.

Brian Johns — Emeritus Professor, Director Bureau of Industry Economics, Department of Industry and Commerce, Edmund Barton Building, Kings Avenue, Canberra, ACT 2600 Australia.

Dennis R. Leyden — Dean, College of Business and Industry and Professor of Economics, Mississippi State University, P.O. Box 5288, Mississippi State, MS 39762, USA.

Leif Lindmark — Assistant Professor, Department of Business Administration and Economics, University of Umeå, S-901 87, Umeå, Sweden.

Philip Neck — Director, International Labour Organization, 7 Sardar Patel Marg, New Delhi – 110021, India.

David Storey — Senior Research Associate, Centre for Urban and Regional Development Studies, University of Newcastle upon Tyne, England.

Tan Thiam Soon — Senior Lecturer, Business Administration, National University of Singapore, Kent Ridge, Singapore 0511.

James H. Thompson — Professor of Economics, Bureau of Business Research, College of Business and Economics, West Virginia University, Morgantown, West Virginia 26506, USA.

INTRODUCTION

The small firm is, and probably always will be, the typical unit of production. Until recent years there had been a tendency amongst economists concerned with promoting economic growth, both in developed and in less-developed countries, to assume that a high proportion of output produced by small enterprises was indicative of low levels of economic development. The increase in industrial concentration, frequently associated with an increase in average plant size, whilst it may have led to higher profits through restricted output and to higher prices, also provided many benefits. It gave greater stability to markets, it enabled scale economies to be reaped (again at the plant level) and most importantly it ensured that large corporations were able to undertake research and development. It was this function which, it was agreed, was vital to future growth and could only be undertaken by large corporations with access to risk capital on a large scale.

Economists in the 1960s, whether they were discussing developed or less-developed economies, spoke with a perhaps surprising degree of unity on these matters, but by the mid-1970s this consensus was no longer apparent. The emphasis upon capital intensive projects in stimulating growth in developing countries became the subject of strong criticism, primarily because of the high capital costs per job created. The shortage of available capital, and the increases in the labour force which the areas experienced, meant that labour, rather than capital-intensive methods of production were viewed more favourably. Empirical research[1] also showed that there were considerable opportunities to substitute labour for capital without losses in efficiency. The developments in intermediate technology meant that whilst there were fewer 'prestige' projects, a considerable switching towards labour-intensive production methods took place. This served the dual function of releasing scarce capital and enabling more individuals to be employed whilst maintaining output levels.

Several developed countries also undertook a reappraisal of the role of small enterprises. In particular, Britain and Sweden began to recognise that developments in the world economy in the 1970s had led to a relative increase in the importance of small firms. The increases in oil and associated energy prices meant that capital-intensive (and hence energy-intensive) projects became less attractive. It became less beneficial to concentrate productive capacity at a single plant since the increase in distribution costs more than offset scale economies at the plant level. Increased energy prices also led to a slow-down in world trade and, since large firms were more likely to export than small, they were disproportionately affected by the international recession.

Superimposed upon the recession was the growth to industrial maturity of countries such as South Korea, Hong Kong, Taiwan as well as the continued development of Japan. These countries began to export goods which competed directly with those produced in the large-firm sector of Western Europe and North America. The inroads made into these markets by Taiwanese textiles, Hong Kong electrical goods and South Korean steel products is well documented.

Finally, despite the recession, incomes continued to rise at least for those in work, in the developed countries. This had the dual effect of increasing the demand for 'one-off' products, which were more likely to be produced by small firms, and decreasing the demand for 'standardised' or mass-produced goods. But perhaps the major impact of increased wealth was on the greater demand for services at the expense of manufactured goods. This demand was satisfied partly by the provision of public services and partly by private services, but in the private service sector the small firm was significantly more likely to be the 'norm' than in manufacturing.[2]

With eight essays on specific countries or groups of countries, this book attempts to review trends in the small-firm sector.[3] The areas chosen cover the full spectrum of economic development although in practice the majority of the text is devoted to an examination of small firms in developed countries. This comprises Part 1 of the book. The final two chapters on South East Asia and Africa review small-firm trends and initiatives in a variety of countries in those areas, and comprise Part II.

The general approach has been to identify several key topics which each of the authors were asked to discuss, but coverage varies from one chapter to another. In part this reflects differences in the importance of the issues in the countries concerned, or the absence of reportable information (particularly statistical data), but it also reflects the interest of the authors themselves.

Part I deals with case studies of six countries which would

generally be regarded as having modern developed economies – the United States, Japan, the United Kingdom, Australia, the Federal Republic of Germany and Sweden. In Part II countries in South East Asia (Singapore, Philippines, Malaysia, Indonesia and Thailand) and on the African continent are surveyed.

In all cases the authors review the variety of definitions used for the small-firm sector and, given these definitions, present such data as are available on the changing importance of the sector. This is followed by a review of the roles of small firms in each of the economies. In most cases the small firms' direct role in providing employment is discussed but its economic functions, notably in acting as a source of potential or actual competition with large firms and in research and innovation, are also reviewed.

The problems which face the small firm vary between countries but difficulties over raising finance, in dealings with government and in reacting to recession are common to all areas. Of perhaps greatest interest, are the initiatives which the respective governments have taken (or not taken) to assist the small-firm sector. Why, for example, have certain initiatives been undertaken in some countries yet ignored in others, and why have initiatives been relatively recent in some countries, yet have been clearly successfully in operation elsewhere for many years? Perhaps the reader may choose at the end to speculate on these matters.

Notes

1. D. Morawetz, 'Employment Implications of Industrialization in Developing Countries', *Economic Journal*, September 1974, pp. 491–542.

2. For a full discussion of these issues see D.J. Storey *Entrepreneurship and the New Firm*, Croom Helm, London, 1982.

3. There are relatively few such studies available, with G. Bannock *Small Firms: A Seven Country Study* Shell UK, 1980 and P. Ganguly 'Small Firms Survey: the International Scene', *British Business*, 19 November 1982, pp. 486–491 being important exceptions.

PART ONE

PART ONE

1 INTRODUCTION: ADVANCED INDUSTRIAL ECONOMIES

In Chapter 2 Thompson and Leyden state that small business – like motherhood and apple pie – has always occupied a specific place of esteem in the United States. The other chapters, notably those by Cross on the United Kingdom, Johns on Australia and Lindmark on Sweden, shows this to be less true for other developed economies. Johns show that in Australia governments have made only modest efforts to assist the small-firm sector, primarily through attempts to eliminate certain obvious disadvantages, rather than to discriminate positively in its favour. Public financial assistance to the small firm sector in Sweden is documented by Lindmark. He shows that although the amount has grown markedly during the decade of the 1970s there is still a tendency to provide loans to small firms whereas large enterprises are more likely to receive grants. In the United Kingdom, Cross also notes that interest in small firms by government is very recent, and that public expenditure in the form of direct assistance is modest.

The contrast with the USA and Japan is stark. The US Small Business Agency, founded in 1953, has thirty years of experience in providing, directly or indirectly, financial assistance to small firms. It has a substantial programme of management education and has been the vigorous mouthpiece of the small business community during that time. It has succeeded in obtaining statutory positive discrimination in favour of small firms, particularly in the area of tendering for public contracts. Similarly, Japan has a long tradition of interest in maintaining the well-being of the small business sector. Anthony, in Chapter 3, clearly demonstrates that small business is part of the social as well as the economic fabric of Japan, and it is for these reasons that legislation such as the 1965 *Law for the Prevention of Delay in Payments to Subcontractors* is of such importance. As Anthony shows, such laws are actively enforced and in fact were further strengthened in 1972 and 1973.

The quality of the statistical information on small firms seems to be directly related to the esteem in which the sector is held in the country concerned, with the USA and Japan having the most comprehensive data and the poorest data being in the UK and

3

Sweden. The Federal Republic of Germany and Australia occupy intermediate positions. In all countries the variety of definitions of small firms are outlined and it is clear that there are major problems in making comparisons of the importance of small firms in each of these advanced economies. A further source of complication is that data are reported for a variety of different years, with some referring to establishments and some to enterprises. In some cases the upper limit to the number of employees is 500 whereas in others it is only 100. Finally, some of the data refer only to manufacturing establishments whilst some refer to all sectors.

Despite this complexity, it seems clear that, generally, the small-firm sector has provided a reduced proportion of manufacturing jobs over time in most countries. The largest proportionate reduction occurs in the Federal Republic of Germany, where Hull shows that in 1950, 51.4 per cent of manufacturing employment was in firms with fewer than 100 workers. This fell continuously so that by 1977 Hull estimated that only 29.9 per cent of manufacturing employment was in such firms. A similar reduction took place in the importance of small firms in the service sector in the Federal Republic, at least until 1970. Continuous decline in the importance of the small manufacturing firm sector is also shown to have occurred in Australia, Sweden and the USA. Johns shows that in Australia between 1969 and 1979 the proportion of manufacturing employment in manufacturing in small firms employing fewer than 100 workers fell from 32 per cent to 29.4 per cent. In Sweden small (defined as having fewer than 200 workers) firms provided 35.3 per cent of employment in manufacturing in 1969, but by 1979 this had fallen to 32.5 per cent. Similarly, United States enterprise statistics also indicate a small reduction in the relative importance of very small enterprises employing fewer than 20 workers in the period 1958 to 1977.

The exceptions to the above trends are in the UK and Japan. The UK has the lowest proportion of manufacturing employment in small firms of any developed country, with UK small firms providing a decreasing share of employment in manufacturing from the 1930s until the late 1960s, since when the trend has been reversed. In the case of Japan small and medium-sized firms provided a higher proportion of manufacturing employment in 1978 than in 1963, although there appears to have been a sharp drop between 1969 and 1972.

The difficulties which face small firms also vary interestingly between countries. Anthony shows that the importance of small firms as subcontractors in Japan means that they are subject to a powerful financial squeeze when credit is tight. Small Japanese firms are not alone in encountering this problem and financial problems are mentioned by most authors. The one exception is Hull who, quoting the work of Geiser, shows that finance problems for firms in the Federal Republic of Germany were less important than obtaining suitable skilled labour, and lack of space for expansion.

In general however, finance, particularly the inadequate provision of risk capital, is remarked upon by Johns for Australia, Cross for the UK and Lindmark for Sweden. Thompson and Leyden for the USA on the other hand stress that the main problem is the high interest rates at which small companies are required to borrow, although they point out that the high cost and limited availability of capital forces small firms to adopt sub-optimal policies in many aspects of management.

Another problem which is remarked upon by several authors is shortage of suitable premises (Cross, Hull), but the main source of complaint by the small business sector itself is the role of government, particularly with respect to its taxation policy and state regulations. These issues are stressed in the chapters on Australia, USA and the Federal Republic of Germany, and it is the editor's experience that much the same opinions are voiced by small firms in the United Kingdom.

Bearing in mind this lack of empathy between small business and the government bureaucracy it may appear surprising that, in most countries under study, there is a complex web of financial, managerial and other assistance provided by the public sector. As noted earlier this programme of assistance and support varies between the countries, being strongly related to the social status of small businesses within each community.

Each country, however, has its own variations on these themes. One of the features of small firm development in Sweden and in the UK has been the emphasis upon local initiatives particularly in areas of either high unemployment or where substantial re-construction has taken place in basic industries. The Swedes have also encouraged the formation of new forms of business such as employee-owned firms and co-operatives.

The main thrust of government initiatives has been to assist the financing of small firms. In the USA the Small Business Agency was established primarily to provide finance to those entrepreneurs unable to obtain monies elsewhere. Thompson and Leyden show there are currently seven different Loan Programmes including those specifically designed to assist racial or ethnic minorities, and three different types of loans including a Loan Guarantee Scheme. The Swedes have created special credit institutions, such as the Industrial Credit Bank, owned jointly by government and the Swedish commercial banks to provide loans to small firms primarily for fixed capital. In the UK the Industrial and Commercial Finance Corporation, a subsidiary of the main private banks, has a long history of success in lending to relatively few small firms, and in 1981 the UK Government initiated a pilot Loan Guarantee Scheme. In Germany the assistance programme to small firms is also administered jointly by government and the private banks. Loans to small firms made under the ERP Programme generally have a duration of 10 to 15 years and offer rates of interest about two percentage points below market rates. Significantly, this rate is then *fixed* for the period of the loan. The Germans have since 1979 reduced the contribution of capital required by an individual in starting his own business. These loans, for twenty years' duration, give capital repayment holidays for ten years and interest payment holidays for two years. Not surprisingly, Hull reports they have been in great demand by the small business sector. In Australia there have been fewer small firm initiatives, with concessional loans being made by the Commonwealth Development Bank (CDB) only being extended to the service sector generally since 1978. Indeed, at the time of writing, it seems that the Australian Government is debating whether loans through the CDB are the most effective means of providing financial assistance to small firms.

The following chapters illustrate the considerable diversity of performance of the small firm sector in these six developed countries. They also show the difference in terms of approach by government to the sector. Perhaps the only consistency is the cautious optimism expressed by most contributors about the future of the small firm sector.

2 THE UNITED STATES OF AMERICA

2.1. Introduction

Small business – like motherhood and apple pie – has always occupied a special place of esteem in the United States. 'A business of my own' has been the recurring dream of generations of wage earners. Only in recent years, however, has the idea taken hold that small business is a special entity which has some serious, distinctive problems that require governmental assistance if this sector is to survive and prosper.

Identification of small business as a separate entity began with the establishment of the Small Business Administration (SBA) in 1953, though problems of definition persist. The 1960s and 1970s saw a gradual expansion of the lending and counselling activities of this agency. More recently, growing concern about the future of small business led to Congressional hearings on this subject in 1978 and to a White House conference in the following year. These two important sources of small business data will be tapped, along with others, in this chapter. Our purpose is to provide a comprehensive view of the nature, trends, current status, problems and prospects of small business in the United States.

2.2. Definition

An adequate definition of small business is necessary for understanding the sector's role in the economy and for establishing appropriate public policy. Conceptually, small businesses can be characterised in the same way as other businesses, i.e. as entities engaged in the production, distribution and sale of products or services in which land, labour and capital are combined to bring the product or service into existence. Attaching the qualifier 'small', however, leads to the problem of deciding *how* small is small – a very significant problem for those concerned with the formulation and exercise of public policy. Spokesmen for small business argue that it does not fit well into the broader definition of business and should therefore be treated differently. The problem is com-

7

pounded by the fact that the types and size of firms eligible for the advocated different treatment may vary with the policy area under consideration. Among these policy areas are: government loans, management assistance, economic development, minimum wages, taxation, anti-trust law, venture capital, employment and research and development.[1] The result is that different agencies, and different departments within those agencies, define the small business community in substantially different ways.

The federal Small Business Administration defines a small business as 'one which is independently owned and operated and which is not dominant in its field of operation'.[2] The SBA specifies proxy indicators for the market concentration part of this definition, namely: number of employees (employment size) and total assets or annual sales volume. The most recent standards for business size categories are shown in Table 2.1. According to this yardstick, the small business may range from one with fewer than four employees and under $500 in assets to the 'large' small business with up to 1,000 employees and up to $50,000 in assets or annual sales. Assistance eligibility standards are still different, however.

Table 2.1: Business Size Standards for Annual Employment, Sales and Assets

Business size	Employment (no.)	Sales or assets ($000)
Small family	0– 4	0– 499
Small-small	5– 19	500– 2,499
Small-medium (1)	20– 49	2,500– 4,999
Small-medium (2)	50– 99	5,000– 9,999
Small-large	100– 499	10,000– 24,999
Large-small	500– 999	25,000– 49,999
Large-medium	1,000–4,999	50,000–249,999
Government sized	5,000+	250,000+

Source: Adapted from *The State of Small Business: A Report of the President* (Washington, DC, US Government Printing Office, 1982), p. 51.

As shown in Table 2.2, the size limits established by the SBA for this purpose vary from industry to industry. An eligible 'small business' may have as many as 1,500 employees (in manufacturing) or as much as $22 million in annual sales (in wholesaling).

Table 2.2: Limits on Sales or Employment for Eligibility in Assistance Programmes Administered by the Small Business Administration

Major Industry Category	Sales* ($ million)	Employment
Retail or Services	2– 8	
Wholesale	9.5–22	
Construction	1.0–9.5	
Manufacturing		0–1500
Agriculture	1.0	

* Not to exceed limit specified, depending on specific minor industry category.
Source: Edward B. Shils and William Zucker, 'The Impact of Federal Regulation', in Paul W. Houck, *The Status of Small Business in Region III* (Pennsylvania Technical Assistance Program, University Park, PA, 1979, for the SBA), pp. 94–110.

Although the SBA is considered *the* agency for US small business interests, its definitions are not uniformly accepted by state and federal agencies. In a survey of 50 states, the District of Columbia and Puerto Rico, only 29 states reported using any specific definition of small business. Of the 29 that did, 14 used SBA guidelines, while the remainder developed their own definitions.[3]

For example, Section 465.8(c) of the Energy Extension Service (EES) regulations defines the small business as 'an independently owned concern which together with an affiliation is not dominant in its field and either does not have average annual receipts for three years of more than $12 million or does not have more than 400 employees'.[4] Other definitions are used by the various states – for example, the state of Florida defines a small business as 'any business which is owned or operated independently of any other business entity and which has no more than 25 employees or more than $500,000 in receipts'.[5]

Moreover, government agencies within the same state may use different definitions. The state of Minnesota's Department of Employment Security defines a small business as any enterprise employing 500 or fewer employees, but the Minnesota House of Representatives' Task Force on Small Business defines it as 'an enterprise having 20 or less employees'.[6]

This lack of agreement has sparked some criticism. The late

Wilford White, a leading small business analyst, argued that the SBA defined small business in terms of its own administrative needs rather than the needs of those it served. 'Obviously, when you find, in concurrent publications, definitions which would include some 5 million to 13 million small business firms, there is now no agreement on what a small business is. Without some basis for an acceptable definition it is impossible to develop any exact economic studies on this highly specialised subject'.[7] Similarly, Nappi and Vora argue that equitable treatment of and assistance to small business is difficult, if not impossible, without uniformity of definition.[8]

In the absence of a single definition, those who administer the programmes must do what is possible with the data available. The result is that employment size is the criterion used for most analyses because there is no output measure which: (a) can be applied uniformly to all industries, and (b) is not affected, as sales and asset data are, by inflation.[9]

2.3. Current Structure

Since definitions of the small business firm in the United States depend as much on the classification structures used in existing data series as on policy concerns or conceptual purity, it is necessary to examine the principal data series from which current and historic statistics on small business are derived.

A. Sources of Information

Sixteen different statistical series are currently used by the SBA in delineating the scope and impact of small business. These statistics, in turn, are used to develop guidelines and policies pertaining to small business. Three of the series are micro-based (individual firm statistics); the remainder are macro-based (aggregated statistics on groups of firms). The 16 series are derived from eight major data gathering efforts conducted by four government agencies and one private credit agency.[10] Of the eight major data collection efforts, three stand out as most comprehensive in coverage: the Internal Revenue Service's *Statistics of Income*; the Bureau of the Census' *Enterprise Statistics*, and Dun & Bradstreet's *Market Identifier File*. Each of these sources of data is subject to certain limitations which are described below.

Statistics of Income. The Internal Revenue Service, the agency responsible for the administration of federal tax collections in the United States, publishes annual statistics on proprietors, partnerships and corporations. These statistics are the most comprehensive available in terms of number of US firms included – 14.7 million as of 1977, the latest year for which complete data are available. The file is restricted to taxpaying units and does not provide employment or production data. It does report levels of sales and assets for sole proprietors, partnerships and corporations. Of the 14.7 million tax-paying business units that filed in 1977, detailed information is available for only 5.6 million. Of that number, ten thousand were firms which operated on a national scale, with more than 415,000 places of business included. Just over nine million businesses filed tax returns for which detailed information from IRS individual files is not available.[11] More than half of that 9.1 million (55.1 per cent) had gross receipts of less than $10,000, and thus are considered less-than-full-time enterprises.[12]

While these statistics cover the greatest number of enterprises of any of the data series discussed here, important information is omitted. Data on proprietors are limited to sales (receipts) and complete profit and loss items, which were reported in the *Statistics of Income* for the US and the individual states. Data on partnerships consist of sales (receipts) and complete balance sheet items, every other year for the US and the individual states. The corporate statistics report sales (receipts) and assets and balance sheet items for the US as a whole, but not for individual states, due to the difficulty of accounting for the activity of multistate corporations. No employment data are available for any of the *Statistics of Income* series. Those interested in employment data must rely on the *Enterprise Statistics*.

Enterprise Statistics. The Bureau of the Census' *Enterprise Statistics* is the result of a business census conducted every five years, beginning in 1958 (1977 is the latest year for which complete figures are available). This report is the second most comprehensive in terms of number of enterprises surveyed – some 5.6 million in 1977. Of this number, one-tenth of one per cent (6,135) can be considered large – that is, having 500 or more employees. Information is included on number of establishments per enterprise in specific industry groups, and on employment, payroll, sales, value-added and new capital expenditures (manufacturing sector only) and industry (excluding retail sales and wholesale trade). The statistics are reported only for the US as a whole. Agriculture, transportation, communication and public utilities, finance, insurance and real estate sectors are not included, and partial figures are supplied for the service sector.[13]

County Business Patterns. The *County Business Patterns* file, published annually by the Bureau of the Census since 1954, supplies detailed state and local data, but is limited to employment and payroll statistics on an establishment basis. The 4.4 million establishments reported in 1977 overstates the actual number of individual firms surveyed, due to the inclusion of multi-establishment firms. Railroads are not covered in *County Business Patterns*.[14]

Market Identifier File. The only source of information on an individual establishment basis is Dun & Bradstreet's *Market Identifier File.* Dun & Bradstreet is a private firm which compiles information on firms seeking credit ratings. Data on employment size, sales, age of firm, and branch and subsidiary relationships are listed for 4.7 million individual establishments. This file may also be used to generate information at the US, state and county levels for a nine-industry set. This data set excludes the self-employed and does not contain payroll information. Two subsets have been created for the SBA, based on the establishment file. The first (DMI File) is a count of 3.7 million enterprises containing sales and employment data down to the county level. The second (FINSTAT) includes detailed information on 890,000 enterprises, excluding the banking sector. This financial statement file provides up to five years (1976–81) of information on employment, sales, assets and balance sheet items on an individual firm basis.[15]

Analyses which depend on a single data source can only approximate reality, since each source has its limitations, as noted above. In the section which follows, the statistics cited are sometimes based on *Enterprise Statistics*, and sometimes on the IRS *Statistics of Income*.

B. Number of Establishments

By almost any count, it is clear that US business consists predominantly of small firms. If, for example, we define small business as all proprietors and partnerships with sales greater than

$5,000 and all corporations with fewer than 100 employees, we find 9.4 million businesses that fit this description in 1978, compared with a known universe of 14.7 million businesses. If we subtract 5.3 million less-than-full-time businesses from the total, these 9.4 million small businesses represent 98 per cent of the estimated total number of full-time businesses in the USA.[16]

Alternatively, if we define small business using eligibility standards for the Small Business Administration's programmes, we find the number reduced to 7.4 million (eligible for loan assistance) and 3.7 million (eligible for procurement assistance), respectively (see Table 2.3).

The small business share of total sales appears quite different. Despite the fact that almost 99 per cent of all firms are small, the small business sector contributed just a little over 38 per cent to the gross national product (GNP) overall and 44 per cent to the private sector portion of the GNP in 1976. Small business accounted for 47 per cent of employment (1978) and 46 per cent of payroll (1977). These general statistics, however, mask divergences in the relative share of sales on an industry-by-industry basis. Table 2.4 shows the small business share of sales for firms of fewer than 100 employees. In the minerals and manufacturing sectors, such firms contributed only 24 and 12 per cent of total industry sales, while in construction, wholesale trade, retail trade and services they contributed 69, 69, 56 and 65 per cent, respectively.

Table 2.5 shows five industries which have traditionally been associated with small business. There is a close correspondence between the share of employment and the share of sales for agriculture, construction and retail trade. No such relationship is evident, however, in the wholesale trade and service sectors. In the wholesale sector, the percentage of employment contributed by small business is 9.4 per cent greater than the percentage of sales, suggesting the presence of increasing scale economies. Quite the opposite is true of the service sector. Small businesses provide 32 per cent of employment and 45 per cent of sales for service businesses with fewer than 100 employees, and 51 per cent of employment and 62 per cent of sales for those with fewer than 500 employees.

The utilisation of employees and assets by small businesses is illustrated in Tables 2.6 and 2.7, which show sales per employee and sales per dollar of assets by employment size of the enterprise. In general, firms having fewer than 100 employees generate sales per

Table 2.3: Small Firms as a Percentage of Total Firms Under Current Size Standards by Industry Divisions (Number)

Industry Division	Loans			Procurement		
	All firms	Small firms	Small firms as % of total	All firms	Small firms	Small firms as % of total
Mining	NA	NA	–	23,097	22,209	96.2
Construction	1,176,135	1,166,963	99.2	1,176,135	1,167,233	99.2
Manufacturing	299,351	281,127	93.9	299,351	287,111	94.9
Transportation, communication, utilities[a]	120,813	110,312	91.3	120,813	116,359	96.3
Wholesale trade[b]	286,925	273,117	95.2	286,925	282,481	98.5
Retail trade	1,567,071	1,514,687	98.4	NA	NA	–
Insurance and real estate	NA	NA	–	NA	NA	–
Services	1,763,992	1,752,297	99.3	1,763,992	1,753,709	99.4
Total (less agriculture)	5,214,287	5,125,503	98.3	3,670,313	3,626,102	98.8
Agriculture[c]	2,314,013	2,304,013	99.6	NA	NA	–
Total (with agriculture)	7,528,300	7,429,516	98.7	3,670,313	3,626,102	98.8

Notes: NA – Not applicable. There is no current standard for these industries. a. Only those industries in which SBA makes loans are listed. Many industries in the Transportation, communication and utilities group and most of the Finance, insurance, and real estate groups (including all of finance) are not eligible for SBA programmes. b. Merchant wholesalers, wholesale agents, brokers, and commission merchants are included. Sales outlets owned by manufacturers are not included as a wholesale function. c. Agriculture is listed separately because SBA historically has made most of its loans to commercial enterprises rather than family firms.

Sources: Data derived by the Size Standards Branch, Small Business Administration, from the Economic Censuses, 1977, Dun & Bradstreet data for 1977, and the Census of Agriculture, 1974 as reported in Table A1.34 of the *Status of Small Business: A Report of the President* (Washington, DC, US Government Printing Office, 1982), p. 19.

Table 2.4: Sales of Companies by Employment Size and Industry Divisions, 1977 (millions of dollars and per cent)

Employment size of company	All industries millions	Cum. %	Minerals millions	Cum. %	Construction millions	Cum. %	Manufacturing millions	Cum. %	Wholesale trade millions	Cum. %	Retail trade millions	Cum. %	Selected services[a] millions	Cum. %
Total	3,324,551		59,782		239,374		1,409,465		709,773		729,617		176,540	
No paid employees	54,931	1.7	–	–	16,178	6.8	–	–	–	–	23,468	3.2	15,285	8.7
0 to reporting period[b]	27,272	2.5	231	0.4	4,425	8.6	689	–	6,951	1.0	11,025	4.7	3,951	10.9
1–4	197,062	8.4	1,673	3.2	28,345	20.4	10,545	0.8	65,052	10.2	66,712	13.8	24,735	24.9
5–9	212,117	14.8	1,548	5.8	26,240	31.4	14,167	1.8	86,230	22.3	65,027	22.7	18,905	35.6
10–19	262,599	22.7	2,609	10.2	30,408	44.1	26,500	3.7	110,143	37.8	74,210	32.9	18,729	46.2
20–49	364,037	33.6	4,914	18.4	37,718	59.9	58,739	7.9	140,525	57.6	102,419	46.9	19,722	57.4
50–99	238,630	40.8	3,487	24.2	22,454	69.3	58,370	12.0	77,907	68.6	63,940	55.7	12,472	64.5
100–249	244,750	48.2	4,214	31.2	21,229	78.2	84,226	18.0	75,831	79.3	45,287	61.9	13,963	72.4
250–499	146,714	52.6	3,401	36.9	11,240	82.9	63,680	22.5	40,347	85.0	19,365	64.6	8,681	77.3
500–999	142,623	56.9	3,426	42.6	7,716	86.1	66,935	27.2	39,055	90.5	17,992	67.1	7,499	81.5
1,000 and over	1,433,816	100.0%	34,279	100.0%	33,421	100.0%	1,025,614	100.0%	67,732	100.0%	240,172	100.0%	32,598	100.0%

Notes: a. Selected services covered by the economic census are listed in Appendix C of the 1977 *Enterprise Statistics*. b. Companies which reported annual payroll but did not report any employee on their payroll during specific pay periods in 1977.

Source: Department of Commerce, Bureau of the Census, 1977 *Enterprise Statistics, General Report on Industrial Organisation*, Table 3, as reported in Table A1.22 of *The State of Small Business: A Report of the President* (Washington, DC, US Government Printing Office, 1982), p. 205.

employee greater than those of firms with between 100 and 1,000 employees, about equal to those of firms with between 1,000 and 9,999 employees, but less than firms with 10,000 or more employees. There are exceptions, however. For example, finance and service firms with fewer than 100 employees produce more sales per dollar than the largest firms of the same types.

In six of the nine industries shown in Table 2.7, sales per dollar of assets for firms in the fewer-than-100 employee category are greater than or equal to those of their larger counterparts. Smaller firms in three industry groups (mining, manufacturing and transportation communication, public utilities) have sales per dollar of assets about 20 per cent greater than their largest employment-sized counterparts.

These differentials in sales per employee and sales per dollar of assets are not reflected in the statistics of average annual wages.

Table 2.5: Employment and Sales Shares in Traditional Small Business Industry Divisions for Firms with Fewer than 100 Employees and 500 Employees, 1978 (Per cent)

Employ-ment size class	Agriculture, Forestry, Fishing	Construction	Wholesale trade	Retail trade	Services
	Small firms as per cent of total number of firms				
Fewer than 100	95.1	99.3	98.9	99.3	97.2
Fewer than 500	100.0	99.9	99.9	99.9	99.4
	Small firm share as per cent of total employment				
Fewer than 100	66.8	70.0	68.5	56.8	32.0
Fewer than 500	76.6	83.7	83.0	65.8	51.3
	Small firm share as per cent of total sales				
Fewer than 100	62.0	68.9	59.1	56.5	44.8
Fewer than 500	69.7	82.6	74.5	65.5	62.1

Source: Small Business Data Base tabulated by Brookings Institute from Dun & Bradstreet, *Market Identifier File*, as reported in Table 1.8 of *The State of Small Business: A Report of the President* (Washington, DC, US Government Printing Office, 1982), p. 54.

Table 2.6: Sales Per Employee by Employment Size of Enterprise, 1978 (thousands of dollars)

Industry division	1–4	5–9	10–19	20–49	50–99	100–249	250–499	500–999	1000–4999	5000–9999	10,000 or more
					Employment Size of Enterprise						
All industries	57.4	60.2	60.1	57.8	54.9	49.8	46.8	53.5	57.5	62.6	68.0
Agriculture, Forestry, Fishing	58.6	54.1	48.6	50.2	49.4	36.4	38.2	45.0	44.4	51.2	71.5
Mining	96.2	80.6	77.1	59.9	58.9	64.9	57.3	80.4	136.4	69.1	246.2
Construction	61.9	56.0	54.5	53.6	55.5	51.7	51.9	48.8	46.5	57.0	31.7
Manufacturing	47.3	43.1	44.9	44.3	43.7	44.5	43.8	45.3	52.8	58.8	65.8
Transportation, Communication, Utilities	51.4	59.7	48.9	45.5	49.2	50.5	51.3	57.7	95.8	106.5	63.7
Wholesale trade	132.0	138.5	135.1	132.1	134.3	141.6	150.9	244.6	185.9	139.2	82.2
Retail trade	44.6	45.1	47.7	50.7	58.2	50.1	40.3	37.5	48.3	47.6	60.6
Finance, Insurance, Real Estate	145.6	137.0	131.2	123.5	125.2	97.6	80.2	76.6	82.5	63.3	57.8
Services	34.4	36.8	34.2	28.6	22.7	19.7	20.8	20.1	20.1	23.9	13.3

Note: Data exclude subsidiaries and firms without sales.

Source: Small Business Data Base, tabulated by Brookings Institution from Dun and Bradstreet's *Market Identifier File* as reported in Table A2.14 of *The State of Small Business: A Report of the President* (Washington, DC, US Government Printing Office, 1982), p. 238.

Table 2.7: Sales Per Dollar of Assets by Industry Division and Employment Size of Company, 1979

Industry division	Employment Size of company Under 100 (1)	100 or more (2)	Ratio Col. 1/ Col. 2
	(Medians)		
Agriculture, Forestry, Fisheries	1.786	2.395	0.745
Mining	1.227	1.016	1.208
Construction	2.528	2.651	0.954
Manufacturing	2.342	1.912	1.225
Transportation, Communication, Utilities	1.889	1.550	1.219
Wholesale trade	2.847	2.780	1.024
Retail trade	2.411	3.201	0.753
Finance, Insurance, Real Estate	0.785	0.712	1.103
Services	1.985	1.896	1.047
	(Means)		
Agriculture, Forestry, Fisheries	3.565*	3.202	1.113
Mining	2.854*	1.266	2.254
Construction	4.425*	7.585	0.583
Manufacturing	3.240*	3.132*	1.034
Transportation, Communication, Utilities	3.636	3.015*	1.206
Wholesale trade	16.076*	4.167*	3.858
Retail trade	3.585	5.133*	0.698
Finance, Insurance, Real Estate	8.546*	5.029	1.699
Services	4.574*	3.384*	1.352

* Indicates coefficient of variation is greater than 5 and, therefore, the number is less reliable.
Source: Small Business Data Base tabulated by Brookings Institution from Dun and Bradstreet's *Market Identifier File* as reported in Table A1.9 of *The State of Small Business: A Report of the President* (Washington, DC, US Government Printing Office, 1982), p. 195.

Across all industries in 1977, there was a consistent positive differential in the average annual wage favouring employees of larger firms. The average annual wage ranged from $7,500 for the smallest class (1–4 employees) to $13,000 for firms with 1,000 or more employees. Comparable differences occurred within individual industries, except for services, minerals, and wholesale trade. This suggests that while some small firms pay wages comparable to those paid by larger firms, the smallest firms usually pay the lowest wages.

The lack of correspondence between sales per employee and average wage may be attributed to a number of factors. First, hours of work are likely to be more variable among small firms, given their higher proportion of part-time workers. Second, competition among workers is likely to be more keen in the small business sector than among large businesses, which generally deal with labour through union organisations. Third, small businesses are usually shown to be less productive when value-added productivity measures are used, due to the low investment per worker.[17] Thus, while they may generate larger sales per employee, the value of their marginal product is likely to be less – leading to lower potential compensation.

One additional significant difference between small and large businesses requires mention. This is that the small business typically has a higher debt-to-equity ratio than the larger firm, as well as a higher proportion of short-term debt. In periods of slack business conditions therefore, small businesses are likely to be more vulnerable to failure than the larger firms.[18]

In summary, an examination of the current structure of the US economy shows that small businesses comprise well over 90 per cent of all industry sectors by number of firms. Small firms contribute materially to the total health of the economy, and often succeed in 'doing more with less assets' than their larger rivals, as evidenced by higher sales per employee and dollar of assets. Being relatively labour-intensive, they tend to be less highly capitalised than their larger counterparts. Finally, they are particularly vulnerable to slack business conditions, in part because of the high debt-to-equity ratios typical of small businesses.

2.4. Small Business Trends in the US Economy

The purpose of this section is to outline the changes which have occurred in the small business sector over time, thereby demonstrating the contribution of small businesses to the growth of the US economy.

A. *Number of Establishments*

From 1975 to 1979 the total number of business establishments in the US grew by approximately ten per cent – from 4.1 to 4.5 million. The two employment-size classes which showed the greatest expansion were the two largest small business categories. In these two groups, the 50–99 and 100–499 employee categories, the number of establishments increased by 32 and 33 per cent, respectively. With the single exception of the very smallest firms (1 to 4 employees), small businesses increased much more rapidly in number than large businesses in this recent period. Between one-half and two-thirds (depending on size class) of the total growth in number of establishments occurred in the latter half of the period.

B. Gross Product Originating

The changing influence of small businesses on the American economy is reflected in their comparative contribution, over time, to sales, employment and profitability and to gross product, discussed below.

The contribution of small business to the GNP declined almost ten per cent between 1955 and 1976, falling from 43 per cent to 39 per cent. In terms of gross product originating in the private sector only, the percentage decline was smaller, amounting to only 7.7 per cent over this 21-year period. The rate of decline varied from one industry classification to another, with the largest decrease occurring in the mining and manufacturing industries. In the former, the decline was from 50 per cent to 32 per cent of the total; in the latter, from 30 per cent to 19 per cent. Conversely, the smallest decreases occurred in the construction, transportation, communication and public utilities, wholesale trade and services categories, where the decline in the small business share ranged from four to six per cent. In three of these categories, small business remained the dominant form of organisation in 1976: construction, 83 per cent, wholesale trade, 84 per cent, and services, 82 per cent.[19]

C. Sales and Employment

Further insight into the changing fortunes of small business can be obtained by examining the changes which occurred over the period 1958–77 in the sector's shares of sales and employment. In both 1958 and 1977 the small business sector (excluding the 0–19 employee category) enjoyed a 30 per cent share of sales. The share of employment for the 20–500 employee-size class, however, declined from 31.9 in 1958 to 30.9 in 1977, a one per cent difference, or an actual decline of almost three per cent. The very smallest business establishments, those having 0–19 employees, did not fare as well. The sales share for this group declined from about 31 per cent in 1958 to about 21 per cent in 1977, a drop of almost one-third over the 19-year period. But the decline in sales share was not accompanied by an equivalent decline in employment share. The latter declined only 7.3 per cent during the period, from 23.3 per cent in 1958 to 21.6 per cent in 1977. This may be explained by the effects of moving previously larger size firms into the 0–19 employment class and to employees who were laid off starting their own business.

Among the several size categories of small business, only the 20–99 employee class gained both in share of sales (1.7 per cent) and share of employment (2.8 per cent) during the period. In contrast, gains in share of total sales were experienced by all classes of large businesses. Interestingly, these were not accompanied by comparable changes in employment share. Instead, three of the four employee size categories of large businesses experienced reductions in share of employment. This seeming incongruity may be attributed in part to improvements in efficiency with existing capital and/or to a shift to more capital-intensive forms of production. Other causal factors may also have been present, however, considering the sharp decline in productivity gains which occurred during the 1970s.[20] Without a detailed analysis of factor costs at the individual firm level, it is impossible to develop a complete explanation for the decline in employment share for larger firms.

The *Enterprise Statistics* may not accurately reflect employment shares for the small business sector. Other figures gathered from unpublished unemployment insurance data of the US Department of Labor give a somewhat different picture of the relative importance of the small business contribution to employment. This source shows small business as having a 73 per cent share of employment in 1977, in contrast to the 53.5 per cent share indicated by *Enterprise Statistics* data. Furthermore, according to the unemployment insurance data, the small business share of employment appears to have increased over the period from 1975–79, in contrast to the slight decline portrayed by the *Enterprise Statistics*. A partial explanation for this difference is that the unemployment data are establishment-based and do not capture the effect of multi-establishment companies. However, the sectors *not* covered by the *Enterprise Statistics* are the very ones in which employment growth is likely to be greatest, particularly among small firms.[21] Of the 9.5 million new jobs that emerged from 1969 to 1976, 7.4 million were created by the small business sector.[22]

D. Equity

The net-after-tax returns on stockholders' equity for the manufacturing sector increased in the period 1970–81. For all manufacturing corporations, a doubling of the return on equity occurred over that period – from 8.7 per cent in 1970 to 16.1 per cent in 1981. For manufacturing firms with assets under five million dollars, the increase was even more dramatic – from around six per cent in 1970 to 19.6 per cent in 1981.[23] The conclusion follows that during this recent period, the profitability and/or inventory valuation adjustments of the smaller manufacturing firms was more favourable than that of the larger ones.

Of possibly greater long-term importance for both large and small business is the increase in debt-to-equity ratios which occurred over the period 1959–80. In general, capital is less readily available to small than to large businesses. It is not surprising, therefore, to observe that small manufacturers have higher debt-to-equity ratios than large manufacturers. Further, over the period 1959–80 the debt-to-equity ratio nearly doubled for both small and large businesses. The doubling of return on equity has been accomplished at significant risk, since interest rates remain high and corporations are increasingly turning to the short-term market to fund outstanding debt. The longer the combination of high interest rates and inflation continues, the greater the possibility of business failure and bankruptcy. Due to inadequate data and space limitations, this important topic cannot be discussed further here. The reader interested in discussions of business failure and bankruptcy should consult *The State of Small Business* and Star and Massi on business failure among retailers.[24]

The need to 'go the debt route' was even more pronounced for large manufacturers than for small. While the small manufacturers of both durable and nondurable goods increased their debt-to-equity ratios by an average of 75 per cent during the 21-year period, the large manufacturers of durable goods increased their average debt-to-equity ratio by 90 per cent and the large manufacturers of nondurable goods increased theirs by 120 per cent. Part of the trend toward convergence in debt-to-equity ratios between small and large manufacturers may be due to small businesses being crowded out of the debt market as larger corporations increase their demand for short-term loans to cover liquidity needs.[25]

E. Innovation

The obvious importance of small business in providing jobs has been noted. Small business also plays an important part in creating new technology and products. During the last twenty years the roles of large and small business in the development of new technologies and products have differed substantially. Large organisations are more likely to be sources of 'process' innovation. When they do develop new products, these tend to emerge from incremental improvements or refinements. Small business is more likely to strive for the unexpected, 'leap-frog' product innovations.[26]

Over two-thirds of the major inventions developed in the twentieth century were the work of independent inventors and small companies. Examples of such inventions are the airplane, the helicopter, catalytic oil refining, oxygen steel-making, photocopying, the automatic transmission, power steering, air-conditioning, the polaroid camera, the zipper, and dacron-polyester fibre.[27] A study of 310 innovations developed between 1973 and 1975 showed that 24 per cent were introduced by firms with fewer than 100 employees, and an additional 24 per cent were developed by firms with between 100 and 999 employees.[28] As many as 50–60 per cent of today's inventors work outside the organised research groups of the corporate industrial laboratories. Independent inventors took out roughly 40 per cent of the total patents in the US over the past twenty years. Of the 60 per cent of patents held by corporations, one-third came from corporate employees working outside corporate laboratories.[29]

Small businesses have a striking record of innovation, particularly in view of their limited share of economic resources. According to the US Office of Management and Budget, businesses employing less than 1,000 employees accounted for roughly half of the nation's innovations between 1953 and 1973. That figure represents an output four times greater per research and development dollar than for larger firms. Firms with fewer than 1,000 employees produced innovation at about a quarter the cost of middle-sized (1,000–10,000 employees) firms, and at about one-twenty-fifth that of large (10,000 and over employees) firms.[30]

What is it about small firms that seems to encourage innovation? Perhaps smaller, less restrictive organisations provide for more individual initiative.[31] Four other reasons have been suggested. First, in a small technological firm, innovation is necessary to ensure survival, whereas the large firm tends simply to maintain its product market position. Second, managers of small technological companies (in which they often own a share) have more incentive to innovate. Third, large firms may prefer to hold technical improvements to a minimum for marketing reasons. Fourth, researchers and innovators in large firms tend to specialise; those in small firms tend to be technical generalists. Overspecialisation limits innovation: the more knowledge a developer has to draw on, the more original the resulting innovation tends to be.[32]

The inescapable conclusion is that small businesses are a substantial source of innovation and technical change, and that they make their contribution more efficiently and at lower cost than larger businesses. The National Science Foundation reports, however, that private research and development declined by 13 per cent between 1968 and 1978. Patents peaked at 56,000 in 1971; numbers have fallen ever since. (Patents granted in other countries during the same ten-year period increased dramatically.[33]) This recent decline in patents granted in the United States may be due at least in part to the fact that a patent has less than a 50 per cent chance of surviving a court challenge. Another partial explanation for the decline is that federal policy in this country permits government contractors to infringe on patent rights if necessary to meet the terms of a contract.[34] Perhaps the best explanation, however, is offered by Robert Noyce, Chairman of Intel Corporation, a pioneer firm in the semiconductor industry. He concludes: 'The combination of cost-inflating government regulations and higher taxes for all practical purposes killed off the greatest advantage this country once had over foreign competitors: the ability of talented individuals to form their own companies to push outward the frontiers of technology.'[35]

2.5. Problems of Small Business

A. The NFIB Survey

Small businesses face more numerous and troublesome problems today than in any period since the Great Depression. For many years, the National Federation of Independent Business (NFIB) has surveyed its members about the single most important problem which they face as small business persons. This continuing survey covers more than two thousand firms. In January, 1982, it showed the results indicated in Table 2.8.[36]

Table 2.8: NFIB Members' Survey on Business Problems

Problem rated 'Most important'	Per cent of Replies
Interest Rates and Financing	33
Inflation	21
Taxes	13
Inadequate Demand for Product	9
Minimum Wage Laws; Cost of Labour	3
Other Government Regulations; Red Tape	4
Competition from Large Business	6
Quality of Labour	4
Shortage of Fuels, Materials or Goods	a
Other, or No answer	7
Total	100

Note: a. Less than 0.5 per cent.
Source: *NFIB Quarterly Economic Report for Small Business*, January 1982.

The priority given particular problems varied considerably from one industry to another. 'Interest Rates and Financing', for example, was cited by particularly large percentages of respondents in financial services (57 per cent), construction (48 per cent) and wholesaling (40 per cent). Similarly, 'Quality of Labour' was listed as most important by a relatively large proportion of manufacturing firms (9 per cent), 'Government Regulations' by a comparatively large share of transporation firms (11 per cent) and 'Competition from Large Firms' by a disproportionate number of retailers (12 per cent).[37] The proprietors of the very smallest businesses (annual sales less than $50,000) regarded 'Inflation' and 'Interest Rates and Financing' as equally serious problems. Each was rated 'most important' by 27 per cent of this group.[38]

The high ranking given to interest rates and financing in this survey is of recent origin and reflects the tight money policies of the Federal Reserve beginning in October 1979 and the resultant upsurge in interest rates. Through most of the 1974–81 period, respondents listed inflation as the most important problem, with taxes ranking second. As recently as January 1978, interest rates and financing ranked only seventh in importance.[39]

B. Cost and Availability of Capital

During 1980 and 1981, consumer prices in the United States increased at an average annual rate of approximately 11 per cent.[40]

Tight money policies initiated by the Federal Reserve authorities to combat this strong inflationary pressure pushed interest rates to the highest levels in many decades. Thirty per cent of the small businesses responding to the NFIB survey reported that they were paying interest rates of 16–18 per cent, and 56 per cent said they were paying rates of 19–22 per cent on short-term loans in the third quarter of 1981.[41]

High interest rates have a dampening effect on business activity in general, but pose a particularly serious threat to the survival and profitability of small enterprises. There are two principal reasons for this. One is that small businesses must pay significantly higher interest rates than their larger competitors on loans of the same type and maturity. While a large firm of good credit standing is likely to pay the prime rate on its short-term bank loans, small firms typically must pay from 2 to 4 per cent above prime on such loans and from 3 to 6 per cent above prime on loans from finance companies. Costs of borrowing from other sources can run even higher. A second reason why high interest rates have such a great impact on small businesses is that small firms depend much more heavily than large ones upon debt financing, and particularly bank loans, as a source of funds. Not only does the small business have less opportunity than a well-established large firm to draw upon internally generated funds, such as retained earnings or depreciation reserves, but it also has little or no access to capital markets. The public equity market usually does not become available to a firm until it reaches an annual sales level of about $10 million.[42] Consequently, the current lending policies of banks – and of the Federal Reserve authorities – can be a critical factor affecting the ability of small firms to meet their capital needs.

Writing in the *Journal of Small Business Management* several years ago, Chandran, de Salvia, and Young summed up the situation of a small business in a period of tight money:

> When interest rates are high under the Federal Reserve's tight money policy credit becomes more difficult to obtain and the usual sources of loan funds . . . may simply not be available. Commercial banks may be 'loaned up' and the terms of trade credit and its availability are likely to be more rigid than in normal times. Where and when capital is available, it is usually on a short to medium term basis. Loans tend to be smaller and interest rates as high as 18 percent are not uncommon. Small firms cannot pay such high rates of interest and hope to survive

and grow . . . . With high debt-to-equity ratios, the rise in interest rates exacerbates liquidity problems even more. The tight money conditions also suppress even the small amount of venture capital normally coming into small businesses.[43]

The high cost and limited availability of capital may force the small firm to adopt less-than-optimal policies in many areas of management. Because it is forced to buy in smaller than economic quantities, it may be unable to take advantage of quantity and payment discounts and consequently may find its operating costs increased. Because the ˙small firm lacks capital to maintan inventories at the most appropriate level, it may encounter frequent stockouts and lose customers as a result. To conserve its scarce working capital, it may be forced to cut advertising and promotional expenses, with predictably unfavourable effects on sales. Liquidity problems may also lead to sub-optimal capital budgeting decisions. Because of these and other potential ill-effects, the limited availability and high cost of capital combine to form one of the most important causes of business failure for small firms.[44]

C. Inflation

Apart from its role as the root cause of today's high interest rates, inflation affects the operation of a small business in two principal ways. On the cost side, it results in higher prices for raw materials and labour which, in turn, push up operating costs. On the revenue side, small businesses find it difficult to pass on increased costs in the form of higher prices because they usually face strong competition in their product markets. Also, unlike some of their larger counterparts, they are seldom in a position to change processes or update technology to minimise the effects of rising costs and decreased productivity. Nor can they usually emulate larger firms by discontinuing the production of low markup items and shifting production to higher profit lines. Consequently, the earnings of small firms tend to be squeezed and cash flow diminished during periods of severe inflation.[45]

D. Recession

The severe impact of a recession on small business is reflected in the sharp increase which typically occurs in business failures during such a period. According to a recent government report, business failures in the United States have increased substantially in the last fifteen years, but particularly during the recessions of 1974–5 and 1980–2. During such periods, small businesses suffer declines in sales and profits and experience worsened cash flow problems. The ability of the smaller firms to survive a deep recession has been weakened, in recent years, by increased leverage and a heavy debt burden.[46]

As in the case of inflation, small businesses usually experience greater difficulty than their larger competitiors in coping with recession. The big companies usually have larger liquid reserves and better access to working capital, and are usually able to maintain their advertising budgets, while small companies are forced to cut theirs back sharply. Even more importantly, the large firms usually possess the advantage of diversification. A company serving many geographical markets with a variety of products has a better opportunity to average-out random ups and downs in the business fortunes of its units, as compared to the undiversified small enterprise.[47]

When inflation and recession are present simultaneously, as has recently been the case, the differential impact on small business becomes even more pronounced. On this point, John M. Blair, former chief economist of the Senate antitrust committee, comments as follows:

> Smaller firms pay more for money even in the best of times, but inflation has aggravated the difference. The bias against smaller companies applies not only to corporate bonds and bank lending, but also to the equities market. The securities of large companies enjoy higher price/earnings ratios because they are better known, more actively traded, and, therefore, more liquid.[48]

E. Taxes

Spokesmen for small business criticise the federal tax system on three principal grounds. These are:

1. that it discriminates in favour of large, capital-intensive businesses and against small, labour-intensive ones
2. that it is unnecessarily complex
3. that it fails to give enough consideration to the special needs and problems of small business.

Each of these criticisms requires at least some brief explanation.

The charge of discriminatory impact relates chiefly to two taxes – the corporate income tax and the social security payroll tax. According to an estimate by Professor R. A. Schotland of the Georgetown University Law School, the average *effective* rate of the corporate income tax is 15 per cent higher for small firms than for large.[49] This differential is attributed to the presence in the tax law of certain opportunities and concessions which – for all practical purposes – are available only to large firms. Examples include accelerated depreciation, investment tax credit, the LIFO method of calculating depreciation, foreign tax credit and the tax-free exchange of stock. In a recent attitudinal survey of 1,300 small business persons, 95 per cent expressed some level of agreement with the statement that 'larger firms are better able to take advantage of tax regulations'.[50]

Another frequently-cited example of the discriminatory impact of the federal tax system is the heavy burden which social security payroll taxes impose on labour-intensive small firms. There has been a very substantial increase in the level of these taxes over the last several decades. As a result, many of the nation's small businesses now pay more in payroll taxes than in any other kind of business tax. In the attitudinal survey mentioned above, 45 per cent of the respondents indicated that payroll taxes were the most burdensome type of tax in terms of dollar cost.[51]

The criticism that the federal tax structure, as it applies to small business, is unnecessarily complicated, has been summarised concisely by Charles C. Holt, Director of Inflation and Unemployment Research for the Urban Institute.

> The federal tax system is a morass for small business as a result of its complexity, uncertainty, administrative burden and costs for legal, tax and accounting services. Some small business managers are seriously distracted by the burdens from running their businesses.[52]

As noted above, a third criticism is that federal tax laws fail to take into account the special needs of small business. This is particularly true with regard to capital accumulation. Bruce G. Fielding, a certified public accountant and small business advocate, has expressed this criticism as follows:

Our tax laws have neglected to take into consideration that a small business must be allowed to accumulate capital in order to assure a healthy and steady growth. The small businessman is faced with discriminatory tax rates, severe penalties for unreasonable accumulation of surplus, taxation of paper profits, the costly administrative burden of pension and profit sharing plans and crippling inheritance taxes which can force the sacrifice sale of a healthy business.[53]

Like federal taxes, state and local taxes include many features which impact unfavourably upon small business. State corporate income taxes typically have proportionate rates which are regressive in effect, and further discriminate against small firms in their generally complex nature and rigid provisions for filing and payment. Personal income taxes (at all levels, including the federal) impose heavy compliance burdens on small business because of the withholding provisions. In the case of retail sales taxes, rate differentials pose special problems for small firms operating in interstate markets. Also, complicated exemptions, burdensome recordkeeping requirements and other features combine to produce a heavy compliance burden. Broad-based gross receipts taxes usually favour large, integrated businesses and are particularly burdensome to unprofitable small firms. In property taxation, discriminatory assessment practices and the favoured treatment of personal over real property produce a bias in favour of the larger, more capital-intensive firms. Overall, the state-local tax systems appear as vulnerable as the federal system to the criticism that they discriminate against small businesses.[54]

F. Government Regulation

The generally adverse reaction of small business persons to government regulation is described by Hentzell; 'No aspect of government seems to arouse more rage among small business owners than federal, state, and local regulations that are applied indiscriminately to large and small businesses.'[55] To this candid observation, Chandran, de Salvia, and Young add the following warning:

Compared to other causal factors . . . increasing government regulations in the form of occupational safety rules, environmental restrictions, product safety regulations and increased minimum wage regulations may pose the greatest threat of all to the survival of small firms.[56]

In recent years, there has been unprecedented growth in the number of regulatory agencies and in the scope and volume of their regulations. From 1969 to 1976, 26 new regulatory agencies were created, and between 1970 and 1974, 29 major regulatory statutes were enacted. There are now about 90 federal regulatory agencies issuing 7,000 rules each year.[57]

The overall effect of government regulation tends to be regressive, with compliance costs falling most heavily on the smallest firms. As Walker and Gale point out, 'Since the costs of compliance are relatively fixed, those least able to afford them shoulder a greater burden than their more affluent peers.'[58] Lacking the staff and expertise needed to keep up with changing government regulations and cope with the resultant paperwork, small businesses often must turn to the more expensive alternative of contracting for outside assistance. Even so, the amount of time which the small business manager must devote to regulation-related tasks is substantial – about three and one-half hours weekly according to one estimate.[59]

How great a burden does massive government regulation place upon small business? Several years ago, the SBA's Office of Advocacy conducted a study in which 800 owners of small businesses kept a diary of time spent in filling out government forms, together with an estimate of the associated costs. This study showed an average cost of $1,270, with the cost for individual companies ranging from $400 to $72,000 annually. On this basis, Milton Stewart (the SBA Chief Counsel for Advocacy) has estimated the total annual cost of compliance to be $12.7 billion.[60]

Perhaps the most common complaint of small business operators concerning government regulation is that these are usually applied across-the-board, without regard to the size of the firm. Although a few agencies have recently made changes in their regulatory practices in response to this criticism, these fall considerably short of the adjustments which small business spokesmen consider necessary. Other complaints include the complexity of the regulations, unreasonable time delays in the regulatory process, inadequate communication between the regulators and the regulated and conflicting requirements by different agencies and levels of government.[61]

Of the many federal regulatory agencies, the one criticised most often by small business spokesmen is the Internal Revenue Service or IRS. The aspects most frequently cited are complicated and time-consuming reporting techniques and repeated audits by inexperienced personnel.[62]

The Occupational Safety and Health Administration (OSHA) ranks second in volume of criticism. Its regulations are considered by many small business managers to be confusing and contradictory. In one survey of small businesses, several respondents mentioned having been fined by this agency for violating regulations of which they were unaware.[63]

Another much-criticised web of regulations is that associated with the Employment Retirement Income Security Act of 1974 (ERISA). This act established minimum standards for conducting, vesting and funding pension plans, and required such plans to meet strict reporting, disclosing and fiduciary requirements. It has been attacked not only because of its complexity and severe impact on the administrative costs of pension plans, but also because of investment restrictions which have inhibited the flow of private capital into small businesses.[64]

Like pension regulations, minimum wage laws draw heavy criticism from small businesses. In this case, the most common charge is that the minimum wage sets the price of untrained labour unrealistically high in relation to its value.

Other federal regulations regarded as particularly burdensome for small businesses are those relating to food and drugs, equal employment opportunity, consumer product safety, environmental protection and government contracts. Even antitrust laws, originally enacted for the protection of small business, often work to its disadvantage in practice. Because small firms cannot afford the expensive legal talent available to large companies they 'make tempting targets for government attorneys seeking to build their "batting average" of cases won and lost.'[65]

G. Availability and Cost of Labour

A common side-effect of persistent inflation, as it affects wage rates and fringe benefits, is that small companies are unable to hold or attract skilled labour. According to James D. McKevitt of the National Federation of Independent Business, small businesses consistently report that they have vacancies which they cannot fill and that virtually all of these call for some degree of skill.[66]

Meanwhile, payroll tax increases and minimum wage hikes make it increasingly difficult for the small business operator to hire the young, unskilled and marginal workers who form the heart of the nation's unemployment problem. At present, more than one-fifth of the nation's small businesses have teenagers as full-time employees, and more than one-third hire them part-time.[67]

H. Competition from Big Business

Small business approaches, more closely than any other segment of the American economy, the purely competitive model of economic theory. With many competitors, comparatively slight product differentiation, and little control over its buying and selling prices, the typical small business is largely at the mercy of market forces. But far from operating in a wholly competitive environment, such enterprises today represent only the competitive fringe of a national economy which has grown increasingly oligopolistic. The small business manager often must contend with the market power of much larger firms as competitors, suppliers, and customers; with the monopolistic influence of a union in the labour market; and with the frequent intrusions of government as an insistent regulator. As a result, small business has been gradually losing ground in what its advocates regard as an unfair economic struggle.

I. Energy Problems

The increase in energy costs of recent years has affected many small businesses adversely, as they tend to have higher energy expenditures per dollar of sales than large businesses. For example, a recent survey covering midwestern states revealed that firms with less than $50,000 in sales had energy expenses equal to 6.4 per cent of sales, compared to 1.4 per cent for firms with $800,000 or more in sales.[68] Another nationwide survey showed that small businesses were responding to rising energy costs with such measures as reducing temperatures, reducing use of lighting, adding new insulation, and acquiring more energy-efficient equipment. The same study indicated that the average small business was spending more than $1,200 per month for energy in early 1977.[69]

The federal Department of Energy's Office of Small Business has developed an energy cost reduction programme, the central purpose of which is to provide technical assistance to small business people on practical methods of reducing energy consumption and costs.[70] The primary form of assistance consists of guidebooks, keyed to particular industrial categories and based on actual energy audits of representative firms. On this basis, a list of energy cost reduction recommendations has been developed for each industry group.

2.6. Government Assistance

A. The Small Business Agency (SBA)

A growing public awareness of the special problems faced by small business in the United States today is demonstrated not only by Congressional hearings and a widely-publicised White House conference devoted to these problems, but also – and more tangibly – by the activities of the SBA. This federal agency provides a varied array of financial and managerial aid programmes for qualified small firms. (Many private organisations have also been formed to advance small business interests. Among them are the International Council for Small Business, the National Small Business Association and the National Federation of Independent Business, Inc.)

Financial Assistance. The SBA was founded in 1953 for the purpose of providing intermediate to long-term financing for small businesses which could not obtain money on reasonable terms anywhere else. This remains its principal function today, although it also offers managerial assistance and educational programmes. At present, seven different financial assistance programmes are available. These include:[71]

1. *Regular (7a) Business Loans.* Loans authorised under Section 7a of the 1953 Small Business Act account for the bulk of SBA lending activities (93 per cent of all loans made or guaranteed by the agency in 1977 were of this type). Maturities range from six years for working capital loans to ten years for intermediate and twenty years for real estate loans.

2. *Economic Opportunity Loans (EOLs).* The purpose of this programme is to establish and strengthen the small businesses of the socially and economically disadvantaged. The maximum maturity is 15 years; ten years for working capital loans. In 1977, 3,845 EOLs were approved; average amount: $28,764.

3. *Community Development Company Loans.* This pro-

gramme provides funds for small businesses for equity capital, construction or conversion of physical facilities, and construction of shopping centres. The funds are channelled to qualifying firms through state or local development companies.

4. *Displaced Business Loans*. This programme was established to help small businesses displaced by federally aided construction projects (e.g. new highways, urban redevelopment). The loans may be used to establish a new business, reestablish an existing business, continue a business at an existing location, or to purchase an existing business.

5. *Seasonal Line of Credit Loans*. The SBA's newest loan programme provides funds for periods of heavy seasonal need, such as planting time for small farms or the Christmas season for toy manufacturers.

6. *Small Business Investment Company (SBIC) Loans*. The SBICs are specialised lending institutions which are privately owned and operated, but are licensed, regulated and sometimes financed by the SBA. They provide small businesses with equity and long-term debt financing. Since the start of this programme in 1958, some 50,000 small businesses have received $2.8 billion of SBIC financing.

7. *Minority Enterprise Small Business Investment Company Loans*. These SBA-related institutions specialise in assisting small businesses of the socially or economically disadvantaged. Most of the recipients are members of racial or ethnic minorities.

Three different types of loans (as distinct from loan programmes) are provided under SBA auspices. These are Guaranteed Loans, Immediate Participation (IP) Loans and Direct Government Loans. The Guaranteed Loans are made by private lenders, but carry an SBA guarantee of up to 90 per cent or $50,000, whichever is less. The private lender controls the loans and sets the interest rates, within limits established by the SBA. In recent years, more than 80 per cent of all SBA business loans have been made with a government guarantee of private lender funds. Immediate Participation Loans come partly from public funds and partly from private lenders. The upper limit is $50,000, except for Economic Opportunity Loans, for which the limit is $100,000. Direct Government Loans are made from public funds without a bank's participation. The dollar size limits are the same as for IP Loans.[72]

Management Assistance. Although commonly regarded as a lending agency, the SBA has also emphasised management counselling in recent years. This is provided by the agency's Office of Management Assistance and three SBA-sponsored programmes: (1) the Service Corps of Retired Executives and Corps of Active Executives (SCORE/ACE); (2) the Small Business Institutes (SBIs); and (3) the Small Business Development Corporations (SBDCs). The SBA's Office of Management Assistance, with a staff of about 300, coordinates these programmes nationally. All counselling provided under the several programmes is free to both borrowers and nonborrowers.[73]

SCORE/ACE has approximately 11,000 counsellors, who assisted more than 100,000 small businesses in 1977. Under this programme, experienced executives provide services vital to the SBA Financial Assistance Division, which requires evaluation of all loan prospects by someone other than the loan officer. SCORE/ACE volunteers evaluate applicants' management ability and may continue to advise after a loan is granted.[74]

More than 400 colleges and universities are now participating in the SBI counselling programme. Under this programme, teams of undergraduate business or engineering students, working under the supervision of a faculty member, advise small businesses on specific management problems. In return, the SBA contracts to give each participating school $250 per case each semester.[75]

Another SBA-funded, university-based management assistance programme is that provided through Small Business Development Centers (SBDCs). The SBDC programme draws upon the faculty and other resources of eight selected universities to provide a wide range of management assistance services to small businesses.[76]

While the SBDCs are concerned chiefly with aiding existing small businesses, four university-based Innovation Centers are dedicated to helping new, innovating enterprises get off the ground.[77] Funded by the National Science Foundation, these centres assisted in more than two dozen company formations in a recent five-year period. The NSF also funds a small business innovation research programme which provides grants of up to $25,000 for the first six months of product development. If a product shows promise at the end of this period, second-phase grants of $100,000 to $400,000 may be obtained for additional development and determination of market feasibility.[78]

In the case of minority-owned small businesses, management

and technical assistance can also be obtained, without charge, from many local organisations sponsored by the federal Office of Minority Business Enterprise. This agency works closely with the SBA in attempting to generate more business opportunities in both the private and public sectors for minority-owned firms.

Other Services. Other services provided by the SBA include the publication and distribution of pamphlets and monographs on small business opportunities and problems, the sponsorship of training courses, conferences, and workshops, and occasional research projects dealing with small business problems.

B. State and Local Assistance

State and local governments, as well as many privately-funded industrial development groups, provide financial assistance to new or relocating business establishments as part of their efforts to attract new industry. Among the types of subsidies most commonly offered are tax concessions, provision of plant facilities under liberal lease-purchase arrangements, free extension of access roads and utility lines and interviewing of prospective employees. Historically, however, these organisations have given comparatively little assistance to 'home grown' small businesses.

C. Evaluation of Public Assistance

SBA loans have been the salvation of many small enterprises and the agency enjoys widespread support within the small business community. Nevertheless, it has a rather controversial image. Its reputation as a lending agency has been tarnished, through the years, by the disclosure of a number of instances of corruption or political abuse.[79] Critics have also charged that the agency 'lacks a sense of purpose', tends to make most of its loans in sectors of the economy already overpopulated by small firms, and – in seeking to make an impressive quantitative showing – has sometimes failed to investigate loan proposals sufficiently.[80] The agency's defenders argue that it has made highly significant contributions to the survival and growth of small business in this country. For example, on the basis of a 1976 statistical survey, an agency spokesman concluded that an average of one new job was created and three existing jobs maintained for each $10,000 in loans made to small businesses.[81]

A relatively low-budget endeavour, the sponsorship of Small

Business Institutes on college and university campuses has
developed into one of the SBA's most highly regarded
undertakings. From a small beginning, the programme has
expanded rapidly until it now encompasses more than 400 schools.
Various studies have been conducted to measure its effectiveness,
with generally favourable results. In one study of more than two
hundred SBI projects at two West Coast universities, two-thirds of
the clients reported that they had benefited from the experience and
about half indicated that they expected to make significant use of
the students' work. An SBA survey found that 87 per cent of the
surveyed clients rated the programme either 'good', 'very good', or
'excellent'. A third study, conducted nationwide for the SBA by a
private consulting firm, found that the SBI programme was one of
the most effective programmes offered by the SBA during the
period of study (fiscal 1978).[82]

Other management assistance programmes provided or
underwritten by the SBA have received less enthusiastic reviews. In
the same national survey which resulted in highly favourable ratings
for the SBI programme, other SBA programmes, such as
Management Assistance Officer Counseling, were found to be
'rather ineffective'.[83] Although counselling by retired executives is
viewed favourably by many observers, one critical article contends
that SCORE volunteers usually lack small business experience and
that client's needs and consultant's talents are not always
matched.[84]

2.7. Future of Small Business

The economic seers who have sought to predict the long-range
future of small business in the United States have come up with
sharply conflicting conclusions. Perhaps this should come as no
surprise, for their 'crystal balls' have been clouded by the absence of
reliable statistics pertaining to this sector of the economy.

A. Pessimistic Predictions

It can fairly be said that pessimistic forecasts of the small business
future considerably outnumber the optimistic ones. The consensus
view which one obtains from a transcript of the Congressional
hearings of a few years ago is that the small business sector, which
contributed so much in the past, is in a state of crisis today – its

future is in jeopardy unless prompt and adequate legislative relief is forthcoming. A leading small business spokesman, John Lewis, President of the National Small Business Association, expressed these sentiments in the following gloomy summation:

> The small business community is being squeezed more and more by those forces that have come to dominate our economic system – big business, big labor, and big government. Recent trends in the small business community have shown the small business owner losing more and more ground to forces beyond his or her control. Taxes, paperwork, overregulation, scarce capital, and general governmental indifference to the small business person's plight have eroded the small's ability to compete with the economic and political muscle of big business . . . The very survival of the small business community will be decided in large part by you, the members of Congress, as you enact the laws of this country to govern and protect the rights of its citizens.[85]

A somewhat different, though scarcely brighter, picture was painted by the staff of *Business Week* on the occasion of the fiftieth anniversary of that magazine (September, 1979). These writers predicted that in another fifty years the nation's economic landscape would be dominated by 'super-industries' – multinational conglomerates exploiting a particular economic base or a broad services market. Small business would continue to exist only in clusters of small cottage industries which would act as feeders to the industrial giants, supplying them with equipment, parts and support services.[86]

B. More Optimistic Views

Other writers have challenged these pessimistic predictions. Writing in the *Harvard Business Review*, David E. Gumpert argued that the overall situation for small business is not as bleak as was portrayed in the 1979 Congressional hearings. The facts and figures relating to small business health, he stated, were 'open to varying interpretation'. Some of the statistics presented before the Congressional subcommittee would, in his opinion, seem to demonstrate the 'continuing vitality and good health of small business'. As a prime example, he cited a study, mentioned several times at the hearings, which concluded that companies other than the '*Fortune* 1000' (the nation's largest firms) had accounted for 7.4

million of the 9.6 million new jobs created in this country between 1969 and 1976. Among other favourable factors, he listed an 'uneven but definite decline' in business failures since the early 1960s, a steady upward trend in business incorporations, and the greatly increased number of small business courses being taught in American universities.[87] He concluded that owners of small businesses and their representatives were 'pleading crisis' as a means of getting action on some legitimate complaints which had long been ignored by the politicians.[88]

Similarly, the pessimistic view of the small business future presented in *Business Week* was criticised in a White House Conference paper by Ernest Walker and Lawrence D. Gale. This portrayal, they argued, 'simply illustrates the blind spot that has characterized the conventional wisdom of economic organizations in the 20th Century'. Walker and Gale concluded that our economy will continue to be a two-tiered one, with the small business sector as 'an extremely viable and dynamic tier'.[89]

C. Critical Areas for the Future

In an article published in *Nation's Business* in March 1976, Carter Henderson identified seven critical areas of management planning for small business in the next 25 years. Briefly summarised, these were:[90]

> 1. *Capital.* This will become more difficult and expensive to obtain and could become 'virtually unavailable to many small businesses at almost any price'.
>
> 2. *Raw Materials.* These will also become increasingly costly and far more subject to cutoffs, as has been the case with petroleum and a few other raw materials in recent years.
>
> 3. *Labour.* The most plentiful future resource, it will be substituted increasingly for scarce capital. A moderation of union wage demands is foreseen, as high-level structural unemployment continues. Labour productivity, however, is likely to stagnate as large-scale capital investment ends.
>
> 4. *Technology.* This factor is seen as less important to small business than in the past. Capital and labour constraints will make unlikely the continued introduction of new technology at the rapid rate of the last few decades.
>
> 5. *Markets.* Those based on products which consume large

amounts of scarce, expensive materials will decline. Conversely, those based on products which make smaller demands on irreplaceable resources – or substitute for them – will flourish.

6. *Government Regulation*. This is seen as almost certain to increase further, as elected officials struggle to keep the nation prosperous, while mediating conflicts among opposing economic power blocs.

7. *Management*. Executives 'will have to exhibit greater professionalism and foresight' if they are to succeed in guiding American small business 'through the transition from abundance to scarcity'.

Henderson avoided a direct prediction of the future condition of small business in this country, but his analysis implies that difficult times lie ahead.

2.8. Conclusion

The presence of sharply divergent views concerning the future of small business in the United States is understandable, considering the many uncertainties now confronting independent owner-managers. Through the years, small businesses have exhibited a tenacious will to survive in the face of adversity. During the course of this century, the small business sector has managed to achieve a modicum of growth in absolute terms. Its relative shares of total business activity, assets and employment, however, have gradually but steadily declined. The section of this chapter on the small business sector's share of sales and employment, however, suggests that, depending upon the data used, its share of employment may actually have increased in recent years. The small independents of today face a daunting mix of problems – inflation in combination with recession, unequal tax treatment, oppressive regulation, high energy costs and others. Their ability to deal effectively with these problems has been seriously weakened by the highest interest rates in many decades. While the survival of the small business sector is not seriously jeopardised as yet, the decline in its relative importance appears likely to continue and even accelerate unless adequate corrective measures are taken by the federal government.

42   *The United States of America*

Acknowledgements

The authors would like to thank Lenley Lewis and Deanna Jefferson, both of the Bureau of Business Research at West Virginia University, for editorial assistance and for typing and proofreading. Thanks also to Dr William Whiston, Research Director, Office of Advocacy, US Small Business Administration, for his helpful advice and counsel.

Notes

1. For a comprehensive treatment of defining small business in the US, UK, Israel and the People's Republic of China, see Leah Hertz, *In Search of a Small Business Definition* (Washington, DC, University Press of America, 1982).

2. US Congress, *The Small Business Act of 1953* (Washington, DC, US Government Printing Office).

3. Andrew T. Nappi and Jay Vora, 'Small Business Eligibility: A Definitional Issue', *Journal of Small Business Management*, vol. 18, no. 4 (1980), p. 23.

4. L. Peter Lobo and Owen D. Osborne, 'The Impact of the Energy Situation on Small Businesses in Nothwest States' in Karl H. Vesper *et al.* (eds.), *Small Business Entrepreneurship in Region Ten: The Pacific Northwest* (Eugene, Oregon, The University of Oregon for the SBA, 1980), p. 64.

5. Nappi and Vora, 'Small Business Eligibility', pp. 23–5.

6. Ibid.

7. Wilford White, 'What's New in Washington', *Journal of Small Business Management*, vol. 16, no. 2 (1978), p. 35.

8. Nappi and Vora, 'Small Business Eligibility', p. 25.

9. *The State of Small Business: A Report of the President* (Washington, DC, US Government Printing Office, 1982), pp. 50–1.

10. Ibid., pp. 259–60.

11. Ibid., pp. 38–9.

12. Ibid., pp. 43–5.

13. US Bureau of the Census, *Enterprise Statistics*, (Washington, DC, US Government Printing Office, 1977).

14. US Department of Commerce, Bureau of the Census, *County Business Patterns* (Washington, DC, US Government Printing Office, 1977).

15. *Small Business Data Base* tabulated by the Brookings Institution from Dun and Bradstreet's *Market Identifier File*. See *The State of Small Business*, Chapter 1.

16. *The State of Small Business*, p. 271.

17. Ibid., p. 61.

18. Ibid., pp. 124–5.

19. Ibid., p. 229.

20. Ibid., p. 92.

21. Ibid.

22. *Future of Small Business in America*, Hearings Before the Subcommittee on Antitrust Consumers and Employment of the Committee on Small Business, House of Representatives (Washington, DC, US Government Printing Office, 1978), p. 39.

23. *The State of Small Business*, pp. 241–2.

24. For discussions of small-business failure and bankruptcy, see *The State of Small Business*, pp. 122–32, and Alvin D. Star and Michael Z. Massi, 'Survival Rates for Retailers', *Journal of Retailing* (Summer 1981).

25. *The State of Small Business*, p. 115.

26. O.J. Krasner and M.L. Dubrow, 'The Role of Small Business in Research and Development, Technological Change and Innovation in Region IX', in S.W. Hentzell (ed.), *The Environment for Small Business and Entrepreneurship in Region IX* (Menlo Park, California, SRI International for the SBA, 1979), p. 96.

27. Leonard E. Smollen and Molly Apple Levin, 'The Role of Small Business in Research Development, Technological Change and Innovation in Region I' in Jeffry A. Timmons (ed.), *A Region's Struggling Savior: Small Business in New England* (Walthma, Massachusetts, SBANE Foundation, for the SBA, 1979), p. 74.

28. Smollen and Levin, 'The role of Small Business', p. 75.

29. Krasner and Dubrow, 'Technological Change', p. 100.

30. Smollen and Levin, 'The Role of Small Business', pp. 75–9.

31. Samuel I. Doctors and Richard E. Wokutch, 'Impact of State and Local Policies' in Paul W. Houck (ed.), *The Status of Small Business in Region III* (University Park, Pennsylvania, the Pennsylvania Technical Assistance Program for the SBA, 1979), p. H-17.

32. Smollen and Levin, 'The Role of Small Business', p. 80.

33. 'Small Business Beset, Bothered and Beleaguered by Five Big Problems', *Business Week* (February 1980), pp. 23–6.

34. *The State of Small Business*, pp. 170–1.

35. Testimony in *Future of Small Business in America*, p. 221.

36. *NFIB Quarterly Economic Report for Small Business* (San Mateo, California, National Federation of Independent Business, Inc., January 1982), p. 8.

37. Ibid.

38. *NFIB Quarterly Report*, July 1981, p. 2.

39. Ibid., p. 2.

40. The increase in the Consumer Price Index was 12.6 per cent for the twelve-month period ending in November 1980, and 9.6 per cent for the twelve-month period ending in November 1981. *Federal Reserve Bulletin* (Washington, DC, Federal Reserve Board, January 1982).

41. *NFIB Quarterly Report*, January 1982, p. 5.

42. Ernest Walker and Lawrence D. Gale, 'A Two-Tiered Economy' in *The Regional Environment for Small Business and Entrepreneurship: A Profile of Region VI* (Dallas, Texas, Southern Methodist University for the SBA, 1979), p. 14.

43. Rajan Chandran, Don de Salvia and Allan Young, 'The Impact of Current Economic Forces on Small Business', *Journal of Small Business Management*, vol. 15, no. 1 (1977), p. 32.

44. Ibid., pp. 32–3.

45. Ibid.

46. *The State of Small Business*, p. 132.

47. The editors, *Business Week*, 30 June 1975, p. 99.

48. Ibid.

49. Dennis R. Leyden and James H. Thompson, 'Small Business Taxation in Region III: A Structural and Empirical Analysis' in Paul W. Houck (ed.), *The Status of Small Business in Region III* (University Park, Pennsylvania, The Pennsylvania Technical Assistance Program for the SBA, 1979), p. E-20.

50. K. Mark Weaver, 'Taxation of Small Business in Region IV' in William A. Haffer *et al.*, *The Environment for Small Business and Entrepreneurship in SBA Region IV* (Atlanta, Georgia, Chair of Private Enterprise Foundation, Inc. for the SBA, 1979), p. 237.

51. Ibid., p. 228.

52. Leyden and Thompson, 'Small Business Taxation', p. E-20.

53. Ibid.

54. Ibid., p. E-7.

55. Shirley W. Hentzell, 'The Environment for Small Business and

Entrepreneurship in U.S. Region IX' in S.W. Hentzell (ed.), *The Environment for Small Business and Entrepreneurship in Region IX* (Menlo Park, California, SRI International for the SBA, 1979), p. 3.

56. Chandran, de Salvia and Young, 'The Impact of Current Economic Forces', p. 34.

57. Alvin L. Puryear and Catherine P. Wiggins, 'The Impact of Federal Regulations on Small Business in New England' in Jeffry A. Timmons (ed.), *A Region's Struggling Savior: Small Business in New England* (Waltham, Massachusetts, SBANE Foundation, Inc. for the SBA, 1979), p. 246.

58. Walker and Gale, 'A Two-Tiered Economy', p. 19.

59. Edward B. Shils and William Zucker, 'The Impact of Federal Regulations' in Paul W. Houck (ed.), *The Status of Small Business in Region III* (University Park, Pennsylvania, The Pennsylvania Technical Assistance Program for the SBA, 1979), p. D-13.

60. 'Small Business Beset', *Business Week*, p. 26.

61. Shils and Zucker, 'The Impact of Federal Regulations', p. D-4 and Hentzell, 'The Environment for Small Business and Entrepreneurship in Region IX', p. 3.

62. Ibid., p. D-15.

63. Ibid.

64. *The State of Small Business*, p. 145.

65. *Future of Small Business in America*, p. 82.

66. Ibid., p. 37.

67. Ibid., p. 42.

68. David Bivin and William C. Dunkelberg, 'The Effects of the Shortage of Energy on Small Business in Region V' in Arnold C. Cooper and William C. Dunkelberg (eds.), *The Regional Environment for Small Business and Entrepreneurship, Region V*, (Milwaukee, Wisconsin, The Center for Venture Management for the SBA, 1979), p. 235.

69. Lobo and Osborne, 'The Impact of the Energy Situation, p. 83.

70. Ibid., p. 85.

71. Mary Jane Whistler and Henry Wichman, Jr., 'Providing Economic Opportunity to Small Business Minority Businesses', *Journal of Small Business Management*, vol. 17, no. 4 (1979), pp. 4–7.

72. Ibid., pp. 2–4.

73. Ibid., pp. 7–8.

74. Ibid., p. 7.

75. Ibid.

76. Ibid.

77. At Carnegie Mellon University, University of Utah, University of Oregon and Massachusetts Institute of Technology.

78. Robert H. Brockhaus, Sr., 'The Role of Small Business in Research and Development' in Bruce Kirchoff *et al.* (eds.), *The Regional Environment for Small Business and Entrepreneurship: Region VII* (Denver, Colorado, Denver Research Institute for the SBA, 1979), pp. 187ff.

79. Bonnie Goldstein, 'Abolish the SBA', *The Washington Monthly* (April 1979), p. 44. (See also 'The Small Business Administration: Still Under Siege', *Encore* (2 April 1979), and 'A Box Score on the Controversial SBA', *Business Week* (30 June 1975), p. 100.

80. Goldstein, 'Abolish the SBA', p. 46.

81. *Future of Small Business in America*, p. 198.

82. Matthew C. Sonfield, 'Can Student Consultants Really Help a Small Business?' *Journal of Small Business Management*, vol. 19, no. 4 (1981), p. 4.

83. Ibid.

84. J.C. Hafer and D.M. Ambrose, 'Fit or Misfit, Restructurintg SCORE for

Effectiveness in Managerial Assistance', *Journal of Small Business Management*, vol. 19, no. 4 (1981), pp. 15ff.

85. *Future of Small Business in America*, p. 54.

86. 'New Growth Industries – and Some Dropouts', *Business Week* (3 September 1979), p. 188.

87. David E. Gumpert, 'Future of Small Business May Be Brighter than Portrayed', *Harvard Business Review*, vol. 57, no. 4 (1979), pp. 164ff.

88. The seeming discrepancy between this statement and others as to recent trends in bankruptcies in the USA may be the result of the time period selected for analysis. 1960 and 1961, for example, were recession years with a comparatively large number of business failures.

89. Walker and Gale, 'A Two-Tiered Economy', pp. 8–9, 13.

90. Carter Henderson, 'What the Future Holds for Small Business', *Nation's Business*, vol. 64, no. 3 (1976), pp. 26–8.

3 JAPAN

3.1. Introduction

The debate over whether the small firm can survive and prosper has continued intermittently in the literature on economics since at least the time of Alfred Marshall. In recent years interest in the question has been rekindled in countries like the United States and the United Kingdom with the coming to power of governments with strongly-held beliefs in the ability of private enterprise to restore a lost dynamic to flagging economies. An aspect of this general faith is that small firms, freed largely from the restraining hand of over-bureaucratic state intervention would become the seed-bed of new ideas and new technologies and, in addition, would provide sources of new employment large enough to significantly ameliorate a growing economic and social problem.[1]

Some of these beliefs have undoubtedly been reinforced by an acquaintance – though generally a superficial one – with the Japanese economy. It is well known that the Japanese economy has performed better than those of all other advanced nations through the 1960s and 1970s, and that it has adapted with remarkable flexibility to the shortage of raw materials and their rising prices (particularly oil) which has taken place since the early 1970s. Many factors have been adduced to explain these successes, but the presence of a large and dynamic small firm sector figures, in one way or another, in most people's list. Whilst the main purpose of this chapter is to describe from a variety of angles the size of the small firm sector, how its fortunes have varied over the last two decades or so, and the problems it now faces, an additional important task will be to show how, through the relationship between the large firm and the small firm sector the Japanese economy is indeed given an important degree of flexibility it would otherwise lack.

3.2. Defining the Small Firm

The 'correct' way to define a small firm presents considerable problems. Whilst one has considerable sympathy with the 'economic' definition of the small firm produced in the Bolton Report, a definition based on what the committee regarded as the three essential characteristics of a small firm, two points need to be made with regard to it.[2] Firstly, in the end, the size limits chosen for use in the Report were dictated by the availability of statistics. Secondly, the third of the characteristics identified in the 'economic' definition given in the report (see note 2), namely the independence of the small firm from ownership and control of decision-making by a larger firm of which it forms a *de facto* part, presents particular problems in the Japanese context. As will be explained later in this chapter, subcontracting, which forms such a large proportion of the business of the majority of small firms in Japan, is frequently accompanied by ties based on ownership or part ownership of the small firm by its larger customer. Thus to stress the third of the Bolton characteristics in defining the small firm in Japan would be to exclude the majority of small firms from the discussion altogether. Instead, a strictly legal approach to defining the small firm has been followed, which has been pragmatically relaxed in cases of particular industries or particular problems where a different definition seems to be required.

The standard term used to describe small firms in Japan is *chūshō kigyō*, which in fact translates as small and medium-sized firms. Since the passage in 1963 of the Basic Law Relating to Small and Medium-sized Firms, firms belonging in the *chūshō kigyō* category do so according to strict and legally defined criteria.[3] These are two in number, and are based on the value of a firm's capital and the number of its employees. If either the value of a firm's capital or the number of its employees is less than the prescribed maximum, it legally qualifies as a small or medium-sized enterprise. Table 3.1 summarises the position.

However, there is in practice some variation in the definition adopted for certain specific purposes. For example, where legislation designed to produce certain forms of co-operation between firms is put into operation (such as that encouraging firms to locate together on industrial estates), small firms in the ceramics industry are defined as those with fewer than 900 employees, and not the 300 employees of the Basic Law of 1963. This is obviously a reasonable response to the fact that the average size of plants varies quite widely amongst industries. Again, where legislation designed to help with the financial problems of small (as opposed to medium-sized) firms is concerned, 'small' in manufacturing refers to firms with 20 or fewer employees, and to firms with 5 or fewer in the commerce and services sectors. This too is an eminently practical recognition of the fact that the financial problems besetting such firms may be quite different from those facing firms of a size enabling them to employ several hundreds of persons. Variations in the basic definition of a small firm will be discussed further in the section on the subject of government efforts to assist small firms.

Table 3.1: The Legal Definition of Small and Medium-sized Firms in Japan

Industrial category	Capital	Employees
Manufacturing and Mining	100 million yen or less	299 persons or fewer
Wholesaling	30 million yen or less	99 persons or fewer
Retaling: Services	10 million yen or less	49 persons or fewer

Note: Before the Basic Law of 1963 was revised in 1973, there was no separate category for wholesaling; it was included under Commerce and Services.

3.3 Trends in the Small Firm Sector

Next, let us try to throw some statistical light on the trend in the number of small firms in Japan, particularly over the last decade or so. It will be instructive at the same time to try to gain some idea of the proportion of all firms which enter the chūshō kigyō (small and medium-sized firm) category, and to see what contribution they make to total employment in Japan. It may also further later discussion if we can distinguish the very small from the not so small (that is, small from medium) within the chūshō kigyō definition of the Basic Law Relating to Small and Medium-sized Firms of 1963.

Table 3.2 shows the number of establishments, and Table 3.3 numbers employed therein by broad sectors of the economy (mining, manufacturing, building and construction, and so on), whilst Table 3.4 shows for the same broad sectors the number of establishments which meet the definition given earlier of what constitutes small and medium-sized firms (chūshō kigyō), on the sweeping but temporary assumption (later to be modified) that the firm and the establishment are one and the same thing. Table 3.5

Table 3.2: Number of Establishments by Sector

Sector	1963	1966	1969	1972	1975	1978
Mining	10,312	10,112	9,394	8,376	7,287	6,846
Building and Construction	245,074	294,707	347,579	409,518	447,772	495,603
Manufacturing	619,703	668,744	738,094	791,281	813,812	841,311
Wholesaling and Retailing	1,962,327	2,086,129	2,297,528	2,490,271	2,635,991	2,868,173
Finance and Insurance	55,570	58,223	58,639	61,812	66,617	75,660
Real Estate	81,581	115,601	129,083	154,117	177,327	214,089
Transport and Communications	100,865	109,364	111,370	120,509	131,665	141,966
Electricity, Gas, Water and Heating	12,103	13,165	13,793	12,303	11,653	11,088
Services	925,968	992,612	1,074,237	1,150,222	1,232,352	1,335,228
Total	4,013,503	4,348,657	4,779,717	5,198,409	5,524,476	5,989,964

Source: *Jigyōsho Tōkei Chōsa Hōkoku (Establishment Census of Japan, Vol. I, All Japan)*, 1963, 1966, 1969, 1972. 1975 and 1978 (Bureau of Statistics, Office of the Prime Minister).

Table 3.3: Number of Persons Employed by Sector

Sector	1963	1966	1969	1972	1975	1978
Mining	370,426	319,080	258,939	186,712	146,693	133,639
Building and Construction	2,423,218	2,978,740	3,365,074	4,024,595	4,220,915	4,638,059
Manufacturing	10,462,406	11,337,551	12,630,821	13,305,694	12,699,232	12,543,776
Wholesaling and Retailing	7,996,895	9,112,914	10,388,642	11,635,869	12,368,240	13,599,173
Finance and Insurance	963,341	1,173,409	1,253,749	1,410,780	1,521,584	1,645,082
Real Estate	184,986	261,972	312,856	402,205	468,719	531,163
Transport and Communications	2,494,190	2,765,888	2,982,069	3,107,316	3,132,837	3,256,430
Electricity, Gas, Water and Heating	234,660	250,804	265,245	274,512	303,671	311,181
Services	4,910,062	5,923,130	6,719,631	7,539,405	8,295,980	9,275,083
Total	30,040,184	34,123,488	38,177,026	41,887,088	43,157,871	45,933,586

Source: *Jigyōsho Tōkei Chōsa Hōkoku* (*Establishment Census of Japan, Vol. I, All Japan*), 1963, 1966, 1969, 1972, 1975 and 1978 (Bureau of Statistics, Office of the Prime Minister).

gives the number and proportion of workers in small and medium-sized firms in these same sectors, and also the number and proportion of those employed in *small* firms as defined (see note b to Table 3.4).

Table 3.4 clearly shows that in all sectors of the economy the overwhelming proportion of establishments are small or medium-sized according to the definition of the 1963 Basic Law. In addition, it shows that, with the exception of the utilities sector (gas, electricity, water supply, and so on), transport and communications, finance and insurance and wholesaling, the large majority of establishments are very small. That is, they employ 19 or fewer people in mining, building and construction and manufacturing, and 4 or fewer people in the six other broad sectors identified. Even in these four sectors well over one-third of establishments are small as defined above.

Turning to Table 3.5 we observe the same broad pattern with reference to the numbers employed in small and medium-sized establishments. Whilst the proportion of employees working for small and medium-sized establishments in utilities, transport and communications, and finance and insurance is substantially lower than the other seven sectors, even here around one-third to one-half of all workers are employed in small or medium-sized establishments as legally defined. In the other sectors of the economy the proportion is two-thirds or more. It is clear that in the sectors which are the large employers of labour, namely building and construction, manufacturing, the retail and wholesale sectors and in services, the small establishment is where the overwhelming majority of workers are likely to find employment.

However, the establishment and the firm are not necessarily one and the same thing, and it is necessary to distinguish between the two. This is not altogether a straightforward statistical task, as the plenitude of data on establishments is not matched by that on multi-establishment firms. Clearly firms with more than one establishment may belong in the large firm category even though each of their individual establishments is small or medium-sized according to the definition used up to now. Such firms are unlikely to experience the problems of the genuine small firm to the same degree, in particular perhaps the acute problem of finance for new investment and the characteristic Japanese problem of attracting a skilled workforce. (In Japan most recruits to a firm come from the current cohort of school or university graduates. The pick of these

Table 3.4: Number of Establishments in the Small and
Medium-Size Category (*Chūshō Kigyō*)

		Number of Establishments	Per cent[a]	Number of Establishments	Per cent[b]
(i)	Mining				
	1963	10,090	97.8	8,143	79.0
	1966[f]	9,955	98.4	7,956	78.7
	1969[e]	9,278	98.8	8,188	87.2
	1972[d]	8,305	99.2	6,673	79.7
	1978	6,811	99.5	5,584	81.6
(ii)	Building and Construction				
	1963	244,468	99.8	219,847	89.7
	1966	296,055	99.8	263,367	88.8
	1969	346,909	99.8	325,777	93.7
	1972	409,520	99.8	367,984	89.7
	1978	495,123	99.9	447,192	90.2
	1981[g]	550,044	99.9		
(iii)	Manufacturing				
	1963	616,025	99.4	531,592	85.8
	1966	664,804	99.4	572,152	85.6
	1969	733,538	99.4	670,764	90.9
	1972	788,619	99.4	684,231	86.2
	1978	837,222	99.5	733,874	87.2
	1981[g]	868,334	99.5		
(iv)	Wholesaling[c]				
	1963	294,109	99.3	155,158	52.4
	1966	325,726	99.3	160,941	49.0
	1969	322,304	99.2	159,210	49.0
	1972	358,041	99.1	174,410	48.3
	1978	418,890	99.3	201,950	47.9
(v)	Retailing				
	1963	1,662,558	99.8	1,454,341	87.3
	1966	1,753,353	99.8	1,502,889	85.5
	1969	1,966,085	99.7	1,656,588	84.0
	1972	2,148,601	99.7	1,803,320	83.6
	1978	2,437,053	99.6	1,995,855	81.6
(vi)	Finance and Insurance				
	1963	51,735	93.1	26,813	48.3
	1966	53,422	91.8	25,450	43.7
	1969	53,548	91.3	23,719	40.4
	1972	55,898	90.4	23,104	37.4
	1978	69,209	91.5	29,340	38.8
(vii)	Real Estate				
	1963	81,336	99.7	76,664	94.0
	1966	109,464	99.7	102,667	93.5
	1969	128,656	99.7	119,386	92.5
	1972	153,398	99.6	139,851	90.8
	1978	213,551	99.7	194,202	90.7

(viii)	Transport and Communications				
	1963	90,435	89.7	45,766	45.4
	1966	98,216	89.3	48,308	43.9
	1969	98,846	88.8	46,209	41.5
	1972	85,795	90.1	42,762	44.9
	1978	128,313	90.4	63,214	44.5
(ix)	Electricity, Gas, Water and Heating Supply				
	1963	11,170	92.3	6,925	57.2
	1966	12,179	92.5	7,652	58.1
	1969	12,729	92.3	7,858	57.0
	1972	5,610	88.0	3,482	54.6
	1978	9,710	87.6	4,322	39.0
(x)	Services				
	1963	915,234	98.8	718,259	77.6
	1966	985,454	98.6	753,773	75.4
	1969	1,056,336	98.3	800,888	74.6
	1972	1,053,880	98.8	833,475	78.1
	1978	1,308,641	98.0	962,088	72.1
	1981[g]	1,334,709	98.5		

Notes: a. The figures in this column give the percentages of all establishments which fall legally into the small and medium-sized enterprise category as defined in the Basic Law Relating to Small and Medium-sized Firms (*Chūshō Kigyō Kihonhō*) of 1963. The assumption that the firm and the establishment are one and the same is still, for the moment, in operation.

b. The figures in this column give the percentages of all establishments which can be defined as *small*, as opposed to medium-sized. For simplicity, the definition used is that in the Basic Law Relating to Small and Medium-sized Firms, and also in other legislation governing small firms, e.g. The Small Firm Mutual Aid Law (*Shōkibo Kigyō Kyōsaihō*). In Mining and Manufacturing, Building and Construction, the small firm is defined as having fewer than 20 employees; in all other industries (wholesaling, retailing, etc.) as having fewer than five employees. However, see note e to this table.

c. Wholesaling also includes agencies and brokers.

d. In 1972 there occurs a slight discrepancy between the total number of establishments and total persons engaged given in Table 6 of *The Establishment Census of Japan*, which gives the size breakdown of establishments and which is used to calculate the percentages in Table 3.4 and Table 3.5 and the total number of establishments given in Table 3.2, and total persons engaged given in Table 3.3. The figures in Tables 3.2 and 3.3 are taken from Table 1 in *The Establishment Census*. This discrepancy does not occur in the Censuses for other years.

e. Unlike every other year covered by *The Establishment Census for Japan*, the 1969 census fails to distinguish the size category 10–19 persons, using only the size category 10–29 persons. For this reason, I have classified the small firm for 1969 only as employing 29 or fewer workers in the Mining, Manufacturing and Building and Construction sectors. In all other sectors the small firm remains as defined in note b to this table.

f. The total number of establishments used to calculate the figures for 1966 in this Table is 4,352,137 which differs slightly from the total of 4,348,657 of Table 3.2. The latter is a revised figure, the revision being confined to the categories of Building and Construction, Wholesaling and Retailing, Real

Estate, Transport and Communication and Services. Since a breakdown by
size category of establishment was only possible for the former, unrevised
figures, these were used for 1966.

  g. The data for 1981 are abstracted from A. Nishikiori 'Drawing up a Public
Policy of Support for Small Business', paper presented at International
Congress on Small Business, Torremolinos, Spain, Oct 23–26, 1982.

Source: *Jigyōsho Tōkei Chōsa Hōkoku (Establishment Census of Japan)*,
Bureau of Statistics, Office of the Prime Minister, Tokyo, 1963, 1966, 1969,
1972, 1975 and 1978.

are attracted by the larger firms who are able to offer higher wages
and better conditions of employment, often in the form of bonuses
and fringe benefits such as health care and company leisure
facilities.)

Fortunately, in practice much of the firm/establishment problem
disappears on closer examination. We find that in 1978, of the
5,849,321 privately owned establishments in the ten sectors of
industry identified in Table 3.4, 4,864,048 or 83.2 percent are
single-establishment enterprises. Moreover, the single-establishment enterprise (firm) is found almost exclusively in the
small and medium-sized firm category as defined above. Thus we
can conclude, with very little damage to the truth, that the figures
for small establishments given in Table 3.4 very accurately reflect
the numbers of small firms, since the terms firm and establishment
can almost be used synonymously in the small firm sector of
industry. For the same reason, the figures given in Table 3.5 for
numbers engaged in small and medium-sized establishments are an
equally accurate guide to the numbers who work in small and
medium-sized firms.

These conclusions can be demonstrated for some important
sectors of the economy in 1978, which is the latest year for which
comprehensive figures are available to the author. The paper by
Nishikiori, cited in Footnote g in Tables 3.4 and 3.5 does, however,
provide some data for 1981. Of the 841,132 private establishments
in manufacturing industry, 496,436 or 59 percent were individual
proprietorships, defined in Japan as unincorporated enterprises
managed by an individual on his own account. Since there are
recorded only 489,978 individual proprietors, a small minority
obviously manage more than one establishment, but most are
single-establishment firms. All of the 496,436 establishments
employ fewer than 300 workers. Only 4 establishments employ
between 200 and 299 persons, whilst most (375,369 or 75.6 per cent)
establishments employ between 1 and 4 persons. Therefore, very

few individual proprietorships can realistically be thought to belong outside the small or medium-sized category, although it is just possible that a few may, by owning more than one establishment.

Most of the remaining establishments in maufacturing (339,253 out of 344,696) belong to companies (*kaisha*), which include joint stock companies (*kabushiki kaisha*), limited companies (*yūgen kaisha*), limited partnerships (*gōmei kaisha*), unlimited partnerships (*gōshi kaisha*), mutual companies (*sōgo kaisha*) and foreign companies. The remainder are corporations other than companies (for example, registered religions, schools, foundations and so on), and unincorporated associations. Of the 269,591 companies recorded in the *Establishment Census for Japan 1978*, 216,681 or 81.6 per cent were single-establishment companies, whilst the remaining 52,910 were multi-establishment companies. Of the 216,681 single-establishment companies in the manufacturing sector, only 292 employed more than 300 persons and therefore fail legally to qualify as small or medium-sized firms, whilst 181,330 or 83.7 per cent employed 19 or fewer people and enter the small firm category as previously identified. Therefore it is clear that in the incorporated sector, too, the overwhelming majority of firms are small or very small, single-establishment organisations.

In the building and construction industry there were 495,345 private establishments in 1978, of which 325,099 were individual proprietorships run by 324,040 proprietors. None of the establishments employed more than 299 persons, although it is possible that a few firms fell outside the small and medium-size category by dint of consisting of more than one establishment. Of these establishments, 319,977 (98.4 per cent) employed 19 or fewer persons.

Of the remaining 170,246 establishments in this industry, 169,559 belong to companies of one form or another. There were 134,493 companies recorded in 1978 in the *Establishment Census*, and of these 113,534 (84.4 per cent) were single-establishment companies. 100,338 of these single establishment companies (88.4 per cent) employed 19 or fewer workers. The very small, single-establishment firm clearly predominates in the building and construction industry too.

Turning next to the retail sector which employed over nine and a half million people in 1978, of the 2,444,448 establishments recorded in the Census, 1,953,313 were individual proprietorships

Table 3.5: Persons Engaged in Small and Medium-Sized
Establishments by Sector

		Numbers engaged[a]	Per cent[b]	Numbers engaged	Per cent[c]
(i)	Mining				
	1963	160,842	60.4	46,243	12.5
	1966[f]	158,251	49.6	47,813	15.0
	1969[e]	138,959	53.7	63,794	24.6
	1972	118,518	63.5	42,951	23.0
	1978	80,721	60.4	40,622	30.4
(ii)	Building and Construction				
	1963	2,066,606	85.3	789,135	32.6
	1966	2,699,256	88.2	1,035,036	33.8
	1969	2,984,495	88.7	1,601,113	47.6
	1972	3,594,206	90.3	1,606,444	40.4
	1978	4,359,090	94.0	2,258,812	48.7
	1981[g]	4,714,338	95.3		
(iii)	Manufacturing				
	1963	7,254,735	69.3	2,753,816	26.3
	1966	7,966,334	70.3	3,034,065	26.8
	1969	8,686,384	68.8	4,191,962	33.2
	1972	8,049,635	60.5	3,503,082	26.3
	1978	9,200,377	73.3	3,760,360	30.0
	1981[g]	9,551,914	74.3		
(iv)	Wholesaling[d]				
	1963	2,277,266	84.7	358,958	13.4
	1966	2,681,560	84.5	384,136	12.1
	1969	2,696,966	82.9	383,886	11.8
	1972	3,050,264	81.1	429,488	11.4
	1978	3,461,721	85.4	517,947	12.8
(v)	Retailing				
	1963	4,833,433	91.0	2,931,969	55.2
	1966	5,327,528	89.7	3,012,137	50.7
	1969	6,334,175	88.8	3,434,456	48.2
	1972	7,005,774	88.3	3,767,092	47.5
	1978	8,442,435	88.4	4,292,511	45.0
(vi)	Finance and Insurance				
	1963	491,988	51.1	53,730	5.6
	1966	577,037	49.2	51,499	4.4
	1969	623,865	49.8	47,627	3.8
	1972	686,212	49.2	47,434	3.4
	1978	822,952	50.0	63,377	3.9
(vii)	Real Estate				
	1963	157,162	85.0	107,600	58.2
	1966	213,727	83.9	139,937	54.9
	1969	260,899	83.4	163,671	52.3
	1972	332,510	83.1	195,746	48.9
	1978	472,380	88.9	287,388	54.1

(viii)	Transport and Communications			
	1963	791,028	31.7	100,164	4.0
	1966	888,990	31.7	104,685	3.7
	1969	954,140	32.0	98,584	3.3
	1972	797,811	39.0	77,837	3.8
	1978	1,173,137	36.0	126,437	3.9
(ix)	Electricity, Gas, Water and Heating Supply			
	1963	73,642	31.4	13,600	5.8
	1966	80,262	32.0	15,122	6.0
	1969	86,286	32.5	15,086	5.7
	1972	39,762	21.6	6,818	3.7
	1978	92,082	29.6	9,265	3.0
(x)	Services			
	1963	3,711,550	75.6	1,359,745	27.0
	1966	4,220,472	72.6	1,454,027	25.0
	1969	4,659,658	69.4	1,566,106	23.3
	1972	4,039,149	71.9	1,599,279	28.5
	1978	6,122,640	66.0	1,850,970	20.0
	1981[g]	5,579,852	69.2		

Notes: a. The total of persons engaged includes family workers and temporary workers engaged at the date of the census, as well as permanent employees, owner proprietors, etc.

b. As in Table 3.4, the figures in this column are the proportions (percentages) of people engaged in small and medium-sized firms as defined by the Basic Law Relating to Small and Medium-sized Firms (*Chūshō Kigyō Kihonhō*) or 1963. See Table 3.1.

c. As in Table 3.4, the figures in this column are the proportions (percentages) of people engaged in *small* firms as defined in the Basic Law, as well as in other legislation relating to the small firm.

d. Including agencies and brokers.

e. Unlike every other year covered by *The Establishment Census for Japan*, the 1969 census fails to distinguish the size category 10–19 persons, distinguishing only the size category 10–29 persons. For this reason, I have classified the *small* firm for 1969 as employing 29 or fewer workers in the Mining, Manufacturing and Building and Construction sectors. In all other sectors the small firm remains as defined in note b. to Table 3.4.

f. The total number of persons engaged to calculate the figures for 1966 in this Table is 34,128,490, as opposed to the figure of 34,123,488 in Table 3.3. The latter is a revised figure, the revision being confined to the categories: Building and Construction, Wholesaling and Retailing, Real Estate, Transport and Communications and Services. Since a breakdown by size category of establishment was only possible for the former, unrevised figures, these were used for 1966.

g. The data for 1981 are abstracted from A. Nishikiori 'Drawing up a Public Policy of Support for Small Business', paper presented at International Congress on Small Business, Torremolinos, Spain, Oct 23–26, 1982.

run by 1,906,486 proprietors. Only 896 of these establishments employed more than 50 workers, whilst most – 1,770,936 or 90.7 per cent – employed 4 or fewer people. Most of the remaining establishments (473,086 out of 491,135) belonged to companies, and of the 230,530 companies registered in retailing, 180,941 were single-establishment enterprises. Whilst 392 of these employed

Table 3.6: Bankruptcies Amongst Small and Medium-Sized Firms, 1971–80

Year	(A) Total bankruptcies	(B) Bankruptcies amongst small and medium-sized firms	(B)/(A) Per cent
1971	9,206	9,147	99.4
1972	7,139	7,101	99.5
1973	8,202	8,159	99.5
1974	11,681	11,586	99.2
1975	12,606	12,544	99.5
1976	15,641	15,577	99.6
1977	18,471	18,404	99.6
1978	15,875	15,825	99.7
1979	16,030	16,003	99.8
1980	17,884	17,842	99.8

Notes: a. Figures for bankruptcies amongst small firms from 1975 onwards are given in *Chūshō Kigyō Hakusho, 1981* (The 1981 White Paper on Small and Medium-Sized Enterprises), The Small and Medium-sized Enterprise Agency (ed.), Attached Statistical Materials, p. 38. For 1971–4 figures were not published in this form, but figures were available in earlier White Papers for bankruptcies by size-category of firm using the value of the firm's capital to determine its size-category. All firms with capital of 50 million yen or less have been placed into the small and medium-sized category, although firms with capital up to 100 million yen or less are defined as small or medium-sized in the manufacturing and mining industries. Since the White Paper does not distinguish firms at the larger end of the small and medium-sized range in its bankruptcy figures, identifying only the size-category 50 million yen or more, this means it was not possible to isolate the small number of firms becoming bankrupt in those years whose capital was between 50 million and 100 million yen. Thus, figures and proportions for 1974 and earlier do not strictly compare with those from 1975 onwards, although the discrepancy is very slight since the number of firms involved is very small.
    b. The figures cover only legally incorporated firms.
Source: Small and Medium-sized Enterprise Agency (ed.,), *Chūshō Kigyō Hakusho* (White Paper on Small and Medium-sized Enterprises) 1979, 1980 and 1981, Attached Statistical Materials Section.

more than 50 people, a large majority were very small, employing 4 or fewer people (141,200 or 78.0 per cent).

Taking one last example, the services sector as identified in Tables 3.4 and 3.5 which employed 6,957,608 people in 1978, shows the same overall pattern. 858,693 or 69.7 per cent of all establishments were individual proprietorships run by 841,632 proprietors. Of these establishments, 934 employed 50 or more people, but 733,078 (85.4 per cent) employed 4 or fewer. Of the remaining 373,015 establishments only 181,794 belonged to companies, a rather smaller proportion than in the other sectors examined. However, the single-unit enterprise continued to predominate since 123,926 (80.8 per cent) were single-establishment companies. Some of these were large by service sector standards since 1,674 of them employed 50 or more workers, but most were small, with 67,808 (54.7 per cent) being very small, employing 4 or fewer people.

Table 3.4 enables certain broad conclusions to be drawn about how the numbers of small firms and the proportion of the total of all firms that they represent have changed since the early 1960s. Table 3.5 permits equally broad observations to be made about numbers employed in the small and medium-sized firm sector (and the small firm sector), as well as the proportion of all employees who obtain their livelihood in this sector.

Firstly, it is clear that in most of the ten broad sectors of the economy identified in Tables 3.4 and 3.5, the number of small firms has increased markedly during the period of 15 years covered, whilst the proportion of small and medium-sized firms amongst all firms has changed little in most of these sectors. This is not unexpected in an economy which, over most of the period, grew very rapidly by international standards, and where entry for the small firm is not economically (or administratively) difficult. It is true that in many sectors of manufacturing, as well as in wholesaling and other industries, high degrees of concentration were reached in the 1960s according to the standard three, six or ten firm measures of concentration.[4] Nevertheless, a relatively small proportion of a constantly *growing* market was always shared amongst a very large number of small and medium-sized firms. This situation clearly persisted through the 1970s. As can be seen from Table 3.4 an exceptional industry is mining, where geological and technical difficulties, together with a centrally-made decision to plump for imported oil as Japan's major source of industrial energy, led to a marked contraction in the hitherto quite large coalmining industry which bulked very large in the mining industry as a whole. Thus the number of firms contracted markedly, although the proportion of workers engaged in small mining firms rose.

Another exception to the general rule is the utilities sector, where the numbers of small firms declined and where they also accounted for a diminishing proportion of total employment in the sector. This is chiefly explained by the massive construction programme of new types of dwelling, mainly large complexes of high-rise flats, whose methods of heating in particular marked a radical departure from those traditionally employed in Japanese houses, and whose needs are best serviced by the large, semi-public utilities companies.

Why is it that small and medium-sized firms have been able to survive and even to increase their numbers in most sectors so as to defend their proportional position amongst all firms? And how have they been able in key sectors of the economy such as manufacturing secularly to increase their share of total employment? These questions are particuarly apposite when it is remembered that small-scale industry spread widely through an economy has often been taken as an indication of economic backwardness. A complete treatment of this dual structure of the Japanese economy must be sought elsewhere, although a part of the answer may be found later in this chapter in the section on the relationship – particularly the subcontracting relationship – between large and small firms.[5] However, at this point it would seem helpful to explain briefly and in simplified form the dual nature of the labour market in Japan.

On the supply side of the labour market most workers in Japan want secure employment contracts (or an equivalent unwritten promise since written contracts are rare in Japanese industry), wages or salaries which fluctuate little and whose trend is upward in real terms, security of tenure and fringe benefits which range from recreation facilities through company-provided housing to medical services and pensions which are underprovided by the state. These benefits are usually only provided by the large firm (in the case of the fortunate minority of workers in some, but not all, large firms, security of tenure is absolute – lifetime employment – and promotion, and hence remuneration, depends solely on seniority). It is clear from Table 3.5 that with one or two exceptions (transport and communications and the utilities, for example) the majority of workers find employment in the small firm sector where few of the above advantages can be expected. In the small firm sector total remuneration (including fringe benefits) is lower, job security less and inter-firm mobility higher.

On the demand side of the labour market, large firms traditionally recruit almost exclusively from the ranks of new high-school and university graduates, and to a very limited extent from middle-school graduates, which is the point at which compulsory education ends. They take the cream of each successive cohort, whilst small firms find themselves in competition for the rest. Until 1973 and the first oil crisis, Japan's economy had grown rapidly and almost continuously for nearly a decade and a half, led by growth in the output of large manufacturing firms. As a result of this there arose a comparative shortage of labour which manifested itself in a rise in the proportion of workers engaged in the large firm sector and a fall in the proportion employed in small and medium-sized firms, which Table 3.5 shows to have occurred between 1969 and 1972. Another manifestation was a diminution in the wage differential between small and large firms, in manufacturing in particular, as small firms found they had to compete harder for workers. The slowing down of migration out of rural areas into urban/industrial areas because of the by-now much depleted agricultural labour force, together with the effects of a birth rate which had fallen rapidly after the early postwar rise, compounded the problem of comparative labour shortage.

However, growth almost ceased in the years immediately after the oil crisis of 1973, and resumed at a much slower pace in 1976. Large firms found themselves facing the need to reduce costs, particularly energy costs and labour costs which often had features not unlike fixed costs because of the lifetime employment system and its associated features. Therefore, after 1973, they embarked on a programme of 'rationalisation', which involved a lower rate of new recruitment and attempts to transfer workers to subsidiary or affiliated companies which were often located in the small and medium-sized firm sector. At the same time small firms often found it easier to reduce energy costs and thus remain viable, whilst the new technology of the 1970s was eagerly adapted to the needs of smaller firms. Thus, despite slower growth in the gross national product, small firms increased in number in the manufacturing sector and elsewhere, and also increased the proportion of all workers they employed. Table 3.5 shows that these trends continued between 1978 and 1981. In this they were helped as large manufacturing firms found it increasingly advantageous to subcontract to them those parts of the production process where the extra flexibility of the small firms, both technical and managerial, enabled costs of production to be lowered. Thus the continued large size of the small firm sector is not to be equated with backwardness; rather the explanation is to be found in Japan's somewhat unusual 'dual' industrial structure and in the peculiarities of its labour market.

The above sections have demonstrated the dominance of the small firm in the Japanese economy, in terms of both employment and numbers of enterprises. These facts may contrast with the casual observer's view of the Japanese economy, whose impressions are formed from Japan's export performance where large manufacturing firms figure very prominently. But the fact is that the small firm is responsible for much of Japan's production of goods and services, and the large majority of workers are employed in small firms, in contrast with the economy of the United Kingdom for example.[6] It is the very size and importance of the small firm sector which accounts for the longer history and deeper concern shown for it amongst social scientists as well as economic bureaucrats and politicians in Japan. The health of the small firm sector has, in a variety of ways, a very great deal to do with the

Table 3.7: Bankruptcy Rates by Sector of Industry, 1975–80

Year	Building and Construction	Manufacturing	Commerce	Services etc.	All Industry
1975	2.14	0.72	1.03	0.66	0.98
1976	2.88	0.93	1.16	0.61	1.16
1977	3.08	1.12	1.39	0.60	1.31
1978	2.36	0.94	1.15	0.50	1.07
1979	2.23	0.86	1.21	0.46	1.04
1980	2.31	0.91	1.31	0.52	1.11

Notes: a. The bankruptcy rate is calculated by:

$$\text{bankruptcy rate} = \frac{\text{Number of bankrupted firms}}{\text{Total of all firms}} \times 100$$

b. The figures cover only legally incorporated firms.

Source: Small and Medium-sized Enterprise Agency (ed.), *Chūshō Kigyō Hakusho* (White Paper on Small and Medium-sized Enterprises), 1981, Attached Statistical Material, p. 38.

health of the domestic economy as a whole, and difficulties in the small firm sector can assume the dimensions of a major economic as well as a social problem.

Against this background let us now look at some of the problems which face the small firm in Japan, examine the reaction of the small firm sector, and also the response of the government.

3.4 Problems of the Small Firm

A. Sub-contracting

Whilst the collapse of a large firm which is a household name in Japan is a rare but not unheard of event, and whilst a number of firms which are too large to be defined as small or medium-sized do go bankrupt each year, to a very large degree bankruptcy is the province of the small and medium-sized firm. Table 3.6 gives figures for bankruptcies over the last decade for legally incorporated firms only and the proportion of bankruptcies occurring amongst small and medium-sized firms. Table 3.7 provides a sectoral break-down of bankruptcies. Throughout the last decade, bankruptcies amongst small and medium-sized firms never accounted for less than 99 per cent of total bankruptcies. Small and medium-sized firms accounted for a somewhat smaller proportion of the debts involved, but this proportion rose from around three-quarters in 1975 to nearly 92 per cent in 1980, averaging about 84 per cent over this period.

Tables 3.6 and 3.7 cover only incorporated firms, whilst data on the collapse of firms in the vast individual proprietor sector are very difficult to obtain. However, numbers are commonly acknowledged to be very high, and there is no reason to suppose that trends in total collapses in this sector have not followed those discernible in Table 3.6 or that the degree of riskiness in each of the broad sectors identified in Table 3.7 does not apply amongst individual proprietorships.[7] From Table 3.7 it can be seen that whilst in the economy as a whole the chances of a firm going bankrupt have been a little more than one in a hundred over the period 1975–80, there are significant sectoral variations, with firms in the building and construction sector facing the highest degree of risk and firms in services the lowest. The 1980 White Paper on Small and Medium-sized Enterprises also reveals that bankruptcies were particularly common amongst firms engaged in or connected with the production and sale of textiles, both fibres and cloth. In 1972 there were 569 bankruptcies in this area of industry, rising to 1,388 in 1979. Textiles is, of course, an industry which has suffered particularly badly from foreign competition, notably from the developing countries of South East Asia, such as Taiwan, South Korea and Hong Kong.

The production and sale of metals and machinery has also been a peculiarly risky area in the last decade, with bankruptcies rising from 1,858 cases in 1972 to 2,988 in 1979. Here the causes may be sought amongst factors such as rising energy costs, since Japan relies almost entirely on high-cost imported oil, and the coming of new technologies based on the micro-chip, as well as the forces of foreign competition.

It is clear that the number of business failures has greatly increased in the last decade or so, and that the basic causes for this are to be found in the process of adjustment to slower rates of economic growth which began in 1971 with President Nixon's measures to curb Japanese exports to the United States. The first of the oil crises in late 1973 signalled the end of the period of cheap raw materials, the sudden increase in the price of oil being of particular significance to Japan whose indigenous energy resources are small and whose reliance on imported oil is consequently very high. The process of adjustment in the mid-1970s was followed by renewal of economic growth, but the second oil crisis of 1978–9 has meant that conditions on the cost side continue to be very difficult, whilst at the same time the onset of world depression has meant firms have also been faced with difficult market conditions of falling or stagnant demand.

However, whilst the above considerations are generally taken to explain the increase in the number of failures in the last decade, they do not explain why failures are almost wholly confined to the small and medium-sized firm sector, and why they have run at a high rate throughout Japan's postwar history. To discover the causes of this phenomenon we should need to examine the structure and operation of large-scale industry in detail, a task which is beyond the scope of this chapter. Instead, what we can do is examine in a little more detail some of the factors which have traditionally made life difficult for the smaller entrepreneur.

The first of these factors concerns subcontracting amongst small and medium-sized firms and the problems which the subcontracting relationship has traditionally posed.

It is not easy accurately to gauge the extent of subcontracting in Japan.[8] It is generally accepted to be very widespread, and on occasions to involve several layers of subcontracting with sub-contractors themselves subcontracting out work. The peculiar problems it poses are of sufficient gravity to involve government intervention at the legislative and other levels, in order to work for their amelioration.

It is possible to gain some idea of the extent of subcontracting from the *Establishment Census*. The 1978 Census divides the production activities of establishments into three categories. These are, firstly: those producing 'mainly according to estimated production' (*omo ni mikomi seisan*). That is to say, firms utilising their current capacity to produce at the rate which they estimate the market will bear at or near the current price, but at least in part in advance of specific orders for that output. Secondly, the census distinguishes those establishments which produce 'mainly according to orders from others' (*omo ni juchū seisan*). That is to say, firms which have rather more safely guaranteed outlets for the products they are currently producing. Lastly, the census distinguishes firms which mainly 'process raw materials supplied by others' (*omo ni shikyū genzairyō de kakō*). It is of course in this last category of firm that most, though perhaps not all, subcontracting firms will be found. Therefore it may be worth while to attempt to describe, with the aid of statistics, some of the salient features of this sector, confining ourselves in the first instance to manufacturing industry only.

It is clear from Table 3.8 that even using the narrowest definition of subcontracting – that is, where the material for processing is supplied to the subcontractor and the completed produce returned to the firm placing the order – that it is a widespread practice throughout manufacturing industry. Moreover, in the table only the broad, two-digit classification of industries has been used. Had the narrower, three-digit definition been used it would have been possible to locate more exactly those areas where subcontracting was commonest. For example, under transportation equipment (JSIC No. 36) the proportion of subcontracting establishments is higher in the bicycle and bicycle parts industry (JSIC No. 363) at 49.5 per cent of all establishments, than in the shipbuilding, repairing and marine engines industry (JSIC 364) where the proportion of subcontracting establishments is 21.3 per cent. Had it been possible to go to the four-digit level (as it unfortunately is not

Table 3.8: Subcontracting in Various Sectors of Manufacturing Industry, 1978

	A Total establishments	B Total workers engaged	C Subcontracting establishments	D Numbers engaged therein	C/A%	D/B%
All manufacturing	841,132	12,509,106	310,111	1,999,890	36.9	16.0
20[a] Textiles (excluding Clothing and other Finished Products)	122,537	979,815	90,435	407,897	73.8	41.6
21. Clothing and other finished textile products	59,636	694,392	38,207	329,162	64.1	47.4
31. Iron and steel	8,995	477,866	2,543	38,483	28.3	8.1
32. Non-ferrous metals and Products	6,460	202,336	1,676	19,812	25.9	9.8
33. Fabricated metal products	106,717	1,035,624	46,328	261,765	43.4	25.3
34. Industrial machinery (except Electrical)	64,485	1,102,317	23,270	120,948	36.1	11.0
35. Electrical machinery and equipment	35,442	1,366,179	13,913	203,306	39.3	14.9
36. Transportation equipment	23,913	1,013,137	10,624	101,066	44.4	10.0
37. Precision machinery	14,481	318,613	5,478	47,937	37.8	15.0
26. Chemicals	8,493	537,276	739	13,569	8.7	2.5

Notes: a. Figures in this column refer to the two-digit industry number of the Japan Standard Industrial Classification (JSIC), adopted in 1967.

Source: *Jigyōsho Tōkei Chōsa Hōkoku* (Establishment Census of Japan, 1978), vol. 1, Results for Japan, Bureau of Statistics, Office of the Prime Minister, Tokyo, Table 20.

using the Establishment Census) and separate, for example, the large motor vehicle assemblers from the motor vehicle parts makers, then it is likely that an even larger proportion of subcontracting would have been isolated in certain specific areas of industry.

However, it should already be apparent from Table 3.8 that most subcontracting firms are small. In fact of the 310,111 manufacturing establishments recorded as relying mainly on subcontracting work, only 133 employed 300 or more people and therefore fall outside the *chūshō kigyō* category. Moreover, 210,701 of these establishments (67.9 per cent of the total) employed four or fewer people. In terms of ownership, 239,401 of all subcontracting establishments, employing 799,563 people, were individual proprietorships, whilst 69,032 establishments belonged to companies, and were on the average larger in size, employing 1,176,741 people. Nevertheless, all but 132 of these establishments employed 299 or fewer people. Since, as we have seen earlier, the terms 'firm' and 'establishment' can be used more or less synonymously for small organisations, whether they be in the form of individual proprietorships or whether they take on company form, it is evident that the small, single-establishment firm dominates the subcontracting sector of industry. Furthermore, the lower the layer of subcontracting that is uncovered the smaller will be the firm found operating there.

The time has come to ask the question: in what ways does this widespread network of subcontracting affect the health of the small firm sector of Japanese industry? The answer in general is that it presents a situation where the potential for exploitation of the small by the larger is great and is frequently exercised. From the time when the Japanese Government regained control over the economy in the early 1950s it pursued an industrial policy which, with the aim of rapid reconstruction, granted special privileges to large firms in heavy industries such as shipbuilding, iron and steel, electrical power, chemicals and so on. This policy was continued through the 1950s and into the 1960s, whilst rapid economic growth founded on this platform led to the growth of a large domestic market for manufactured consumer goods. In the new, mass-production technology area of this market, such as cars and household electrical goods, large-scale consumer goods firms achieved positions of dominance. Without equal access to imported technology which was selectively apportioned through the agency of the government, and without the resources to develop new technology of its own; without equal access to foreign sources of raw materials and largely excluded from the chief sources of finance for investment which were selectively controlled by the major financial institutions in favour of large firms, it is little wonder that a wide gap opened between large and small firms which has proved very difficult to bridge.

The gap manifested itself in the form of wide differentials in productivity and wages between large and small firms. The differences in productivity reflected capital scarcity and hence differing capital intensities between 'modern' and 'traditional' (largely synonymous with large and small) sectors of industry. There also developed in Japan a set of labour market institutions which served to reinforce differentials in wages founded originally on productivity differentials. These were the arrangements, found only in large firms, whereby employment was granted for life to an élite core of workers, and whereby promotion and payment was based largely on seniority and only to a limited extent on merit. This meant that wages and the wages bill remained high and fundamentally irreducible in the large/modern firm sector, even in the face of the overall labour surplus which the economy experienced until about the middle of the 1960s.

The reaction of many large firms was to subcontract to small firms those parts of their manufacturing process which would not suffer unduly from sometimes lower technical and supervisory standards. There unions were absent and wages lower, and thus the large firm effectively reduced its own labour costs at one step removed. This was of course, a rational response to an industrial structure and conditions within the labour market whose origins were to be found in the history of the economy. If that were the whole of the story it would not be reasonable to describe these arrangements as containing any element of exploitation, at least as judged by the tenets of neo-classical economic theory. However, small firms willing to take on subcontract work were and are very numerous, enabling the large firm placing the order not only to pick and choose amongst potential subcontractors, but also to have the major say in fixing the terms on which the work was to be done, or even to fix the terms unilaterally in many cases. Each subcontractor would be of minor importance to the large firm placing its orders, and subcontractors prone to complain about the terms on which deals – frequently without written contracts – were made, or who otherwise proved troublesome, could easily be replaced. By contrast, the subcontracting firm's very livelihood frequently depended on the goodwill and continuing custom of its large 'patron'.

Furthermore, it is a source of grievance in the small firm sector, as well as a matter of public and governmental concern, that in times of slow activity, or in response to government monetary policy which raises the cost of borrowing to firms, large firms attempt to, and succeed, in passing on a larger proportion of their costs to their subcontractors. This they achieve mainly in two ways. The first is by raising the costs of the materials they supply for their subcontractors to work on. The second is by a combination of reducing the cash element in the payment of their debts to subcontractors, and simultaneously and unilaterally lengthening the period over which they receive work on credit from their subcontractors. That is to say, payment is made in the form of a trading bill whose maturity date may be arbitrarily extended by weeks or months.

This practice was of sufficient concern to provoke legislation seeking to curb it as long ago as 1956, when the Law for the Prevention of Delay in Payments to Subcontractors (*Shitauke Daikin Shiharai Chien Hō*) was passed. The law was subsequently strengthened in 1962 and 1963 when the period within which payment to subcontractors had to be made was fixed by law, and the minimum size of firms offered protection by the law was raised. Although the law was designed to regulate delays in payments, unilateral lowering of the prices paid to subcontractors, the fixing of unfairly low prices to subcontractors, and so on, it has never been an unqualified success. It was recognised at the outset that subcontracting firms might well be loath to lodge the report which would initiate an investigation under the law, and accordingly the authorities themselves can initiate investigations where they have reason to believe the practices described above occur. However, limits on time and resources have restricted the number of cases which could be investigated over the years, whilst fear of losing orders from his main customers to one of their numerous competitors has restrained many a subcontractor from initiating the investigation process himself. Moreover, where conduct in violation of the law has been found to have occurred, the erring firm is not penalised as such. Instead, measures towards the reform of the patron firm's conduct are 'recommended' under clause seven of the law, or else the firm becomes the recipient of 'administrative guidance' (*gyōsei shidō*), a common and all-embracing term in Japan which signifies the influence exerted by economic bureaucrats of the Ministry of International Trade and Industry in particular (but in this case also of the Small and Medium-size Enterprise Agency, and the Fair Trade Commission), in order to encourage firms to follow the course desired of them by the government. In other cases it is reported that firms 'spontaneously' reformed their actions on receipt of the report which precedes an on-the-spot investigation.

In these circumstances it is perhaps not too surprising that the practice of passing on costs (*shiwayose*) to the subcontractor has continued to flourish. This is known not only from the recurrent attention it has received from economic commentators of one description or another, but also from government figures of investigations conducted. For example, up to the end of November, 1963, patron establishments requiring a report numbered 1,269, and the figure was expected to exceed 1,800 by the end of the year. Of these, 152 cases required further investigation which was said to have resulted in reform of the behaviour of the offending firm. Eight took measures of reform recommended under article 7 of the Law, 113 received 'administrative guidance' towards reform while 31 altered their behaviour of their own accord.

In 1970 there were 14,802 cases of preliminary documentary investigation, whilst in the cases of 878 of the establishments involved, fears of violations of the law were sufficiently strong to justify further, on-the-spot investigations. These fears were probably well-founded, since in the previous year 26 establishments were recommended to take specific measures to reform their conduct towards their subcontractors under article 7 of the Law, 704 establishments were pressed to modify their behaviour via 'administrative guidance', whilst 427 'spontaneously' reformed themselves. By 1975, significantly a period when the economy was stagnant after the 1973 oil crisis and the deflationary measures taken in its aftermath, 36,466 establishments were reported as having been the subject of preliminary investigation, exceeding the total of 35,804 of the previous year. As a result of the previous year's investigations, specific recommendations under article 7 of the Law were made in four cases, whilst administrative guidance towards more acceptable behaviour towards subcontractors resulted in 778 cases investigated. 994 'spontaneously' mended their ways after the official spotlight had fallen on them.

By 1980 the number of establishments that were scrutinised had risen to 59,158, which again represented an increase on the total of 41,937 of the previous year, whilst the establishments singled out for the strongest measure for rectifying an undesirable state of affairs under the Act, the application of Article 7, numbered only two. Cases of reform as a result of administrative guidance numbered 2,718, while numbers who responded of their own accord are no longer recorded.[9] It is difficult to draw hard-and-fast conclusions from these figures, except that whilst cases where presumption of guilt exists have been growing, cases of concrete action have not increased at the same rate. Suspicion is strong in the small firm sector as well as amongst observers, that rectification of the grievances felt by small firms towards unfair subcontracting arrangements is not high on the list of official priorities.

It should be noted in passing that a closer examination of the incidence of *shiwayose* – defraying of costs by passing the burden on to subcontractors – would reveal the following pattern. Up to about 1968 when Japan entered an era where balance of payments surpluses were the norm, pressure on subcontractors, and consequently numbers of bankruptcies increased in times of recurrent balance of payments deficits. These were met by monetary policies of a deflationary kind designed to make finance, especially all-important bank credit, harder and dearer to obtain for the large firms which patronised the subcontracting sectors of industry. Since the early 1970s the main underlying causes of *shiwayose* have become pressure on the costs of larger firms from rising imported energy and raw material prices, together with more slowly growing domestic and external demand due to the general recession in the world economy.

Despite these factors the government insists that the situation facing subcontractors in their relations with the larger firms from whom they receive their orders has not markedly worsened in recent years. Payment terms have apparently remained stable with the cash component in payments averaging 44 per cent, while the maturity of the bills used to complete payment for work done is about 119 days on average, which is barely within the official standards laid down in 1970. It is also admitted that bills of much longer duration are still used in a large number of cases. The same source is guardedly optimistic about trends in the way contract prices are fixed, stating that the involvement of subcontracting firms in the process has increased in recent years, although no evidence is presented. Official sources also claim that there is a distinct upward trend in the number of subcontractors who are made privy to the future ordering plans of patron firms at the time when orders are placed, thus reducing a major source of uncertainty and enabling subcontractors to plan their production in a way not hitherto possible. It is reported that the proportion of subcontracting firms now receiving such advance notice has risen to 64 per cent, although the virtual absence of written contracts means that subcontractors still operate in conditions of high uncertainty despite these marginal improvements.[10]

Before leaving the subject of the problems faced by small subcontracting firms, brief mention should be made of other forms of government intervention. Late in 1970 the Law for the Promotion of Small and Medium-sized Subcontracting Firms (*Shitauke Chūshō Kigyō Shinkō Hō*) was passed. The stated object of this measure was to raise the general standard of technology and capital equipment of small subcontractors and thus attempt to ensure them a greater measure of independence. As with other measures affecting the welfare of the small firm, the general method of procedure under this law is via 'administrative guidance'. That is, promotional standards or norms (*shinkō kijun*) are set which companies using subcontractors extensively are 'required' to meet, although the methods appear only to consist of written 'advice' or 'guidance' from officials. At the same time there exists a national Association for the Promotion of Subcontracting Firms. Since 1965 this organisation has been subsidised by national government, as have the 47 regional Associations with which it is connected. The chief function of these Associations is to advise subcontracting firms or societies of subcontracting firms on all aspects of their business with the general aim of raising their technical and managerial standards and helping them to cope better with the problems they confront in a changing business environment. The advice is again provided by officials of the government agencies whose area of concern is chiefly the small or medium-sized firm.

B. Finance for Small Firms

The other main persistent problem which confronts the small firm is that of obtaining finance, both for day-to-day operations and for investment in capital and equipment. This is a problem faced by small firms the world over. Nor is it a new problem, having been pointed out, for example, as long ago as 1931 in the United Kingdom in the report of the Macmillan Committee. Funds tend to be difficult to come by or even unavailable, or else available only on terms which put the independence of small firms in jeopardy. The problem is more acute for the new enterprise. In general these difficulties are ascribed to the risks associated with small firms, risks which are based ultimately on size as well as the quality and experience of management. These general observations apply to small firms in Japan too; in addition, for the historical reasons outlined above, they lag behind large firms in technology, capital intensity and hence productivity and wage levels.

There may well be another peculiarity in the Japanese case. In the two decades up to about 1973, the Japanese economy grew very rapidly and the total demand for funds exceeded the total supply. However, the large firm sector of the economy was almost always able to satisfy its demand for finance, not by resorting to the new issues market, but chiefly by borrowing from the main commercial banks (the 14 city banks). In supplying this massive, recurring demand for loans the city banks frequently over-extended themselves, at least as judged by the canons of orthodox banking practice as they are understood outside Japan. They were able to do this – to accept other than in rare cases the demands put upon them by the large firm sector – because they themselves could rely on being able to borrow at will from the Bank of Japan.[11] Up to the early 1970s only in times of serious balance of payments deficit would a programme of monetary stringency be operated. From the early 1970s a more concerted attempt has been made to take the decision on the rate at which the money supply was to increase out of the hands of the large firm sector, and to determine it according to a more orthodox and wider set of criteria than the demand for investment and operating funds of large private firms.

Nevertheless, the observation remains broadly true that large firms still face a situation where, in all probability, their demand for bank loans will be met, even though they have tried in recent years to rely less heavily on this source of finance than throughout the rest of the postwar period. The obverse of this must also, of necessity, be broadly true. That is, that although the commercial banks have widened their range of activities somewhat in recent times they still do the bulk of their business and make the greater part of their profits from lending to the large-firm sector, particularly in maufacturing industry.[12] When allotting their funds the banks did, and still do, regard small firms as marginal borrowers at best, especially when the money market is tight.

The small firm sector has had to cope with this situation as best it could. Small firms in Japan, like their large counterparts, rely heavily on outside sources of finance and relatively little on internal sources such as depreciation allowances and retained earnings. However, small firms rely more heavily on inter-firm credit or trading accounts and on trading notes payable, in addition to short-term borrowing from financial institutions. The difficulties of these arrangements are similar to those caused by the subcontracting relationship. The high risk of deferred payments, accompanied by a high level of arbitrariness in the fixing of prices by large customers, compound the small subcontracting firms' financial problems.

When the managers of small or medium-sized firms have succeeded in obtaining bank loans, they frequently encountered two further problems. The first concerns the terms on which loans were made. The interest rates charged on loans to smaller firms were significantly higher than those charged to large borrowers. Moreover, the differential in real interest rates was wider than that in nominal rates. The reason for this was that in times of very heavy demand for funds – the period of very rapid economic growth up to 1973 in particular – even with the cooperation of the government through the Bank of Japan, the commercial banks had to adopt some form of rationing. The device they chose, although officially frowned upon, was compensatory deposits. A borrowing firm was required to keep a certain minimum ratio of deposits to loans with the lending bank, and firms whose ratio was on average highest would receive better terms on their loans. That is, firms least likely to use a high proportion of the loan nominally available to them were given favourable treatment. It is not hard to imagine that such firms were more likely to be large ones with more successful records and securer futures than small firms.

The second problem was that of negotiating long-term loans from financial institutions. Quite simply, banks over most of the postwar period had little desire and little need to indulge in this sort of business because of the combination of reasons outlined above. However, both these problems have shown signs of easing over recent years as banks have become less able to rely for their profits on loans to large, private manufacturing companies to supply their massive need for funds to invest in new capital and technology. Coupled with this, many small and medium-sized firms have attracted the sympathetic ear of the banks through their own efforts at modernisation and rationalisation. The relatively high energy efficiency of small firms has also played a part in this process in the newly energy-conscious Japan.[13]

In addition, the efforts of the government to improve the financial stability and the ease of access to funds by small firms should not be overlooked. The principle adopted by the government over the question of finance for small firms is that it should supply directly only the marginal demand for funds left unfulfilled by private financial institutions. Thus, it lends less when the private funds market is slack and more when it is tight. Nevertheless, the three most important of the financial institutions created by the government to aid small firms account on average for around 12 per cent of the annual total demand for funds of small and medium-sized firms. These institutions are: the Small Business Finance Corporation, the People's Finance Corporation and the Central Bank for Commercial and Industrial Cooperatives. There are two other organisations, one for providing finance to help small firms invest in means of reducing the environmental pollution they cause (Environmental Improvement Finance Corporation), and another specialising in the problem of the small firm on the island prefecture of Okinawa. It should be emphasised that each of the five institutions mentioned are products of government concern over the financial problems which bedevil the small and medium-size firm sector, and that they are in receipt of government subsidies.

These institutions are prepared either to lend directly to small firms or to guarantee the creditworthiness and security of the small firm in a variety of ways so that it can obtain access to private sources of funds. The Small Business Finance Corporation makes ordinary and special loans. The use to which the first category of loan is put is not restricted, but the length of the loan seldom exceeds 5 years; there is an upper limit on loans of 120 million yen for investment in capital equipment and 60 million yen for working capital. In 1978 the interest rate stood at 7.6 per cent, which compared well with loans from private institutions. Special loans are used partly as a means of enforcing government policy and therefore are tied to certain specified uses. For example, for modernising production or distribution, for promoting specific industries, for improving safety or helping firms to change their sites as a part of regional policy.

The People's Finance Corporation concentrates on very small firms, chiefly individual proprietorships where the livelihood of the proprietor and his family are inextricably tied to the fortunes of the firm. The most usual loan is the ordinary loan where no restrictions are placed on the use to which it is put in the business. The upper limit on this sort of loan is small, being only about one-tenth of the size of loans made by the Small Business Finance Corporation. However the terms are fairly good and up to five million yen can be borrowed without security. This organisation also makes special loans where government policy plays a large part in the uses to which funds are put. In addition, the People's Finance Corporation lends to very small businesses (20 or fewer employees in manufacturing, 5 or fewer in commerce and services) without security where the money is used to improve managerial standards. This has to be done by securing the services for six months of a managerial training instructor from an approved society or chamber of commerce.

As its name implies, the Central Bank for Commercial and Industrial Cooperatives deals with associations of small firms, and its activities cover the discounting of bills, receiving deposits, the issue of bonds, supplying foreign exchange, and so on, as well as the making of loans. The Bank lends both to the co-operatives and to associations of firms which use the funds in joint ventures, or pass them on to member firms. The bank also lends directly to firms which are members of cooperatives. As a rule the upper limit on loans is 1,200 million yen in the former case, and 120 million yen in the latter. Loans have a maturity of up to 12 years, and the range of interest rates is between 7 and 8 per cent depending on the maturity date. Figures for the amount of and the proportion of all loans provided by government affiliated organisations, as well as private institutions are given in Table 3.9.

Lastly, the government has also established a credit guarantee scheme to help with the troublesome problem of the creditworthiness of small firms. Briefly, the system operates through credit guarantee associations which are applied to by small firms seeking loans from private institutions. These associations then investigate the applicant's reasons for and planned use of the loan, and if it is found to be satisfactory, guarantees the loan from the private institution. In return for this service it charges a guarantee fee. In order to guarantee itself against losses in cases of default, the association normally reinsures itself in advance with the

Table 3.9: Outstanding Loans to Small and Medium-Sized Firms from Various Financial Organisations (thousand million yen)

Year	Commercial banks[a]	Mutual banks and credit associations[b]	Government affiliated financial institutions[c]	Total (100 per cent)[d]
1973	25,715 (51.1)	18,951 (37.7)	5,625 (11.2)	50,291 (100.00)
1975	28,895 (47.3)	23,962 (39.3)	8,184 (13.4)	61,041 (100.00)
1977	44,017 (52.9)	28,481 (34.2)	10,698 (12.9)	83,196 (100.00)
1979	54,114 (53.0)	34,993 (34.3)	12,933 (12.7)	102,040 (100.00)

Notes: a. Figures in this column refer primarily to loans made to small and medium-sized firms by the City Banks and the Regional Banks. b. The institutions in this column do the bulk of their business with small and medium-sized firms, but they belong in the private sector of financial organisations. c. The four institutions represented in this column are government affiliated (and subsidised) institutions. Their titles and the nature of their activities is described on p. 75 of this chapter. d. The figures in brackets are the percentage contributions which the financial institutions of the different kinds identified made to the total of loans received by small and medium-sized firms.

Source: Small and Medium-Sized Enterprise Agency, *Chūshō Kigyō Hakusho* (*White Paper on Small and Medium-Sized Enterprises*), (Ministry of Finance Publishing Bureau, Tokyo, 1981), Statistical appendix, p. 30.

Small Business Credit Insurance Corporation. The credit guarantee associations number fifty-two in total and are in large cities and in the seats of the prefectural governments. They receive financial assistance from local and prefectural government, while the Small Business Credit Insurance Corporation is subsidised by central government. By 1982 its guarantee obligation outstanding was 7,635 billion yen. In total, these measures amount to a substantial contribution towards the amelioration of the financial difficulties of small firms.

Nevertheless, it is clear that small firms find on average nearly nine-tenths of their finance for investment and working capital in the private sector. It is true that the proportion they receive from the commercial banks has grown a little over the last decade, whilst that provided by the Mutual Banks and Credit Associations which were hitherto more closely identified with the small firm sector has declined somewhat. Table 3.9 bears this conclusion out and supports the contention made earlier that the powerful commercial banks have begun to take a slightly closer interest in lending to small firms. It is also true that the 12 per cent or so of the financial needs of small and medium-sized firms provided by the government affiliated financial institutions plays its part in mitigating the worst of the financial difficulties faced by the small and medium-sized firm sector. However, it also remains true that difficulty of access to financial resources remains the main problem facing even the most efficient of small firms in the Japanese economy.

3.5 Other Government Measures

Lastly, it should be mentioned that the government has instituted a range of measures other than financial ones which are designed to further the health and efficiency of small and medium-sized firms. These measures can be grouped into two broad categories: those which are designed to promote the reorganisation of small firms, and those whose primary aim is to provide the small firm with expert advice and guidance.

The main thrust of government policy towards the reorganisation of small firms is the promotion of cooperation and joint action. Two laws are particularly important in this respect. They are: the Law Relating to Cooperatives of Small and Medium-sized Firms and the Law for the Promotion of Industrial

Associations of Small and Medium-sized Firms. The rationale of these laws is that the superabundance of firms whose average size is very small renders them incapable alone of modernising their methods and strengthening their competitive position and ability to survive. Therefore, the first of the two laws provides for the setting up of industrial cooperatives where small firms are grouped in order to share common facilities, provide each other with orders, share a common brand name, and so on. Site rents are generally reasonable where cooperatives are located, whilst government subsidised infra-structure and access to transport facilities is also of a reasonably high standard. Firms participating in these cooperatives are also afforded preferential tax treatment.

The second of the two laws is chiefly designed to organise industry or trade associations of small firms in selected industries. Organisation and clerical staff are provided by the government to encourage the establishment of such organisations, and the central and prefectural governments combine to meet a part of the costs of running the prefectural federations of small business associations, and the National Federation of Small Business Associations located in Tokyo. The two laws complement each other by the way in which they work, since, for example, the managerial guidance provided to cooperatives and the full-time clerical staff furnished to them come through the various federations of small business associations.

It is difficult to generalise about the success of these particular efforts to strengthen the small firm sector of industry. The number of small firm industrial cooperatives is not negligible; 157 were set up between 1966 and 1972 in the first flush of enthusiasm for the movement, although thereafter some of this impetus was lost. However, at least one commentator attributes no more than partial success to these initiatives, chiefly because of a confusion of aims.[14] Cooperatives are normally located inland, in newly-developing areas away from the crowded pacific coast industrial belt where the vast majority of Japan's industrial firms, both large and small, are located. The result has sometimes been to remove firms from their immediate markets, raise transport costs and attenuate the personal relationships so important in Japanese society and industry. In other words, the attempt to use the industrial cooperative movement and its associated measures also as an arm of regional policy has at least partially and in the short-run blunted its effectiveness.

Measures aimed at providing small firms with advice and

guidance have quite a long history in Japan, dating back to the formation of the Small and Medium-sized Enterprise Agency in 1948. The central government and the regional authorities provide a wide range of managerial and technical consultancy services, usually through the agency of specialists based in the offices of the prefectural and city authorities. The services of these specialists are available upon request by the small firm, but in addition consultancy concerning the managerial practices of the small firm is required when firms borrow funds from the prefectural authorities for purposes of modernising their capital equipment.

Prefectural and city authorities also provide training courses for managers and engineers in the small firm sector, which is in addition to the more advanced training available from the Small Business Promotion Corporation. This latter organisation is also chiefly responsible for the training given to the specialists in the problems of the small firm employed in central and regional government.

It is difficult to estimate the cost of the impressive array of measures employed by the authorities in Japan to protect and stimulate the small-firm sectors of industry and commerce. The reason lies in the fact that it is difficult to extract from the various special accounts contained in official financial statistics, and from the figures on loans and investments in the annual budget, the proportion of total expenditure directed towards the small-firm sector. However, if we look only at the General Account in the annual budget where expenditure on small firms is clearly set out, it can be seen that, whilst the absolute amount spent has risen steadily, the proportion of total expenditure changed little throughout the 1970s, averaging around 0.6 per cent of the General Account.

3.6 Conclusion

It is clear from the foregoing discussion that the small firm is exceedingly important in almost all sectors of Japanese industry and commerce (as indeed it is in agriculture, which has been omitted from consideration). Numbers of small firms are exceedingly large and they form a high proportion of all firms. The sector is, in addition, an extremely important employer of labour, indeed the most important employer in the great majority of industries, including manufacturing. Nor is there any secular tendency for the small firm sector to decrease in size or importance. As regards its role as an employer of labour the opposite is found to be true; and had there been space to examine the role of the small firm as an exporter and as a direct investor overseas the same conclusion would probably have been reached.

It is no more than a truism to say that the reasons for the greater importance of the small firm in Japan are to be found in the way its industrial structure has developed since the hesitant beginnings of industrialisation a century or so ago. However, it is helpful to stress that large-scale, 'modern' firms have never formed more than an enclave in an economic landscape populated largely by small firms, and that this is still largely true. It is unhelpful to regard this as a sign of economic backwardness, although there are sections of small-scale industry where productivity, wages and conditions lag behind to an extent which justly causes concern in Japan. Rather we should seek lessons from such things as the relationship between large and small firms and the way in which the totality of the production process is divided between the two. This points *inter alia* to a closer examination of the subcontracting system in Japan, which admittedly has problematical aspects for small firms, but which is also the reason for the survival of so many of them. It is, in addition, a source of strength and flexibility for so many large firms, particularly in the important manufacturing, exporting sector.

Lastly, there are important lessons to be learnt from the policies of the government with regard to the small firm sector, and a closer study of this area would undoubtedly be of value. Whilst it is undoubtedly market forces which in the main govern the fate of small firms, one is left with the strong impression that government intervention *at a comparatively low cost* does much to ensure that the birth rate of small firms consistently exceeds the death rate, and that the innovative, technically aware small firm is given a significant degree of assistance towards survival and prosperity. In addition, the more traditionally-minded small firms found in such large numbers in domestic commerce and services (but also in manufacturing) which do so much to enrich the variety of Japanese life are at least given a measure of official protection and assistance.

Notes

1. Recent research has served to temper enthusiasm with regard to this conclusion. It has been shown that, whilst the small manufacturing firm sector has demonstrated its ability to increase the number it employs even when the economy as a whole is relatively stagnant, extravagent claims for its ability to create new jobs based on studies carried out in the United States are not to be accepted without qualification. For other countries, such as the UK, see D.J. Storey, *Entrepreneurship and the New Firm* (Croom Helm, London 1982).

2. The characteristics identified were that: a small firm should have a relatively small share of its market; that it be managed by its owners or part-owners in a relatively 'personalised' way; and that it is relatively independent in that it does not form part of a larger enterprise and that owner managers have the freedom to make their own major decisions. *Small Firms: Report of the Committee of Inquiry on Small Firms*, (Cmnd 4811, HMSO, London, 1971), p. 1.

3. In this respect, as in many others (for example, anti-monopoly legislation), Japanese practice has followed that of the United States rather than the United Kingdom model. In the United States, small firms are defined in rather general terms by the Small Business Act of 1958, whilst specific definitions by area of activity (industry) are the responsibility of the Small Business Administration. In the United Kingdom, as in West Germany and France, there is no legal definition of the small firm. See Chapter 4, page 89.

4. See for example, K. Yamaura, 'Structure is Behaviour' in I. Frank (ed.), *The Japanese Economy in International Perspective* (Johns Hopkins, Baltimore, 1975).

5. See for example, S. Broadbridge, *Industrial Dualism in Japan* (Cass, London, 1966).

6. The median size of establishments in Japan for all manufacturing is 6.2 persons per establishment. To take some examples from the light industries sector, it is 4.8 persons in the food industry, 2.5 persons in the furniture industry and 2.8 persons in the leather industry. In the heavy-industries sector, it is 5.5 persons in vehicle production, and 9 persons in iron and steel. These figures were calculated from frequency tables on the assumption that plant sizes were log-normally distributed. This method has been used by S.J. Prais, *Evolution of Giant Firms* (National Institute of Economic and Social Research, 1976), and also in his more recent *Productivity and Industrial Structure* (National Institute of Economic and Social Research Economic and Social Studies XXXIII, 1982). The latter book provides interesting comparative data on plant size in the United Kingdom, the United States and Germany (see particularly pages 10–13). It is apparent even without full-scale comparison, that the average plant size throughout manufacturing, and probably in most other sectors too, is significantly smaller in Japan than in the three countries examined by Prais. One reason for this is certainly the ubiquitous nature of small firms in Japan and their very large numbers.

7. If the same one or so chance in a hundred of business failure were applied to the individual-proprietor sector of the non-agricultural economy, the number would have been in the range of 40,000–50,000 most years through the 1970s.

8. In 1976 the Small and Medium-sized Enterprise Agency of the Ministry of International Trade and Industry estimated that 60 per cent of small and medium-sized firms in the manufacturing sector engaged in subcontracting work. It observed that the proportion of subcontracting firms was particularly high in the machinery maufacturing industry (general machinery, electrical machinery, machinery for use in transportation, etc.), and the textile trades. See *Chūshō Kigyō Hakusho* (White Paper on Small and Medium-sized Enterprises), 1979, p. 206.

9. All the figures relating to the application of the Law for the Prevention of

Delay in Payments to Subcontractors are taken from *Chūshō Kigyō Hakusho* (White Paper on Small and Medium-sized Enterprises), The Small and Medium-sized Enterprise Agency, Tokyo, various years.

10. The information in this section is from *Chūshō Kigyō Hakusho* (White Paper on Small and Medium-sized Enterprises), 1979 and 1981.

11. This process is described in Y. Suzuki, *Money and Banking in Contemporary Japan* (Yale University Press, 1980), and at shorter length by the present author in 'Financial Problems in Japan' in R. Shiratori (ed.), *Japan in the 1980's* (Kodansha International Ltd., Tokyo, 1982).

12. In fact, banks have traditionally taken into account an additional criterion which has made for an even higher degree of exclusivity when they determine how to apportion their funds. They have tended when required to give priority to borrower firms which belong within the group of firms (*keiretsu* is now the term most commonly used) which they themselves are a part.

13. It was officially estimated that in 1978 small and medium-sized enterprises in manufacturing accounted for 34.4 per cent of all energy used in this sector. However, the efficiency with which they used energy (measured by the ratio of the money value of energy used to the value of output produced multiplied by 100) was significantly higher with a figure of 2.78 as opposed to the 3.88 of large manufacturing firms. Ministry of International Trade and Industry, *White Paper on Small and Medium Enterprises 1981* (Tokyo, 1981), pp. 25–6. However, it should be borne in mind that this in part only reflects the fact that small firms are more numerous in areas of industry with low energy consumption requirements.

14. Y. Miyagawa, *Regional Development and Small Industries in Japan – Industrial Estates and Regional Structure* (Nagoya International Training Centre, Japan International Cooperation Agency, Nagoya, 1976).

Further Reading

Ministry of International Trade and Industry, *Background Information: Japan's Small and Medium Enterprises*. (These booklets have appeared annually since 1963 and are short, English-language summaries of the annual *White Paper on Small and Medium-sized Enterprises* (*Chūshō Kigyō Hakusho*).

Osaka International Training Centre: Japan International Cooperation Agency, *Evolution of Policy for Changing Conditions of Small and Medium Enterprises in Japan* (Osaka, 1978).

M. Shinohara, 'A Survey of the Japanese Literature on Small Industry' in B. Hoselitz (ed.), *The Role of Small Industry in the Process of Economic Growth* (Mouton, The Hague, 1968).

K. Takizawa, *A Comparative Study on the Problems of Small Business in the United Kingdom, the United States and Japan*. (This book was originally published in Japanese, but a complete English translation is available in ten successive issues of the journal *Keizai Kagaku (Economic Science)*, Nagoya University, beginning with vol. 21, no. 3, 1974)

T. Uyeda, *Small Industries of Japan* (Institute of Pacific Relations, Tokyo, 1937)

T. Yamanaka, *Small Business in Japan* (The Japan Times Ltd., Tokyo, 1961).

4 THE UNITED KINGDOM

4.1. Introduction

Interest and more importantly support for new and small firms in the United Kingdom arises from a number of diverse parties and for a number of diverse reasons. The small firm lobby groups range from the outwardly political to those seeking a complete change in society and a return to a more traditional and rural based economy. It would be wrong to presume that these different groups have become merged in their common support for small firms. In fact, and quite understandably, there is now emerging an almost counter-lobby to the pro-small firm lobby, if only to introduce greater balance into the current small firms debate.[1]

Identifying the starting-point of any economic, social or political movement is almost always doomed to failure, witness the attempts to date the beginning of the industrial revolution. For the purpose of this discussion, one of the most significant developments for small firms in the United Kingdom since the Second World War was the establishing of the Bolton Committee in 1969 and its subsequent report published in 1971. Much of the current debate on small firms in the UK has been based on this document up until and including very recent times. The past two or three years has seen a rapid increase in the volume of published empirical research examining issues relating to new and small firms. It is on the bulk of this most recent material which the present discussion is based.

Before embarking on a catalogue of the developments in the small firm sector, it is informative to consider the sources and range of arguments which have currency in the small firms debate in the UK. In all, there are six broad major themes which the supporting arguments take and these are: political; economic; emotional; technological; ecological/environmental; and knowledge based. A brief word is needed to indicate what form each of these themes take.

Political support has come dramatically to the fore with the change in governments in 1979 when the present Conservative Government took office, replacing the previous Labour administration. Deeply rooted in the philosophy of the

84

Conservative Party in the UK is that of self-help and personal initiative. In office this philosophy finds its form in the desire to denationalise or privatize major industries, to trim back the degree of intervention in the economy, and to remove barriers to free enterprise and competition. They believe in the efficacy of free market forces, even when its invisible hands appear to be stricken with arthritis. It is therefore to be expected that small firms would find a favoured slot in the economic policy initiatives of any Conservative administration in the UK. However, there is an element of irony in that a political party which stands by a free market philosophy seeks to intervene and to assist (and possibly to subsidise) that very bastion of free enterprise, the small firm. That being said, the present political climate in the UK is certainly favourable for the introduction of measures seen to aid small firms either by directly aiding their formation and growth, or the removal of barriers and discrimination which may exist.

Intertwined with the political arguments in favour of the small firm, there are a number of economic and social arguments which are usually offered as the prima facie case for supporting small firms. However, the necessary supporting evidence is either of a partial nature, or is lacking altogether, and comment on this fact is reserved mainly for the third and fourth sections of this discussion. The main economic and social argument in favour of small firms, and hence support for them in some manner, usually takes the following form. With the depth of the present recession and the consequent rise in measured unemployment to more than three million there is the ever-pressing need to find new employment opportunities from somewhere; the initial assumption being that society in the UK remains work-orientated.[2] It is further added that the major providers of employment, the large national and multi-national corporations, are not only cutting back on manpower drastically but that this is part of a long-term trend, and that such organisations are unlikely ever to return to their previous establishment levels of employment.

Allied to this is the inability of the service sector to continue its previous role as an absorber of displaced labour from manufacturing industries and of the increasing size of the economically active population – that is, a large youth element and a large number of female entrants and re-entrants to the labour market. The solution to the problems of the recession, at least in part, might be found in encouraging, and possibly harnessing the vitality of the small firm sector. At the same time, with the shrinking manufacturing base, the move to support small firms, especially small manufacturing firms, was seen as one way to help bolster the manufacturing economy.

Further dimensions can also be added to this line of argument, the most important of which is the spatial element. Increasing numbers of local authorities have sought ways in which they can aid and influence the economic prosperity of their immediate areas. As a result of their limited power and resources one of the most readily available audiences for any locally directed aid is the local small firms population. This trend has been most acute in most inner-city areas and in the less prosperous regions of the UK, for example, the Northern Region of England, Scotland and Wales. At a regional level the move towards supporting the local small firm population has drawn support from the failure of successive regional policy measures to ensure either a constant supply, or at least a supply of stable jobs for the assisted regions. Furthermore, the move to support small firms in the less-prosperous regions also stems from the political and economic desire to develop indigenous potential rather than rely on the fortunes of a branch factory economy in decline.[3]

Two of the other themes for the supporting of small firms can be taken together and these are the emotional and the ecological/environmental arguments. The emotional arguments paint a picture of the small family unit in which the quality of workmanship is of paramount importance, and where profits are of little, if any, significance. As a place to work, the small firm offers seemingly perfect working conditions where industrial relations problems do not arise because of the open communications which exist in small firms. Unfortunately, while these arguments are obviously true in part, all of the available evidence would tend to suggest that small firms are not the perfect employers some people would suggest that they are. Furthermore, despite the increasing amount of evidence to the contrary, many of the myths of the working environment offered in small firms are still perpetuated.

In a similar vein the ecological/environmental argument draws on emotions and the appeal of a new lifestyle rather than any empirically derived information. The kind of issues usually raised by the ecological and environmental lobby are of the need to reduce energy consumption, of the collapse of the current methods of production and of their inhumanity, of the need to integrate work and living more to explore and develop one's own potential, and of the need to reduce pollution. Allied to these arguments are desires to develop a new society drawing its main strength and direction from local roots, and by extending democracy via a commune or co-operative system using bartering as a basic means of exchange. The support given by the ecological/environmental lobby is mainly one of an indirect nature as the main focus is upon developing an alternative lifestyle, part of which is based on a small firm economy, rather than moving from a small firm economy to an alternative lifestyle.

There are three main strands to the technological arguments for small, and especially new firms. First, with the development of new manufacturing methods there is the possibility that markets which were previously the preserve of medium and large firms may now be entered by small manufacturing firms. Second, in many of the new and emerging industries small firms have a vital role to perform in the invention-innovation process, and should therefore be encouraged. Third, small firms often provide the vital infra-structural support necessary for the diffusion and successful application of inventions, and the further development of existing innovations. Here, one is specifically concerned with the service role offered by many small firms which can provide the necessary back-up services required with the introduction, and successful operating of, a new piece of manufacturing or office equipment.

The final element in the themes from which support for small firms has been drawn over the past decade is the increasing amount of knowledge and understanding of small firms themselves. When the Bolton Committee presented its report to Parliament in 1971 it was not able to provide any *accurate* national or regional assessment as to the trends in the small firm population. This situation, while far from being completely rectified, has improved beyond all previous recognition. Today there are comparable figures for the birth and death rates of firms using the registration of firms for Value Added Tax as its data base for analysis. More detailed regional and metropolitan accounts of the fortunes of small firms are also available. On the whole they would tend to suggest that there are quite distinct regional differences in the performance of the small firm economy (in terms of the births and deaths of firms) and that the contribution of small firms to employment is a long-term process and is unlikely to be the most immediate route to solving the present high levels of unemployment. However, there are still many questions to be answered concerning small firms.

There are then a series of arguments which are currently being voiced in the UK to support the government's aid programme for small firms. The main purpose of this chapter is to examine some of these arguments in greater detail and to present as comprehensive a catalogue as possible of the small firm population in the UK. In order to achieve these two main aims, the chapter has been divided into six further sections. The first section presents the definitions used to delimit the extent of the small firm population in any specific sector or for any specific assistance programme. The second section examines the stock of small firms and the trends in the small firm sector. In the third section the role of small firms is examined drawing on the small amount of information which is available. The difficulties faced by small firms is considered in the fourth section, while in the fifth section the initiatives adopted by central government to aid small firms are described and commented upon in terms of their effectiveness. In the final section a view to the future is presented based upon the established and developing trends in the small firm sector in the UK.

4.2. Definitions of a Small Firm in the UK

How many small firms are there? To what would appear a relatively straightforward question, there is no simple answer because there is no agreed definition of a 'small firm'. What might be a small firm in the chemicals or cement industry would be a large firm in the engineering industry, yet within their respective industries they will probably face many common problems because of their 'lack' of size relative to the size of the industry itself and the market it services. It is therefore important to have a clear objective in mind before one asks how many small firms there are. At the present time the definitions used by government departments vary from being based mainly on employment and on turnover (both of which *need* to vary through time) to the size of the premises and the size of exports or profits. Some appreciation of the range of definitions currently in operational use can be gained from the listing contained in Table 4.1. Whether these definitions actually mean anything in the respective trades and industries to which they are applied is not seen as important, and the main consideration is to have an agreed definition which can be commonly and readily applied. This also

Table 4.1: Definitions of Small Firms in the UK

(i)   Statistical definitions of small business

Industry	*Definition (upper limits)*
Manufacturing	200 employees
Retailing	£185,000 p.a. turnover
Wholesale trade	£730,000 p.a. turnover
Construction	25 employees
Mining and Quarrying	25 employees
Motor trade	£365,000 p.a. turnover
Miscellaneous services	£185,000 p.a. turnover
Road transport	5 vehicles
Catering	All except multiples and brewery managed public houses

(ii)   Specific definitions relating to government assistance

Type of assistance	*Definition (upper limits)*
European Investment Bank Loans	500 employees
Proprietory Company (proposed)	50 employees
Employment Act Exemptions	20 employees
Council for Small Industries in Rural Areas (CoSIRA) aid	20 employees (skilled)
Export award	200 employees
Export visits	200 employees
Employment subsidy	200 employees
Computer aided production management	500 employees
Industrial Liaison Service	500 employees
Consultancy Scheme	500 employees (min. 25)
Collaborative Arrangements (manufacturing)	200 employees
Manufacturing Advisory Service	1,000 employees (min. 100)
Companies Act disclosure exemption	£1 million p.a. turnover
Proprietory Company (proposed)	£1.3 million p.a. turnover
Value Added Tax registration	£15,000 p.a. turnover
Price code exemptions	£1 million (manufacturing) p.a. turnover
	£250,000 (distribution, services) p.a. turnover
	£100,000 (professions) p.a. turnover
Competition Act exemptions	£5 million p.a. turnover
European Investment Bank Loans	£20 million (fixed assets)
Industrial Development Certificates (exemption)	50,000 square feet
Office Development Permits (exemption)	30,000 square feet
Proprietory Company (proposed)	£650,000 (bal. sht. total)
Small Exporter Policy	£100,000 (export value)
Corporation Tax reduced rate	£80,000 (profits)

Source: M.E. Beesley and P.E. Wilson (1981), *Government Aid to Small Firms in Britain*, UKSBMTA Conference Paper, London.

applies to the now large number of research projects undertaken to examine small, and especially new firms. Invariably the size of a firm (or plant in some cases) is based on the number of employees which will over the next decade become an increasingly poor indicator of a firm's or plant's size. Greater effort is needed at the present time to derive a new measure of size based on output rather than on part of the production process, employment. Furthermore, it is the quality, and not necessarily the quantity of the stock of small firms which is important and it is therefore also important that in the derivation of the new measure of size that a quality measure also be derived.[4]

All of the definitions offered in Table 4.1 are the upper limits for the various categories concerned, no mention is made of the lower limit. Do they include the self-employed who operate on an own account basis? For example, two recent reports examining the same issue, at least in part, came to the conclusion that there were either 2.3 or 1.3 million firms (or businesses) in the UK. The first report drew on data provided by the Inland Revenue[5] whilst the second used the register of those businesses paying Value Added Tax[6] by Ganguly. Both reports started with the same operational definitions of 'the small firm'. It is therefore not only the definition adopted to delimit what is, and what is not a small firm, but also, the data base to which the definition is then applied. The debate of the merits or otherwise of small firms in the UK is therefore littered with provisos and qualifications, and it is vital to establish where the data were derived from, and why and how the data were compiled in the first place. Many of the accounting exercises undertaken to establish the number of small firms, such as the two mentioned above, have been forced to use data which were compiled for another reason other than the counting of the number of small firms.

4.3. Size, Nature and Trends in the Small Firm Sector in the UK

Just as it is extremely difficult to define a small firm, attempting to establish trends within the small firm sector is almost impossible. The only method which is likely to produce anything approaching a reliable description of the trends in the small firm sector is by piecing together a whole series of data sources each having its own strengths and weaknesses. The following discussion uses a very broad definition of the small firm sector which includes both the self-employed and the 'black economy'. The discussion itself is divided into three main parts. The first is concerned with establishing the size of the small firm sector drawing on the most recently available information. The second attempts to establish whether the present size of the small firm sector is either increasing or decreasing, and if there are any smaller trends subsumed within the general trend. In the final section some of these smaller trends, often counter to the general trend, are highlighted.

The most recently available estimates of the size of the small firm sector suggest there are approximately 1.5 million small businesses in Britain, 2 million people are self-employed and a further 6 million people are employed in the small-business sector. The self-employed constitute nearly 10 per cent of the working population and contribute 25 per cent to the Gross National Product. These few figures give some idea of the size of the small firm sector. Attempting to measure the exact size of the small firm sector is fraught with difficulties and this section can only go part of the way towards bringing together the various threads.

There are two main ways of measuring the size of the small firm sector in the UK and these are either by counting the actual number of businesses, or by counting the number of people they employ. Both measures are arbitrary and are more the by-product of existing data collection methods rather than representing a specially designed data collection exercise to assess the size of the small firm sector. In establishing the size of the small firm sector it is best to divide the economy into its four main constituent parts: agriculture and extractive; manufacturing; construction; and the service industries. The bulk of the attention on the small firm sector in the UK is focused on the manufacturing sector, the reasons for which will be returned to later when central government assistance for the small firm sector is considered.

To the simple question 'how many small firms are there?', there is no simple answer. Two main sources of information exist which give some indication of the size of the small firm sector. The first is the Census of Production which is concerned with enterprises, published annually for manufacturing industry, and covers all manufacturing establishments with twenty or more employees. Because of its restrictive coverage data drawn from this source excludes many small firms, and will probably therefore understate their importance to production. In terms of employment, the 1978 Census of Production estimated that a little under 23 per cent of employees worked in small enterprises. However, when the second major source of information on the size of businesses is consulted the numbers employed in small establishments (those employing fewer than 200 employees) in manufacturing industry was 37 per cent in 1977. In fact, according to the Annual Census of Employment, the bulk of the working population in the UK in 1977 were employed in small establishments (58 per cent). The use of these two data sources serves to illustrate the difficulty of establishing the number and relative importance of small firms in the UK.

The situation is further complicated when the move is made from considering small firms as places of employment to representing independent trading concerns. It is quite possible, and in fact quite likely, that a single small firm will trade under several different names for a wide range of commercial, financial and legal reasons. Thus the single small fish-processing firm might trade in its own right and then develop new outlets, say, in Europe, or develop new product lines and will exploit these new opportunities by establishing a new company. Often the proliferation of the number of associated or subsidiary companies operating on the behalf of a single producing unit will be the result of the problem of rewarding individual employees sufficiently. Hence, moves can be made to make an employee a director of the existing company, or to establish a number of other companies of which employees can be made directors. The relationship, therefore, between the registration of a company and the existence of a trading concern is not exact. Furthermore, with the development of the 'ready-made-company-business' still more 'new firms' are being generated only to be left on the shelf as convenience companies, and which can be bought off the shelf to speed up the process of going into business. Much of the existing national data in the UK can therefore be best used for describing very broadly the present stock and trends in the small firm sector. It is doubtful even if a workable registration system could ever be devised, and its administration could possibly only be handled at the local level via the chambers of commerce which exist in most towns and cities.

A further possible indication of the size of the small firm sector can be gained from the numbers of unquoted and unincorporated businesses which stood at about 2.3 million in 1980. Working on the assumption that all large firms are incorporated and probably quoted (the latter assumption does not hold in some exceptional cases), it would seem reasonable to suggest that most of the remainder are 'small firms'. Taking these three data sources together, the Census of Production, the Annual Census of Employment and evidence of Inland Revenue Schedule D (sole traders and partnerships) assessments, a broad estimate of the number of small firms can be gained. A further source which will, with further analysis, also prove a useful indicator of the size of the small firm sector is the Value Added Tax register. As yet only sectoral and regional analyses have been undertaken on these data by Ganguly.[7]

Even when the number of small firms can be stated, depending on the definition adopted and the data base used, no indication is gained as to the dynamics of the small firm sector. How many new firms are being generated? How many small firms are closing? Taking both of these components together, it should be possible to indicate whether or not the small firm sector is either increasing or decreasing. There are, of course, other complicating factors (as shown by Cross) such as the rise in the number of small firms due to previously medium and large firms shedding labour and directly entering their ranks.[8] Similarly, the relative importance of small firms will also increase with the colossal numbers of employees who have been shed from many of the UK's largest manufacturing and commercial companies – for example, the British Steel Corporation (and the iron and steel industry as a whole) has halved in size since 1977. Thus, even if the small firm sector were to remain static in size in absolute terms, it would in relative terms continue to grow in importance.

There are also technological and financial factors favouring the construction of smaller production units and so adding at least to the stock of small establishments, if not small firms. It is now possible technologically to produce far greater volumes of output with greatly reduced numbers of employees. Notions, and fears, of the unmanned factory are with us, and by present-day definitions these firms would not be registered as they do not employ anybody! Allied to this trend has been one ensuring the maximum utilisation of productive capacity which has tended to favour small units especially during a period of relatively slow or static growth conditions. This trend is reinforced by the present financial and investment outlook of many companies which is short-term. Companies are therefore unwilling to set aside large sums of money for lengthy periods with the possibility of not seeing a return on the capital invested for 5 to 10 years. Again this favours the construction of the smaller unit with its invariably shorter building times and hence its ability to contribute to the company more rapidly. Another element of this argument is the notion of flexibility which can be more easily accommodated in a number of small, new units than one huge production unit. This move also fits in with the new economic philosophy that economies of production are only part of the answer to successful production. Often, it is possible to compete on price, quality and time of delivery from a small unit as it is from a large one especially during a period of deeply depressed demand when the large units still have to bear all of the manufacturing service costs associated with any large unit.

This being said, it is possible, using a range of data sources as indicators, to suggest that the numbers of small businesses (it is assumed that nearly all new firms are small firms) would appear to be increasing. Again, this must be qualified for two reasons. First, the conclusion one draws as to the trends in the small firm sector depend on the data source(s) used. Second, the periods of time over which data are available are probably not sufficient, nor consistent enough to allow unequivocal statements to be made on the trends and direction of the small firm sector. With these two provisos in mind, along with the general trends which are contributing to the 'size' of the small firm sector, the discussion proceeds.

The present discussion initially draws on four sources of information: company liquidations and registrations; business name registrations; and the register for Value Added Tax. The last named data source indicates that in 1981 the number of births slightly exceeded the number of deaths (Table 4.2), with this being a reverse of the findings for 1980 – the first year for which such information is available. In 1981 the largest net decline occurred in the retail and catering trades which are directly dependent on consumer spending with transport also registering a deficit. On the plus side, increases were seen in production (manufacturing), construction, wholesaling, professional and other services. This data set is available only for two years which may, or may not be representative of those preceding, or succeeding. Beneath these aggregate changes, there are, however, a number of trades which are performing well. Similarly, the national trend is not mirrored exactly by the stocks of businesses in each region.[9] For example, in 1980 births exceeded deaths in the prosperous Regions of the South East, East Anglia, West Midlands, East Midlands and the South

Table 4.2: Provisional Estimates for 1981: Births and Deaths of Firms by Sector in the UK

Sector	Births	Deaths	Excess	Stock of businesses registered for VAT	Births as % of stock	Deaths as % of stock
Agriculture	5,500	45,00	1,000	180,300	3.1	2.5
Production	12,300	10,100	2,100	127,600	9.6	7.9
Construction	18,200	12,800	5,400	198,500	9.2	6.4
Transport	5,200	5,300	–100	56,000	9.3	9.5
Wholesale	11,600	8,200	3,400	100,500	11.5	8.1
Retail	27,000	30,800	–3,900	263,900	10.2	11.7
Finance property professional services	7,300	5,700	1,600	83,200	8.7	6.8
Catering	12,000	13,100	–1,100	116,600	10.3	11.2
Motor trades	7,200	6,100	1,100	71,300	10.1	8.6
Other services	18,600	13,400	5,200	137,900	13.5	9.7
Total	124,800	110,000	14,800	1,335,900	9.3	8.2

Births: All new registrations less voluntary registrations and those following changes of legal identity.
Deaths: Trader going out of business.
Trader going out of business, buyer already registered or in progress of being registered.
Trader falls below exemption limit.
Trader registered voluntarily seeks to be deregistered.
Trader makes zero-rated supplies only and requests exemption.

Discrepancies between certain totals and the sum of their constituent items are due to the rounding of figures.
The figures are subject to revision.

Source: *British Business*, 23 July 1982, p. 512.

Table 4.3: Births and Deaths of Firms by Region in the UK, 1980, 1981

Region	Births		Deaths		Excess		Births as % of stock		Deaths as % of stock	
	1980	1981	1980	1981	1980	1981	1980	1981	1980	1981
South East	41,500	44,200	40,100	37,200	+1,400	+ 7,000	+9.9	+10.5	−9.5	−8.8
East Anglia	3,400	4,000	3,300	3,300	+ 100	+ 700	+7.6	+ 8.9	−7.4	−7.3
South West	10,600	11,900	10,500	10,700	+ 100	+ 1,200	+7.6	+ 8.5	−7.5	−7.7
West Midlands	9,900	11,500	9,500	9,200	+ 500	+ 2,300	+8.3	+ 9.7	−8.0	−7.7
East Midlands	7,500	8,100	7,300	7,300	+ 200	+ 900	+8.0	+ 8.7	−7.8	−7.7
Yorkshire and Humberside	8,700	10,000	9,100	9,200	− 400	+ 900	+8.0	+ 9.2	−8.4	−8.4
North West	11,100	12,800	12,200	11,900	−1,100	+ 900	+8.7	+10.0	−9.6	−9.3
North	4,500	5,300	4,800	4,600	− 400	+ 700	+7.7	+ 9.1	−8.2	−7.9
Wales	5,200	6,100	5,400	5,100	− 200	+ 1,100	+7.0	+ 8.2	−7.2	−6.8
Scotland	7,600	8,000	7,600	6,900	+ 100	+ 1,200	+7.5	+ 7.9	−7.5	−6.7
Northern Ireland	2,900	2,500	2,200	1,900	+ 700	+ 700	+6.3	+ 5.6	−4.8	−4.1
Miscellaneous	400	300	3,400	2,900	−3,000	− 2,600	–	–	–	–
Total	113,300	124,800	115,300	110,000	−2,000	+14,800	+8.3	+ 9.3	−8.5	−8.2

Note: See Table 4.2. 1980 data are corrected, 1981 are provisional.
Source: *British Business*, 24–30 Spetember 1982.

West. Perhaps surprisingly there was also an increase in the stock of businesses in Northern Ireland and Scotland. The traditionally less prosperous areas of Northern England, North West England, Wales and Yorkshire and Humberside showed net declines. In 1981 all Regions showed increases in the stock of businesses but again birth rates were highest in South East England and lowest in Northern Ireland. Hence, whatever the national trend might in fact be, there are many other variants depending on the trade, or region in question. Both of these sources of variation are returned to later.

The question now to be addressed concerns whether what happened in 1980 was a minor interruption of an upward trend, or the beginning, or part of a downward trend. Probably the only means available in the UK of assessing the trends in the small firm sector, and not just parts of the small firm sector, is to use the liquidations and registrations of companies and the additions and deletions of business names. Taking these data sources together would indicate two trends. First, there is a long-term trend in the growth in number of companies and businesses, and the vast bulk of these additions will. in all probability be small firms. And second, the majority of additions are businesses which are trading as unlimited liability operations and this would suggest a trend towards the non-manufacturing sectors. The data upon which these comments are based are presented in Table 4.4. It is not possible unfortunately to further disaggregate these analyses to indicate in any detail which trades are growing and which are declining. It is however possible, using estimates of the numbers who are self-employed (with or without employees) to determine which trades are attracting most new small firms.[10] The available evidence would again suggest a long-term trend in the absolute increase in the number of self-employed people. Over the past twenty years the trend was one of decrease to about 1966 and then, with minor setbacks in 1972 and 1974, one of gradual increase up until the present time. By far the largest decline has been in agriculture, forestry and fishing with the loss of over 100,000 self-employed persons. Most of the manufacturing industries have remained relatively static over the period except in the timber and furniture trades which nearly doubled their numbers between 1961 and 1973 (25,000 rising to 48,000). Other notable increases have occurred in the construction industry with the number of traders increasing from 173,000 in 1961 to 438,000 in 1974. Amongst the service industries only in the distributive trades has there been any decline

Table 4.4: Company Liquidations, Registrations and Additions
to the Business Name Register, UK 1970–80

Year	Company liquidations UK	GB	Company registrations GB	Business name registrations GB
1970	3,905	3,886	29,605	78,786
1971	3,687	3,661	38,862	78,728
1972	3,245	3,231	53,917	95,706
1973	2,688	2,673	66,457	104,825
1974	3,888	3,875	41,535	86,600
1975	5,620	5,602	44,998	97,826
1976	6,217	6,168	55,189	108,333
1977	6,134	6,102	54,520	111,823
1978	5,413	5,360	62,679	133,976
1979	4,809	4,775	65,076	141,156
1980	7,344	7,270	68,256	151,486

Source: G. Bannock, 'The Clearing Banks and Small Firms', *Lloyds Bank Review*, no. 142, 1981, Table 1.

where there has been the loss of about 100,000 traders over the last twenty years. The remaining four service trades; transport and communications, insurance, banking, finance and business services; professional and scientific services and miscellaneous services have all undergone gradual increases in their numbers. The bulk of these increases have occurred in three regions in the UK, those of the South East and West, and of East Anglia. The remaining regions have recorded increases but these have been of a relatively minor nature when compared to those of the three main growth regions for the self-employed. In only one region has there been a decline in the number of self-employed people and that is in Northern Ireland which has suffered severe disturbances to normal trading conditions since 1969.

Before moving to any final statement concerning either the stock or the trends in the small firm sector in the UK it is necessary to consider that part of the small firm sector which is not officially recorded; the informal economy. The informal economy has many other names (e.g. underground, hidden, parallel, irregular, black, dual, cash, moonlight, submerged, twilight, or *travail noir* or *Schattenwirtschaft* or *lavoro sommerso*), but here just one expression – the informal economy – will be used. The definition used here of the informal economy is that of Smith,[11] 'GNP that because of non-reporting or under-reporting is not measured by official statistics'.

As would be expected, estimating the size of a non-reporting part of the economy is problematic, and as a result has attracted estimates from 'the experts'. For example, when Sir William Pile, the former Chairman of the Board of Inland Revenue, gave evidence to the Expenditure Committee of the House of Commons in 1977 he suggested that it was 'not implausible' for the informal economy to have accounted for some 7.5 per cent of GDP. More recent calculations by Dilnott and Morris[12] would suggest that this initial estimate was a little on the high side and that the informal economy accounts for about 2.3–2.4 per cent of GDP in the UK. And, from the detailed analyses of Dilnot and Morris it would appear that much of the informal economy represents an extension to existing self-employed activities. There is still, however, a sizeable element which falls outside this category, and would for some groups, notably the skilled manual worker, be a second job. It is, however, impossible at the present time to allocate the informal economy in any meaningful way between trades and regions, but it is likely that the informal economy mirrors the distribution of the self-employed and is concentrated mainly in the service and construction sectors.

Finally, the informal economy, apart from representing a stock of highly transitory small businesses which probably only trade when work is available and when extra income is desired, may also represent an important seedbed for subsequent full-time, legal small firms. It is often noted for example that before many small firms are established that their founders had traded in some form before becoming employed by the business they establish. It is therefore ironic that the present efforts to reduce the size of the informal economy by more vigorous tax inspection, could mean that the supply of new firms making themselves available for government assistance might decrease. Furthermore, these efforts might force some people to develop part-time businesses into full-time ones when there is still only a market for a part-time business, and all that will be achieved is the encouragement of possibly mediocre and complacent firms which are doomed to fail from the start. Again, this would run counter to the present initiatives to increase the numbers of new business starts because the available assistance will be dissipated by helping firms which should never have been established. This subject will be returned to later when central government assistance for small firms is considered and commented upon.

Despite the lack of reliable information, it would appear from the data which are available that the small firm sector in the UK is increasing in size in both absolute and relative terms. These increases are not occurring across all sectors, nor across all regions of the UK. It would appear that there are favoured regions in the UK which have recorded the bulk of the increases in the numbers of small firms (in the form of the self-employed as in the USA). It is important that these long-term trends be considered when formulating assistance programmes for the new and small firm sector as it would appear that radical differences in form and application will be necessary if all parts of the UK are to gain from such a policy stance. Much of the debate in the UK concerning small firms stops at this point – that is, the interest is in small firms *per se*, and it is assumed that the more that can be created the better it is for the economy. Reference to the role and contribution of small firms to the economy, either locally, or nationally is lacking and still rests, in the main, on anecdotal tales. The following section presents what little evidence there is in an attempt to examine the role of the small firm sector in the UK.

4.4. Role of the Small Firm in the UK

It would appear from the available evidence that small firms in the UK play a number of distinct roles in the economy, and some of the more obvious ones are listed in Table 4.5. While it is relatively easy to provide such a list, it is difficult to find the necessary evidence either to refute or to support each of the suggested roles. In fact, many of the roles ascribed to small firms are the converse of the arguments in favour of large firms and oligopoly. Another source of ideas which give rise to a list of possible roles of small firms is that body of economics literature relating to 'barriers to entry' – articulated by Bain, [13] Mansfield [14] and Steindl. [15] The purpose of this section is to examine briefly those aspects of the role of small firms for which data are available and to comment, where possible, on the remaining ones.

In social terms it would appear that small firms play an important role in a number of ways. There are probably five broad aspects of the social role of small firms which can be mentioned here. First, the setting-up of a small firm offers an outlet for those individuals who for whatever reason have been unable to find work in, or have been forced to withdraw from the formal labour market. The reasons why an individual may regard himself (or herself) as marginal, or society regard them as marginal, are legion, and they may draw their origin from class, ethnic, religious, and political backgrounds. Even within accepted sections of society there are those individuals who 'do not fit'. This may be a result of their upbringing, a failure to become settled because of migration whilst a child, or some other factor which has caused a major disruption to their lives – for example, death of a parent or divorce. That being said, the important point is that small firms do appear to have a role to play in allowing socially marginal individuals to find an outlet for their talents and abilities as demonstrated by Collins,[16] and Stanworth and Curran.[17]

Second, and very much related to the above point, small firms, or more correctly, self-employment, is the natural route for the talents of all artists to find their expression. The pursuit of the 'artists ideal' can only be found by being self-employed, though in many cases artists pursue a number of other sources of employment – for example, teaching art or poetry, and so combine the pursuit of their art with the rather mundane need to have sufficient money with which to live.

Third, small firms for many people represent the preferred state of employment because not only does it mean that you are your own boss, but also gives status and recognition. For the plant manager becoming self-employed might mean becoming a Managing Director and Chairman of his own company. The move into self-employment and the establishment of one's own business can therefore be interpreted as being a means of moving up the social and occupational hierarchy. It offers a route to betterment and of obtaining the fruits of a better lifestyle. Actually how important in quantitative terms the setting-up or the joining of a small firm in a senior position is in accounting for the social mobility which does occur in the UK is uncertain, but it would appear to be of relatively minor significance compared to the gross flows between social groups and occupations.[18]

Fourth, over the past two decades there have been waves of support of varying strength and duration for the move towards finding a new lifestyle. Emphasis being placed in each of the successive waves on the rejection, at least in part, of the existing order, values and attitudes of society allied to which has been the move into usually more rural surroundings. The basis of these

Table 4.5: Summary of the Role of Small Firms in the Economy

1. The small firm provides a productive outlet for the energies of that large group of enterprising and independent people who set great store by economic independence and many of whom are antipathetic or less suited to employment in any organisation but who have much to contribute to the vitality of the economy.

2. In industries where the optimum size of the production unit or the sales outlet is small, often the most efficient form (as measured, say by profitability) of business organisation is a small firm. For this reason many important trades and industries consist mainly of small firms.

3. Small firms add greatly to the variety of products and services offered to the consumer because they can flourish in a limited or specified market which it would not be worthwhile or economic for a large firm to enter.

4. Many small firms act as specialist suppliers to large companies of parts, sub-assemblies, components, or services (contracted-out labour, maintenance, etc.) produced often at a lower cost than the large companies could achieve. Small firms provide an important part of the economic infrastructure upon which the economy depends.

5. In an economy in which even larger multi-product firms are emerging, small firms provide competition, both actual and potential, and provide some check on monopoly profits and on the inefficiency which monopoly might breed. In this way they contribute to the efficient working of the economic system as a whole. Furthermore, big business knows that its chance to continue under private auspices rest heavily upon the presence of many virile, healthy small businesses, and so will aid their survival.

6. Small manufacturing firms, in spite of their relatively low expenditure on research and development in comparison to many sectors as a whole, are an important source of invention and of innovations. Outside manufacturing, small firms may play an important role in innovation because of the generally lower capital costs of development work.

7. The small firm sector is a breeding ground for new industries.

8. Small firms provide a means of entry into business for new entrepreneurial talent and the seed-bed from which new large companies can grow (though their numbers will be very small) to challenge and stimulate the established leaders of industry.

9. Small firms provide a means by which new resources, or resources which would otherwise lie dormant, can be brought into productive use and so increase output at a possibly marginal opportunity cost. At the same time, small firms also provide an outlet for investment goods and investible funds.

10. In a period of economic depression many unemployed people may go

into self-employment (and hence establish a new, small firm) to tide themselves over until new employment opportunities develop. This process would thus reduce the cost to the exchequer in terms of unemployment payments, and so on.

11. Small firms are important employers of skilled labour (e.g. engineering craftsmen) and many, as a result of their labour intensity, may help to maintain a skilled labour base in an area, or in an industry while largely routine semi- and unskilled work is being provided in large companies.

---

alternative societies has been one of self-sufficiency with only the minimum of contact with 'the outside world' at least in the first instances. Such communities have developed in parts of Wales and more recently at Greenham Common in Berkshire. The means of existence of these communities and the strengths and weaknesses of their economies rests on those of the small firm. Small firms can therefore be seen as a way by which marginal groups who wish to isolate themselves from the accepted trading patterns of society can survive and prosper.[19]

Fifth, the creation of employment opportunities is one of the central elements of any social policy. Small firms do play a role by creating and sustaining employment in situations where their medium and large firm counterparts would fail to do so. Hence, in inner-city areas and in rural areas small firms offer a means by which employment levels can be maintained, and possibly increased in some rural areas.[20] However, whilst small firms do provide employment it is often of a highly unsatisfactory nature due to the poor physical working conditions and poor industrial relations practices.[21] In some cases, small firms can provide a high quality of employment in terms of involvement and a generally high level of job satisfaction. Evidence on this topic is weak and is often based on the views of the owner-founder and not of the employees themselves or their unions.[22] Curran and Stanworth suggest that where employee-based information does exist it would appear that the small firm does not offer the supposed superior working conditions that are available in medium and large firms.[23] Small firms in general offer a very restricted range of jobs and promotion prospects and so are unlikely to attract the highly-qualified staff they might require in some cases, especially in manufacturing industry. Evidence relating to small firms in, say, the professional and financial services does not exist, but it would be safe to suggest that such employment is of equal standing to that offered by any other size of firm. It is important to remember that there is a very wide range of working conditions offered by small firms, and it would be wrong either to condemn or condone small firms as places of employment until evidence is forthcoming from settings other than in manufacturing industry. This bias, both in research and assistance available for small firms in manufacturing industry, is commented on later.

One aspect of the role of small firms upon which there is some evidence, again drawn from the manufacturing industries, is the part played by small firms in the innovation process. From the available evidence it would appear that small firms have made, and continue to make a significant contribution to the successful commercial introduction of new products and processes. Over the 1945–80 period small firms have provided between 11 and 17 per cent of all innovations across a variety of industrial sectors (30 in all) and it would appear that through time the small firm sector has managed to maintain its level of contribution whilst the very large firms (10,000 or more employees) have substantially increased their contribution. It is the firms in between these two size-categories which would appear to have missed out and declined in their importance in introducing new products and processes within manufacturing industry (see Table 4.6). In drawing conclusions from these data it must be remembered that they relate to the 1945–80 period and the significance of the innovations over a longer period might either increase or decrease. It is possible, for example, that the importance of the contribution made by small firms might vary through time, and it is not clear how the emergence of one innovation 'opens the door' for a whole range of further innovations. Within this latter process the role of small firms remains unclear, and without much greater research effort an increase in our knowledge is unlikely.

Even when these limitations are recognised, it is undeniable that small firms have played an important role in the introduction of innovations in the UK over the 1945–80 period. There are a number of sectors in which small firms have played a particularly significant role and these are: general and textile machinery; scientific and industrial instruments; timber and furniture; leather and fur; and paper and board. As would be expected there is an equal list of sectors in which small firms made no (apparent) contribution to the introduction of any innovations, and amongst these are: coal; pharmaceuticals; dyestuffs; iron and steel; aluminium; aerospace;

Table 4.6: Significance of Small Manufacturing Firms in the Innovation Process in the UK, 1945–80

Number of employees	1945-9 no.	%	1950-4 no.	%	1955-9 no.	%	1960-4 no.	%	1965-9 no.	%	1970-4 no.	%	1975-80 no.	%	Total no.	%
1-199	15	16	23	12	30	11	45	11	61	13	60	15 (11)	78	17 (12)	312	14 (12)
200-499	8	8	11	6	22	8	24	6	33	7	36	9 (7)	32	7 (6)	161	7 (7)
500-999	3	3	4	2	19	7	20	5	23	5	16	4 (4)	14	3 (3)	99	4 (4)
1,000-9,999	34	36	69	36	67	25	109	27	107	23	67	17 (9)	65	14 (13)	519	23 (23)
10,000 and over	34	36	84	44	136	50	206	51	243	52	221	55 (59)	272	59 (66)	1,197	52 (54)
Total number of innovations	94		191		274		405		467		401		461		2,293	

Note: Numbers between brackets for the periods 1970–4 and 1975–80 are the weighted percentage contributions, assuming the sectoral mix as in the period 1945–69.

Source: J. Townsend, F. Henwood, *et al.*, *Innovations in Britain since 1945*, Occasional Paper, Science Policy Research Unit, University of Sussex, UK.

heavy electrical; glass; cement; and gas. Again, there is probably a relationship between the development of new measurement instruments and the development of new production process, say, in the petrochemical or glass industries. Our knowledge of the innovation process is far from complete, and so, therefore, is our present understanding of the role of small firms in that process.[24]

The remaining roles attributed to the small firm and listed in Table 4.5 are, by and large, not based upon any rigorous analysis. In fact the roles listed form an important part of the arguments for supporting small firms and it is surprising that so much effort should be channelled to the small firm sector without at least some effort being devoted to its monitoring and development. It would, however, appear that small firms do have an important role to play in the economy and in society in general and that their role will probably vary through time, by sector of the economy and by location. Hence, the social importance of small firms might be the prime consideration for supporting relatively labour-intensive firms in rural and inner-city areas, whereas in the suburbs and new towns there might be strong economic arguments for aiding the new, high-technology companies. Consequently, it might be opportune for the government to assist and pump-prime the small firm sector at various times and in various places, but the results of such actions should not be expected to be uniform.

4.5. Difficulties of Small Firms in the UK

Many difficulties faced by small firms in the UK are similar to those faced by their medium and large counterparts. There are, however, a number of areas where small firms do find particular difficulties as a result of their size, and also as a result of implicit biases towards large firms. Probably the key area where small firms face the greatest of their difficulties is that of finance. Raising finance for whatever purposes is always problematic irrespective of the size of the firm concerned. For the small firm these problems are usually compounded by their very size (lack of collateral) or their newness (lack of track record). As a result, the financial institutions, especially the high-street banks, regard loans to small firms as representing a higher risk than, say, making loans to medium or large firms. Furthermore, the latter two categories of firms fund a larger proportion of their investment from internally generated funds, or can raise finance from a number of sources and so spread the potential risk (and loss).

It would appear that the greatest difficulty is faced by the totally new venture which, by definition, has no track record and will therefore have no trading evidence as to the proposed venture's viability. This is the generally accepted state of affairs in the UK, but it should be remembered that such difficulties are not faced by all small firms. For example, farmers, who together make-up a sizeable proportion of the small firm sector, will probably find much less difficulty in raising finance than the working-class housewife wishing to establish a hairdressing business. In the case of the farmer, the bank or potential investor at least has the land as collateral, for which there is always a ready market, whereas investing in a totally new firm represents almost a 'total risk' where there might be no collateral whatsoever. Efforts are being made at the present time to educate those seeking funds and those investing funds on how to communicate. Many of the difficulties of raising finance are caused by the parties concerned not speaking the same language, yet they are both seeking the same end – somewhere to invest the bank's funds and funds to exploit a particular business opportunity. Research to date tends to suggest that this gap still exists despite continued government and banking involvement to reduce the gap, and at the present time much of the assistance programme for small firms is aimed at ensuring a flow of funds into new and existing small firms.

The second most frequently mentioned difficulty of small firms is that of premises.[25] Whatever the business, some form of accommodation is required, be it an office, a shop or a factory. There are several problems relating to premises: the availability of premises, and the availability of premises on suitable terms. Small firms, whilst surviving in large numbers in many inner-city areas, have been forced to leave these areas because of shortage of room for expansion and because of rising rents. The redevelopment of inner-city areas has served to exacerbate this situation rather than being a prime cause of the removal of small firms from these areas. The availability of cheap and often poor-quality premises are important to allow the expansion of existing businesses (small firms move frequently because of their cramped conditions) and to allow new businesses to enter with the minimum of overheads. To combat this situation private developers, local and central authorities have embarked on the conversion of existing premises for small firms and the construction of mini-industrial estates catering specifically for the small firm. Allied to this has been the introduction of highly flexible leasing arrangements whereby a month's notice is all that is required before quitting a given property.

Many of the other problems faced by small firms are a result of their size and often their newness. For example, in attempting to secure supplies of materials or machines the small firm will not be allowed the same credit facilities as those of a large firm. This adds to the costs of the small firm and will invariably cause cash flow problems – a large proportion of funds will be tied up in work-in-progress. Just as it is difficult for the small firm to secure supplies of materials or services without payment in advance or at reduced credit ratings, it is often equally difficult to sell one's goods or services. Often an initially disadvantageous pricing policy must be adopted to secure even the smallest amount of business, and even when such business is secured obtaining payments for goods and services provided is not easy. These problems are often further worsened by the inadequate records system and accounting procedures, though it is possible that the present boom in micro-computers might aid the small businessman in this area.

Possibly one of the biggest difficulties most small firms must overcome is the over-involvement of the owner-manager in the everyday running of the business. Too many small firms have a very limited time horizon and give insufficient attention to development. Little, if any consideration is given to what is the most effective means of supplying this or that service, or from which goods is the largest profit made. In short, one of the largest barriers many small firms must overcome is their own incompetence and generally high level of mismanagement. While it is easy to point to these failings of small firms, which account for their very high mortality rates, it is important to realise that many small firms have the seeds of their own destruction cast within them from the start. Efforts to improve the quality of small business management are long overdue and we are now witnessing the first real attempts to redress the balance away from the dominance of many business management courses by 'big business' thinking. It is likely that this trend will gain some support at least in the short term from many 'big businesses' in the UK as the move towards greater decentralisation of decision-making continues, and there will be the need in many big businesses for many of the skills required to run a successful small business.

Much of the previous discussion concerning the difficulties of small firms again draws upon researches on the manufacturing sector and assumes all small firms wish to grow into medium and large firms. This is patently absurd, many small firms trade at the edge of legality everyday and only just manage to survive. For such firms, growth is not a reality. There are other small firms which are trading successfully and do not wish to grow because the lifestyle obtained by running the business as it is is seen as being commensurate with the efforts and problems which must be faced every day. If the business were to expand the balance between the effort expended and rewards gained would be out of balance, and the owner-manager might as well go and work for somebody else. Thus in classifying and cataloguing the difficulties of small firms, it is important to bear in mind that the difficulties are the ones invariably perceived and voiced by those seeking not to be small firms!

4.6. Government Initiatives to Assist Small Firms in the UK

During the 1960s when unemployment began to rise and show marked regional differences, successive governments introduced a wide range of measures to help attract, divert and develop manufacturing industry in the 'depressed' regions. Much the same has happened with the present assistance programme for small firms which has over the past few years grown beyond the comprehension of probably the most well-informed small businessman. The measures have been introduced so quickly and then modified with equal speed that there has been little opportunity to measure whether a scheme has been successful, or has merely diverted elsewhere the problem it was introduced to solve. In fact, because of the ignorance of the small firm sector the various policy measures could merely be supporting an existing trend, or might be attempting to redirect a trend which might be best left well alone. In practice, the simple premise has been adopted which starts with the belief that some small firms are good, and more small firms are better. Hence, much of the assessment has been in terms of numbers of start-ups (closures are usually ignored), the number of jobs created (the numbers displaced are not considered), the number of loans taken-up, and so on, and because there is so little information on the market to which these

Table 4.7: Classification of Government Measures to Assist Small Firms in the UK[a]

Measure	Examples
Financial	Loan Guarantee Scheme; Business Start-Up Scheme; Investment Interest Relief; Venture Capital Scheme; European Loan Scheme; Development Agencies.
Taxation	Value Added Tax; Redundancy Payments Tax Thresholds; Corporation Tax; Pension Contributions Tax Relief; Sub-Contractors Tax Deduction Scheme; Income Tax; Capital Gains Tax; Capital Transfer Tax; Stock Relief.
Premises	Development Land Tax; Industrial Building Allowances of English, Welsh and Scottish Industrial Estates Corporations (under Development Agencies in Wales and Scotland); Rates; Industrial Development Certificates; Office Development Permits.
Legal and regulatory	Buy Back of Shares; Companies Legislation; Business Forms.
Information	Business Opportunities Programme; Manufacturing Advisory Service; Small Firms Information Service; Small Firms Counselling Service.
Education	New Enterprise Development Programme; Growth Programme; Extra Management Resource Programme; Small Business Courses.
Procurement	Direct Labour Organization Tenders.
Exports	Exports Awards; Exports Educational Visits; Market Entry Guarantee Scheme.
Employment	Employment Subsidy.

Note: a. Measures specifically introduced, or the modification of existing measures to assist, to support and to aid small firms.

schemes apply it is impossible to rigorously assess the magnitude of their penetration and success.

This being said, it is important to note the key elements of the current assistance programme for small firms in the UK, which can be divided into nine elements. Of the nine, which are listed in Table 4.7, three predominate – those concerned with finance, tax and premises. By far the greatest effort has been directed towards getting small firms adequately accommodated and financed both in the setting-up and expansion stages. As with most of the previous comments relating to small firms, these schemes are primarily aimed at small manufacturing firms. There are probably three strands to the government's support for small manufacturing firms. First, manufacturing activity is still regarded as being a 'basic' economic activity and upon which the rest of the economy depends. Second, the multiplier effect of jobs and activity in manufacturing industry is greater than that generated in the service sector. The export potential for manufactured goods is more easily recognisable than it is for services provided, by say, the retail or wholesale sectors. Third, the promotion of small firms is seen as part of the restructuring of the UK economy away from being heavily concentrated upon the fortunes of a hundred or so large firms, and also as part of the need to get more people into manufacturing as opposed to service sector jobs. This latter assumption is based on the belief that the UK economy has become unbalanced, and has too few wealth creating enterprises and too many wealth spending bureaucracies. The truth of these arguments is open to debate. How, for example, the trend towards a shrinking but increasingly productive manufacturing sector squares with moves to increase the size of the manufacturing economy by subsidising possibly inefficient and complacent producers is rarely questioned. If markets were freed many of today's assisted enterprises would disappear and so reveal the present assistance programme for small firms as being more social than economic. Again, without adequate monitoring of the small firm sector no evaluation of the success of small firms policy can be made.

Many of the remaining elements in the small firm assistance programme are concerned with removing any barriers faced by small firms simply because they are small. Hence, assistance is made available to small firms wishing to exploit new markets overseas. Here the government will help with market intelligence, establish contacts overseas, arrange visits, and guarantee the value of any exports secured. Another major part of the assistance programme is the promotion of the idea of becoming self-employed and of the wider philosophy underlying small firms – the wish to be independent, the desire to stand on one's own feet using drive and determination and relying on a profit motive.

The present assistance programme for small firms in the UK can be traced back to the fifty recommendations made in the Report of the Committee of Inquiry on Small Firms in November 1971. And since that time the level and breadth of assistance made available for small firms has increased. For the period up to 1977–8 the assistance programme was modified and marginally added to, and the main upsurge has occurred with the reporting of the Wilson Committee on the functioning of the financial institutions, and especially its report on the financing of small firms in 1979. Thus, the present bewildering array of assistance, allowances and advice for small firms has been introduced over the past two or three years. It is therefore difficult to estimate either the gains or losses as a result of the various strands of the small firm assistance programme especially when they are so intertwined. The key test which would indicate the success or otherwise of any assistance programme is its own demise, and the little evaluatory evidence which is available would tend to suggest the *need* for continued rather than pump-priming or bridging assistance. It could well be that the present support and assistance programme is only succeeding in extending the life of small firms which under free-market forces would fail. There is also the possibility that encouraging and allowing the 'success' of mediocre businesses might only succeed in crowding out, and possibly preventing the development of potentially successful business. Furthermore, the indiscriminate distribution of limited resources might at the end of the day only serve to undermine the vitality and reduce the overall quality of the small firm sector. Thus, just as the regional assistance programme which was rigorously applied during the 1960s and early 1970s has been shown to have in part undermined and further exacerbated the very problems which it was introduced to solve, the present small firms assistance programme might have a similar effect on the small firm sector. Furthermore, the worst effects will probably not be evenly spread throughout the UK and some regions might suffer more than others.[26] The truth of these speculations may never be known, but it is important to note that with the present lack of knowledge of the effectiveness of intervening in the small firm sector, they cannot be ruled out, and should at least form part of the present thinking on small firms in the UK.

4.7. Future Developments and Prospects for Small Firms in the UK

Making predictions of how present trends will unfold is always a precarious task, and often best reserved for the brave and the foolhardy. In this section the view into the future is restricted to the immediate future which might be as much as five to ten years at the outside. There are four sources of influence which will individually affect the small firm sector in the UK, and they are, I would suggest: the emergence of new initiatives; the emergence of new actors in the small firms scene; the emergence of new forms of small firms; and, the emergence of small firms as a force in the current developments and application of 'the new technology' (microelectronics).

Traces of more adventurous means of encouraging the emergence of new firms, and the development of existing ones, is already being witnessed in the UK with the use of business competitions and the development of enterprise zones. Business competitions have until the present time been restricted to a relatively small number, drawing sponsorship from some of the largest firms in the UK, for example, Shell (UK) Ltd and Barclays Bank. It is likely that this means of generating interest in small firms, in encouraging large numbers of people to attempt to develop a small firm at least on paper, to act as a natural self-selecting process (only the winners gaining support), and as a means of attracting small firms to a particular area will continue. Business competitions offer a cost-effective means of organising local support and interest for small firms, and can act at the same time as an explicit gesture of concern in the affairs of the local community by the major employers of the area.

Enterprise zones are a particular manifestation of the belief that if business and commerce are allowed to operate unfettered, growth, success and profits can only result.[27] With this in mind a number of enterprise zones have been set-up in some of the most depressed cities and towns of the UK in an attempt to develop natural foci for the regeneration of each specific area. Existing evidence would tend to suggest that the enterprise zones have only succeeded in siphoning off a proportion of those small firms forced to move by the need for larger premises for reasons of expansion.[28] Hence, the enterprise zones are attracting already growing businesses and are therefore acting as a means of concentrating the growth which may occur as a result of the growth of the small firm sector in a particular area. However, it is too early to condemn the enterprise zones as being the redirectors (and concentrators) rather than the generators of growth. It is possible, for example, that by bringing together the most growth-orientated firms into a restricted area greater growth may result. It is likely that this approach to encouraging small firms will develop over the coming years because of its innate geographic component which is required if some form of regional balance is to be introduced into the present national assistance programme for small firms.

Already there are many agencies and groups helping small firms in some shape or form. To this long list, I would suggest, will be added the names of more and more local authorities and also more and more large businesses. The impetus for the involvement of local authorities will be their increasing need to help their own areas and the emergence of local initiatives finding greater favour from central government. The recent reorganisation of training for young people in the UK is locally based, drawing on local resources to meet local needs. This principle will emerge in an increasing number of areas, and is likely to spill-over into greater assistance being devoted towards small firms (there already exists a high level of involvement in some areas).

It might appear strange, but the other new actor will be large businesses. In the UK there are a number of large firms already heavily involved in helping small firms – ICI, IBM, Shell, Marks & Spencer often through local Enterprise Agencies.[29] This trend is likely to develop as the importance of the social responsibility role of large firms becomes increasingly important.[30] Furthermore, it is important that positive attitudes towards business exist in the UK for the successful operating of large businesses themselves, so that they will continue to appeal to large numbers of people as employers. In short, many large firms are using small firms as a part of the promotion of their public (corporate) image, and as part of the general attitude – formation role of the present assistance programme for small firms in the UK.

In discussing small firms it is all too easy to forget the large number of forms small firms can take. Four forms, not necessarily new forms, are beginning to gain popularity and appeal in the UK. These forms are: spin-offs (large firms hiving-off excess business ideas which are not economically attractive to large firms);[31] co-ops (the co-operative movement has grown, albeit slowly, over the past few years and now gains government support via the Co-operative Development Agency);[32] buy-outs (with the present round of cost cutting exercises in most large firms the option is being given to the employees to raise sufficient funds to buy-out that part of business which employs them) – this is reviewed at length by Arnfield *et al.*;[33] and franchising[34] (whilst such firms have existed in a number of forms for many years – public houses, petrol stations – there has been a rapid increase in the numbers of franchises – ready-made small businesses – on offer). The next few years therefore will not only witness an increase in the numbers of small firms, but also a change in the nature, structure and source of small firms. The role, social or economic, played by the four types of business mentioned above might be different from that of the traditional small firm.

The final area where developments are likely to occur in the UK are in the areas of the development and application of microelectronics in the manufacture of new products or in their introduction into existing products. One of the key features of the microelectronics revolution has been the tumbling cost of the basic building-blocks – microchips. Small firms will probably be able to exploit many of the opportunities created by this new technology and could play an important role in their application to existing products and processes. The general lack of expertise in the microelectronics area in many firms will allow the entry of an increasing number of maufacturing and service firms. Furthermore, because of the rapid expansion and development of the microelectronics industry, and the growth of the market for its goods there will be many market opportunities which can be exploited by new firms. In any new industry small firms have invariably played an important role in its early years, and this is likely to be the case with microelectronics.

This brief discussion of the small firms sector in the UK has attempted to present what the state of the art is in the UK in the 1980s. It would appear from the limited data which are available that the number of small firms is increasing and that these increases reveal a distinct regional and sectoral distribution. Similarly, it would appear that small firms do play a wide range of roles in the economy and that these will probably vary through time, through space and by sector. Small firms face many difficulties purely as a result of their size, but in some cases biases do exist against them. Some of these biases have been removed by the wide range of government initiatives to assist small firms. The effectiveness, and in fact the need of many of these initiatives is open to question, and the evaluation of the schemes adopted to-date has been largely of a cursory nature. For the foreseeable future the indicators would suggest continued support and assistance for small firms in varying a number of forms, from a larger number of helpers, and for an increasing variety of small firms.

Notes

1. D.J. Storey, '*Entrepreneurship and the New Firm*', Croom Helm, London, 1982.
2. R. Darendorf, '*Is the work society running out of work?*' BIM Fellows' Luncheon Address, 8 November 1979.
3. M. Cross, 'Fostering New Enterprise in the North' *Department of Employment Gazette*, Vol. 89, No. 5, 1981, pp. 245–8.
4. J.E. Mitchell, 'Small Firms: a critique', *The Three Banks Review*, No. 126, 1980, pp. 50–61.
5. Report produced by G. Bannock of the Economist Intelligence Unit for the Forum of Private Business, and reported in the *Financial Times*, 17 February 1982.
6. A. Ganguly, 'Births and deaths of firms in the UK in 1980' *British Business*, 29 January 1982, pp. 204–7.
7. ibid., and A. Ganguly, 'Regional distribution of births and deaths in the UK in 1980', *British Business*, April 1982, pp. 648–50.
8. M. Cross, '*New Firm Formation and Regional Development*', Gower, Farnborough, 1981, pp. 85–100, 122–7.
9. There are now a wide range of studies which examine new and small firms in most of the Regions and Metropolitan Areas in the UK. Unfortunately, few, if any, of these studies use either consistent definitions of a new or small firm, nor do they use directly comparable time periods. Some of the main studies are (by region):

Scotland	D. Hamilton, L. Moar and I. Orton, *Job Generation in Scottish Manufacturing Industry*, Fraser of Allander Institute, University of Strathclyde, Scotland, 1981. M. Cross, *New Firm Formation and Regional Development*, Gower, Farnborough, 1981. J.R. Firn and J.K. Swales, 'The Formation of New Manufacturing Establishments in the Central Clydeside and West Midlands Conurbations, 1963–1972: A Comparative Analysis,' *Regional Studies*, Vol. 12, No. 2, 1978, pp. 199–213. Scottish Development Department, *Manufacturing Industry in the four Scottish Cities 1966–1971*, S.D.D. Edinburgh, 1977. Scottish Economic Planning Department, 'Small Units in Scottish Manufacturing', *Scottish Economic Bulletin*, Spring 1980.
Northern Ireland	R.T. Harrison and M. Hart, 'New business formation in Northern Ireland – a preliminary investigation', *Annual Conference of the Institute of British Geographers*, Leicester, 1981.
Wales	N.W.C. Woodward, *The employment characteristics of establishments in South Wales*, Working Paper, Department of Economics, University of Cardiff, 1978.
Northern England	J.F.F. Robinson and D.J. Storey, 'Employment Change in Manufacturing Industry in Cleveland 1965–1976', *Regional Studies*, Vol. 15, No. 3, 1981, pp. 161–72. D.J. Storey, 'New Firm Formation, Employment Change and the Small Firm: The Case of Cleveland County', *Urban Studies*, Vol. 18, 1981, pp. 335–45.

Tyne and Wear County Council, *Manufacturing Employment Change in Tyne and Wear since 1965*, Planning Dept, Newcastle-upon-Tyne, 1982.
P.S. Johnson and D.G. Cathcart, 'New Manufacturing Firms and Regional Development: Some evidence from the Northern Region', *Regional Studies*, Vol. 13, No. 3, 1979, pp. 269–80.

North West England
P.E. Lloyd and P. Dicken, 'New Firms, Small Firms and Job Generation: the experience of Manchester and Merseyside', *Working Paper No. 9*, Department of Geography, University of Manchester, 1979.
R.K.B. Hubbard and D.S. Nutter, 'Service Sector Employment in Merseyside', *Geoforum*, Vol. 13 (3), 1982, pp. 209–35.

East Midlands of England
S. Fothergill and G. Gudgin, *Unequal Growth*, Heinemann Educational Books, London, 1982.
G. Gudgin, *Industrial Location Processes and Regional Employment Growth*, Saxon House, Farnborough, 1978.

West Midlands of England
Firn and Swales, 'The Formation of New Manufacturing Establishments'.

South East England
R. Dennis, 'The Decline of Manufacturing Employment in Greater London: 1966–1974', *Urban Studies*, Vol. 15, No. 1, 1978, pp. 63–73.
C.M. Mason, 'New Manufacturing firms in South Hampshire: Some Preliminary Survey Evidence', *Annual Conference of the Institute of British Geographers*, Southampton, Conference Paper, 1982.
P. Gripaios, 'Industrial Decline in London: An examination of its causes', *Urban Studies*, Vol. 14, No. 2, 1977, pp. 181–9.

UK
R.J. Pounce, *Industrial Movement in the United Kingdom 1966–75*, Department of Industry, H.M.S.O. London, 1981.
R.D. Macey, *Job Generation in British Manufacturing Industry: Employment Change by Size of Establishment and by Region*, Department of Industry, Government Economic Service Working Paper No. 55, London, 1982.
S. Nunn, *The Opening and Closure of Manufacturing Units in the United Kingdom 1966–75*, Department of Industry, Government Economic Service Working Paper No. 36, London, 1980.

10. Using Department of Employment estimates and figures derived from the Labour Force Survey of the Office of Population Censuses and Surveys: Department of Employment Gazette Vol. 84, No. 12, 1976, pp. 1344–9 and Vol. 85, No. 6, 1977, pp. 604–5.

11. A. Smith, 'The Informal Economy', *Lloyds Bank Review*, No. 141, 1981, pp. 45–61.

12. A. Dilnot and C.N. Morris, 'What do we know about the black economy?' *Fiscal Studies*, March 1981, pp. 58–73.

13. J.S. Bain, *Barriers to New Competition*, Harvard University Press, Harvard, 1956.

14. E. Mansfield, 'Entry, Gibrats Law, Innovation and the Growth of Firms', *American Economic Review*, Vol. 52, 1962, pp. 1023–51.

15. J. Steindl, *Random Processes and the Growth of Firms*, Griffin, London, 1965.

16. O.F. Collins, D.G. Moore with D.B. Unwalla, *The Enterprising Man*, Michigan State University, Business Studies, East Lansing, Michigan, 1964.

17 J. Stanworth and J. Curran, *Management Motivation in the Smaller Business*, Gov. ᵣr Press, Epping, 1973.

18. M.G. Scott, *Entrepreneurs and Entrepreneurship: A Study of Organizational Founding*, Unpublished PhD dissertation, University of Edinburgh.

J.H. Goldthorpe (with C. Llewellyn and C. Payne), *Social Mobility and Class Structure in Modern Britain*, Oxford University Press, Oxford, 1980.

19. L. Brown, *Building a Sustainable Society*, Worldwatch Institute Book, W.W. Norton, New York, 1981.

J. Robertson, *The Sane Alternative*, River Basin Publishing Co., St. Paul, Minneapolis, 1981.

20. M. Cross, 'The Components of Employment Change – Rural Growth and Urban Decline', *XIth European Congress for Rural Sociology*, Helsinki: Conference Paper, 1981.

21. W.W. Daniel, *The Unemployed Flow, Stage I Interim Report*, Policy Studies Institute, London, 1981.

22. B.J. Boswell, *The Rise and Decline of Small Firms*, George Allen and Unwin, London, 1973.

R. Scase and R. Goffee, *The Real World of the Small Business Owner*, Croom Helm, London, 1980.

23. J. Curran and J. Stanworth, 'Size of Workplace and Attitudes to Industrial Relations in the Printing and Electronics Industry', *British Journal of Industrial Relations*, Vol. 19, No. 1, 1981, pp. 14–25.

J. Curran and J. Stanworth, 'The Social Dynamics of the Small Manufacturing Enterprise', *Journal of Management Studies*, Vol. 18, No. 2, 1981, pp. 141–58.

24. A. Robertson, 'Innovation Management. Theory and Comparative Practice illustrated by two Case Studies', *Management Decision*, Vol. 12, No. 6, 1974, pp. 330–73.

Confederation of British Industry, *Innovation and Competitiveness in Smaller Companies*, CBI, London, 1979.

25. Coopers and Lybrand (with Drivas Jonas), *Provision of Small Industrial Premises*, Small Firms Division, Department of Industry, London, 1980.

JURUE, *Industrial Renewal in the Inner City: An Assessment of Potential and Problems*, Department of the Environment, London, 1980.

N. Falk, 'Finding a Place for Small Enterprise in the Inner City', in A. Evans and D.E.C. Eversley (eds.), *The Inner City, Employment and Industry*, Heinemann Educational Books, London, 1980, pp. 367–88.

26. D.J. Storey, *Entrepreneurship and the New Firm*, devotes Chapter 10 to constructing a Regional Index of Entrepreneurship.

27. One of the underlying ideas is the creation of small 'economic islands' with some of the characteristics of Hong Kong. This is outlined in A. Rabushica, *Hong Kong: A Study of Economic Freedom*, University of Chicago Press, Chicago, 1979.

28. As reported in *New Society*, 21 January 1981, p. 101.

29. V. Sargent, *Large Firms and Small Firms: A Review of Current Activities*, London Enterprise Agency, London, 1980.

30. L.H. Peach and B.J.A. Hargreaves, 'Social Responsibility: The Investment that pays off', *Personnel Management*, Vol. 8, No. 6, 1976, pp. 20–4.

31. E.G. Fronko, 'One company's cast-off Technology is another company's opportunity', *Innovation*, No. 23, 1971, pp. 52–9.

32. J. Thornley, *Workers Co-operatives: Jobs and Dreams,* Martin Robertson, London, 1981.

33. R.V. Arnfield, B. Chiplin, M. Jarrett and M. Wright (eds.), *Management Buyouts. Corporate Trends for the 80's*, University of Nottingham, Nottingham, 1981.

34. J. Stanworth, *A Study of Franchising in Britain – a Research Report*, School of Management Studies, Polytechnic of Central London, 1977.

5 AUSTRALIA

5.1. Introduction

A government-appointed committee reporting on small business in Australia in 1971 identified management as the principal feature which distinguished small firms from others.[1] The committee's definition of a small firm was 'one in which one or two persons make all the critical management decisions . . . without the aid of internal specialists and with specific knowledge in only one or two functional areas.'[2] This definition recognises that a small firm is an independent business and not a subsidiary or affiliate of a large enterprise. In fact, the vast majority of small firms in Australia are owned and managed by individuals or by members of a single family. The typical small firm remains in the hands of the original founder or members of his family from the time it is established until its eventual demise.

In order to examine the size and scope of the small business sector in Australia, a quantitative rather than a qualitative definition of a small firm is needed. There are some compelling reasons for basing this quantitative definition on the employment size of a firm. First, details of employment are provided by all firms in the annual censuses of Australian manufacturing while information about turnover and value added is no longer being collected from very small firms.[3] Secondly, international comparisons of small business activity are facilitated when employment is used as a measure of firm size. A measure based on annual turnover, for example, is difficult to apply consistently across countries. Exchange rates have to be used to convert turnover to a common currency, and variations in exchange rates may not correspond to the relative changes in the domestic price levels of the countries concerned.

The most widely-used statistical definitions of a small firm in Australia are as follows. In manufacturing industry, a small firm is one which employs fewer than one hundred persons, including the working proprietors. In retailing, wholesaling, construction and other service activities it is a firm employing fewer than twenty, again including the working proprietors, and in agriculture, where employment data is less readily available, it is a firm with an annual

120

value of operations below A$200,000. These definitions of a small firm are used throughout this chapter.

A very large proportion of all firms are classified as small under these definitions. For example, over 95 per cent of manufacturing, retailing and private construction firms have employment levels falling within the size limits just mentioned. The contribution of these small firms to aggregate output and employment in each industry is of course smaller than this proportion would indicate. The latest available data from the Australian Bureau of Statistics show that small firms account for just over 30 per cent of total manufacturing employment, about 55 per cent of retail employment and approximately 63 per cent of employment in private building and construction. The approximate number of small firms in various industries and their total employment is shown in Table 5.1

Official data is not available on the size distribution of firms in many areas of the service sector where small firms are known to be prominent. For example, there has not been a recent economic census covering the road transport industry, financial, property and business services, or such professions as lawyers, doctors, dentists or architects. Limited information about the role of small firms in some of these activities has been collected through sample surveys conducted by individual researchers, but the coverage is far from complete.

Despite these gaps in our knowledge of the small business sector, it is possible to derive an approximate estimate of the number of small firms in Australia and their contribution to employment. In 1980, there were probably about 600,000 active small trading enterprises employing arond 1.8 million persons. This means that employment in small firms accounts for approximately 40 per cent of total private sector employment

The official data, such as that used in compiling Table 5.1 relate to all enterprises falling within the prescribed size limits. Since an enterprise is defined as a single operating legal entity, the subsidiaries of larger firms are often included in the data as separate enterprises. This applies equally to subsidiaries or affiliates of foreign companies operating in Australia and to subsidiaries of large Australian-owned firms. Clearly, it would be desirable in principle to exclude such firms from the small firm category. Although this cannot be done as far as the official data are concerned, any bias resulting from the inclusion of these firms is

Table 5.1: The Small Firm Sector in Australia

Industry	Small firm definition	Number of small firms '000	Employment in small firms '000	Year
Mining	Fewer than 20 persons employed	0.6	2.9	(1980)
Agriculture	Annual value of operations less than A$0.2 million	161.7	n.a.	(1980–81)
Manufacturing	Fewer than 100 persons employed	33.9	363.2	(1980)
Retailing	Fewer than 20 persons employed	122.0	439.6	(1980)
Wholesaling	Fewer than 20 persons employed	21.7	104.9	(1969)
Construction[a]	Fewer than 20 persons employed	49.4	151.5	(1979)
Selected service industries[b]	Fewer than 20 persons employed	31.1	152.5	(1980)
All Industries (estimated)		600 approx.	1,800 approx.	(1980)

Notes: a. Including the building trades, but excluding general government construction. b. Comprising motion picture theatres, cafes and restaurants, hotels etc., accommodation, licensed clubs, laundries and dry cleaners, men's hairdressers and women's hairdressing and beauty salons.

Sources: Australian Bureau of Statistics, *Enterprise Statistics: Details by Industry Sub-Division Australia 1979–80* (Preliminary) (Catalogue No. 8107.0) (Canberra, June 1982); *Enterprise Statistics: Details by Industry Class Australia 1978–79* (Catalogue No. 8103.0) (Canberra, January 1982); *Agricultural Industries, Structure of Operating Units Australia 1980–81* (Catalogue No. 7102.0) (Canberra, August 1982); *Enterprise Statistics: Details by Industry Class Australia 1968–69* (Reference No. 17.15) (Canberra 1974).

likely to be small. They would account for an insignificant fraction of the total number of small firms recorded in each sector and a tiny proportion of small firm employment, except perhaps in manufacturing industry.

In the remainder of this chapter we shall explore a number of facets of small firm activity in Australia. The next section discusses the recent trends in small firm employment and considers whether there has been any decline in the importance of small firms in the economy. This is followed by a review of the limited evidence on the birth and death rates of small firms. The third section considers the role of small firms in Australia as innovators, as suppliers to big business, and as a source of competition to the large established firms. The particular problems facing small firms, which are being highlighted as a result of the present recession, are reviewed in the next section. Finally, we consider what government initiatives have been undertaken to alleviate the problems of small firms and to foster the development of an efficient small business sector.

5.2. Recent Trends in Small Business Activity

During the past decade, small firms have declined in relative importance in manufacturing, mining, retailing and some specific parts of the service sector. Since these are the only individual industries for which trends in small business activity can be reliably measured, it might be thought that there has been a general decline in the importance of small firms in the Australian economy as a whole. However, such an inference would probably not be justified. It is likely that small firms have maintained their share of total private-sector employment in this period, mainly as a result of the continued expansion of the service sector, in which small firms play a major role.

In retailing and in selected parts of the recreational and personal services industry,[4] the number of small firms increased between June 1969 and June 1980, as can be seen in Table 5.2. In manufacturing industry and mining, on the other hand, the number of small firms declined. More importantly, the share of employment contributed by small firms fell in each of these four industries, with the most severe falls taking place in retailing and in the mining industry.

When the four industries are aggregated, it can be seen that the

Table 5.2: Number of Small Firms and Their Share of Employment in Selected Industries, June 1969 and June 1980

Industrial sector	Number of small firms, '000		Percentage of industry employment		Change in employment share, 1969 to 1980 (percentage points)
	June 1969	June 1980	June 1969	June 1980	
Mining	0.8	0.6	7.3	3.8	-3.5
Manufacturing	30.4	33.9	32.0	30.7	-1.3
Retailing	113.6	122.0	60.7	55.5	-5.2
Selected service industries[a]	22.5	31.1	53.2	52.7	-0.5
Total of above industries	167.3	187.6	42.6	40.9	-1.7

Note: a. Comprising motion picture theatres, cafes and restaurants, hotels etc, accommodation, licensed clubs, laundries and dry cleaners, men's hairdressers and women's hairdressing and beauty salons.

Sources: Australian Bureau of Statistics, *Enterprise Statistics: Details by Industry Sub-Division Australia 1979–80 (Preliminary) (Catalogue No. 8107.0)* (Canberra, June 1982); *Enterprise Statistics: Details by Industry Class Australia 1968–69 (Reference No. 17.15)* (Canberra, 1974).

decline in the small firms' share of total employment has been comparatively slight – from 42.6 per cent in June 1969 to 40.9 per cent in June 1980. Put another way, small firms accounted for just under 10 per cent of the increase in total employment in these industries during the period. While the recent growth in small firm employment in these industries has been relatively slow, the performance would have been considerably worse but for the substantial increase in employment in the selected parts of the recreational and personal services industry. Small firms almost maintained their share of employment in this industry during the 1970s, and by June 1980 still accounted for over 52 per cent of the industry's total employment.

However, the industries included in Table 5.2 account for only about 50 per cent of total private-sector employment in Australia. The principal privately-owned industries not represented in the table are wholesaling, finance, property and business services,[5] medical services,[6] construction, transport and storage and agriculture. In nearly all of these industries small firms are thought to occupy an important, and in some cases, a predominant place.[7] Between August 1969 and August 1980 total private employment in Australia grew by just over 660,000 persons, although only about 120,000 of the additional jobs were in the four industries listed in Table 5.2. Since employment in agriculture recorded a small decline during this period, it follows that more than four-fifths of the increase in private employment took place in finance, property and business services and the various other service activities just mentioned. It seems likely that small firms were able to maintain their overall share of employment in these tertiary activities during the period, because the areas of most rapid employment growth were health services, real estate and business services and road transport, in each of which small firms are strongly represented. If this view is correct, there can be little doubt that the share of total private employment contributed by small firms remained constant or even increased slightly between 1969 and 1980.

Two principal conclusions can be drawn from this analysis of the recent broad trends in small business activity in Australia. The first is that, in the industries for which measurable trends can be calculated, the past decade has seen some erosion in the competitive position of small firms. In the case of the mining industry, the further decline in the already tiny share of employment held by small firms is related to the large scale of the recently established export-oriented mining ventures which have become the focal point of Australia's so-called 'resources boom'. In the case of retailing, the declining share of employment in small firms is partly a reflection of the greater concentration of grocery retailing in the hands of the major supermarket chains, and the continued decline in the importance of the small independent corner store.

As we have seen, the share of employment contributed by small firms declined least in the selected service activities comprising hotels, clubs, cafes and restaurants, laundries and hairdressers. This is not surprising, since these are personal services which have to be provided at widely dispersed locations, and consequently the opportunities for economies of large-scale operation are limited. Nevertheless, some large United States companies, including Kentucky Fried Chicken, Pizza Hut and McDonalds have entered the Australian fast-food market in recent years. The impact of their entry upon small firm employment in cafes and restaurants, has been limited by the fact that most of their franchised outlets are operated by small independent businesses.

Finally, in the case of the manufacturing sector a variety of factors has led to the fall in the employment share of small firms. These include technological changes, which have sometimes resulted in an increase in the minimum efficient scale of production; increased import penetration, particularly in some labour-intensive industries; and changes in the pattern of demand for manufactured goods. As the data on manufacturing industry are more extensive than for other industries, a more detailed analysis of the trends in small firm employment can be carried out for that sector. Some results from such an analysis are described in the next section of this chapter.

The second conclusion that can be drawn from the broad employment trends described above is that the apparent deterioration in the competitive position of small firms in primary and secondary industry has probably not been accompanied by an economy-wide fall in the employment share of small firms. This is mainly because the pattern of business and household demand has shifted during the decade towards a relatively greater expenditure on private (and public) services. Small firms enjoy competitive advantages in the provision of many personal and specialised business services and these advantages are not readily eroded by larger businesses. Hence, increased spending on services has favoured the growth of the small business sector, offsetting other factors pulling in the opposite direction.

A. Trends in Manufacturing Industry

As mentioned previously, small maufacturing firms declined in number during the 1970s and this was accompanied by a fall in their share of the industry's employment. What were the reasons for the decline? First, there is no evidence to suggest that it was due to a decrease in new business formations. Indeed, the number of very small manufacturing firms – those with fewer than ten persons employed – increased by almost one-fifth between June 1969 and June 1979. Moreover, aggregate employment in these very small firms also increased, despite the general downward trend in manufacturing employment. The only other size-category of manufacturing firms to increase their employment significantly in this period were the large firms employing 500 persons or more. Thus, it was the medium-size and larger small firms which bore the brunt of the decline in total manufacturing employment.

Secondly, changes in the broad composition of manufacturing output and employment were only partly responsible for the observed decline in the small firms' share of employment. It is true that the most severe fall in employment took place in the clothing and footwear industries, two industries in which small firms are strongly represented. However, other industries in which small firms are very prominent, such as fabricated metal products and wood, wood products and furniture, slightly increased their share of total manufacturing employment in the period.

If the industrial composition of manufacturing employment had not changed over the ten years from June 1969, small firms would have still have experienced a decline in their employment share – from 32 per cent to about 30.2 per cent[8] in June 1979. Since their actual share of employment in the latter month was 29.4 per cent, this implies that approximately two-thirds of the drop in the employment share can be attributed to the gradual erosion of the competitive position of small firms within individual manufacturing industries.[9] Only the remaining one-third of the decline can be explained by the changing pattern of employment among the various manufacturing industries.

Table 5.3 provides some confirmation that small firms have been losing their competitive position in individual industries. In eight of the twelve manufacturing industry subdivisions, there was a decline in the small firms' share of employment between 1969 and 1979. Only in the fabricated metal products and other machinery and equipment industries did the share increase, while in the transport equipment industry it remained steady.

We can throw some light on the factors that may have contributed to the changing employment share of small firms in each industry, by recognising that the employment share in any year can be expressed as the product of three ratios. These are the average employment in the plants operated by small firms relative to the average employment per plant in the industry as a whole; the average number of plants operated by each small firm relative to the average number per firm in the industry; and the number of small firms in relation to the total number of firms in the industry.[10] Changes in any of these ratios will influence the aggregate share of the industry's employment contributed by small firms. Hence by analysing these changes over time, we can offer some explanation for the observed variation in the small firms' employment share.

An analysis of the data for the manufacturing industries listed in Table 5.3 reveals that between 1969 and 1979 the average employment-size of the plants operated by large firms increased in every industry in relation to the average size of the plant operated by the small firms.[11] This suggests that economies of large-scale production were becoming more pronounced during this period. Changes in the average number of plants operated by small firms were relatively unimportant, but in three industries, food, beverages and tobacco, chemicals, petroleum and coal products and other machinery and equipment the average number of plants per large firm declined substantially. This implies that in these three industries particularly, the additional economies of large-scale production arose at the plant rather than the firm level, to the point where large firms found it economic to concentrate their production in fewer plants than before.

If, as we have inferred, the minimum efficient size of plant was increasing in these industries, small firms would probably have found it more difficult to compete. Consequently, a decline in their relative numbers could be expected. This indeed was the case in the food, beverage and tobacco and chemical, petroleum and coal products industries. However, in the other machinery and equipment industry, the number of small firms increased substantially, both in absolute terms and as a proportion of all firms in the industry. A likely explanation is that the small firms in this

Table 5.3: Manufacturing Industries: The Share of Small Firms in Total Industry Employment

	Percentage of industry employment		Change in share 1969 to 1979
	June 1969	June 1979	(percentage points)
Food, beverages and tobacco	26.4	19.4	−7.0
Textiles	19.1	25.9	+6.8
Clothing and footwear	50.5	47.5	−3.0
Wood, wood products and furniture	69.5	62.7	−6.8
Paper, paper products, printing, publishing	39.6	35.9	−3.7
Chemical, petroleum and coal products	19.4	14.4	−5.0
Non-Metallic mineral products	26.3	22.9	−3.4
Basic metal products	7.4	6.2	−1.2
Fabricated metal products	48.3	51.4	+3.1
Transport equipment	13.6	13.7	+0.1
Other machinery and equipment	28.1	30.0	+1.9
Miscellaneous manufacturing	38.6	37.9	−0.7
Total manufacturing	32.0	29.4	−2.6

Source: Australian Bureau of Statistics, Canberra, *Enterprise Statistics, Details by Industry Class Australia 1968–69 and 1978–79* (ABS Catalogue No 8103.0); *Manufacturing Establishments: Summary of Operations by Industry Class, 1978–79* (Cat No 8202.0).

industry are mainly supplying specialised less-expensive items of equipment to customer specifications. Thus, they seldom compete directly with the larger firms which are manufacturing standard lines or more expensive items of heavy machinery and equipment.

Apart from other machinery and equipment, there were only two industries, textiles and fabricated metal products, in which small firms increased their share of total employment between 1969 and 1979. The textile industry suffered a drop in total employment in this period of more than 40 per cent, largely as a result of higher import penetration. It seems that small firms were relatively more sheltered from this stronger competition than the larger firms in the industry, while the number of firms employing 100 persons or more fell by about 38 per cent, the number of small firms declined by less than 6 per cent.[12]

Finally, small firms have traditionally occupied an important place in the fabricated metal products industry, supplying a wide range of goods to households and to meet the specialised requirements of other manufacturers. In the period under review the number of small firms in the industry increased, while the number of large firms fell by more than one-quarter. Although the average plant size of the larger manufacturers increased, this was not sufficient to offset the effect of the reduced number of large firms and consequently the employment share of these firms declined.

The general conclusion that can be drawn from the preceding discussion is that, considering the problems confronting Australian manufacturing industry during the 1970s, small firms producing specialised products and goods-to-order appear to have survived relatively well. The story was somewhat different where small firms were faced with stronger competition from imports in the mid 1970s, as in the case of the clothing and footwear industries.[13] Moreover, small firms found themselves at an increasing competitive disadvantage in some industries producing standard consumer products or producer goods in which the minimum efficient size of plant was increasing. This applied particularly to the food, beverages and tobacco and the chemical industries.

B. Births and Deaths of Small Firms

There is no direct evidence on the rate at which small businesses are being formed in Australia. It is known that new company registrations per year amount to about 8 per cent of the number of companies already on the register.[14] But this is not a reliable guide to the small firm birth rate, because some of the newly-registered companies will never become active trading enterprises. Moreover, the new registrations include firms which have been operating for some time as partnerships or sole traders and are now seeking incorporation.

The indirect evidence, however, indicates that the birth rate of small firms has remained at a high level during the 1970s. First, the number of small retail concerns increased by about 7 per cent between June 1969 and June 1979, while the number in the selected parts of the recreational and personal services industry increased by over one-third. Even in maufacturing industry, where small firms experienced a reduction in their share of employment, the number of small enterprises rose by about 5 per cent during this period. These increases in 'the stock' of small firms suggest that the birth rate was running ahead of the closure rate[15] in the industries for which we have information.

Secondly, two recent surveys of small businesses, one conducted in 1973 and the other in 1978, have shown that 21 to 25 per cent of small non-manufacturing firms in Australia are less than five years old.[16] Since it is more difficult to identify and establish contact with newly-established firms, these percentages could understate the true proportion of young firms in the small business population. However, even if taken at their face value, they point to a relatively high birth rate of small non-manufacturing firms during the past decade.

While the rate of small business formation has not been a matter of serious concern in Australia, politicians and businessmen frequently deplore the rate of small business failure. In fact, data which might be used to calculate small business failure rates are scarce and often unsuitable for the purpose. However, as we shall see later, some useful information is available about the causes of small business failure and how the likelihood of failure varies with the age and size of the firm.

One source of information on small business mortality is the Annual Report on the operation of the Bankruptcy Act.[17] This provides data on business bankruptcies among unincorporated enterprises including sole traders, but does not cover company liquidations. Moreover, voluntary closures, in which the proprietors of a business cease trading and make their own private arrangements with their creditors, are also not included in the data.

It is believed that the annual number of voluntary closures is far greater than the number of business bankruptcies.

In comparison to the number of small firms in existence, the annual total of business bankruptcies is very low – no more than 0.5 per cent in the year ended June 1981, for example. There has been an upward trend in the past five years in the number of business bankruptcies reported annually, but it is difficult to be certain that this reflects a corresponding upward trend in small business closures of all kinds. The doubt arises because of the very limited coverage of the bankruptcy data.

A recent paper by R.A. Price analysed the closures among manufacturing firms in Victoria over the ten years to June 1976.[18] He found that most of the closures were voluntary and that small firm closures per year represented about 5 per cent of all the manufacturing firms employing fewer than 100 persons. While noting that closure rates generally tended to follow the course of the business cycle, he found that closures among very small firms with fewer than five employees did not vary in this way. In their case the rate of closure was several times greater than the average rate for manufacturing industry as a whole and remained virtually constant throughout the ten-year period.

A recently completed study by Renfrew, Sheehan and Dunlop of the Small Firms Research Group at the University of Newcastle, New South Wales, traces the history of over 2,000 manufacturing and non manufacturing small firms from 1973 through to 1978.[19] Their best estimate is that about 19 per cent of the firms in existence in 1973 had closed by 1978, with 29 per cent being the most pessimistic estimate of closures during the period.[20] These estimates correspond to an annual closure rate in the range of about 4 to 6 per cent[21] and therefore are closely in line with the earlier estimate by Price.

Most small business closures involve firms which have been in existence for only a brief period. A.J. Williams investigated a sample of failed businesses in Western Australia and found that two-thirds of the firms were less than five years old when they failed.[22] It appears that by the time a small firm has reached five years of age its life-expectancy has improved considerably.

What are the principal causes of small business failure? The annual statistics on business bankruptcies are very helpful in answering this question, even though the data relate to unincorporated businesses only. In each of the six years to 30 June

1978, lack of business ability, training or experience was found to be responsible for more business bankruptcies than any other single factor. Insufficient initial working capital and adverse economic conditions affecting industry (including credit restrictions and severe competition) were identified as the next most important causes of failure in that period. However, in the years 1978–9 and 1979–80, adverse economic conditions replaced lack of business ability as the prime cause of business bankruptcies. While it may be inferred from these figures that many small businesses are established on the basis of over-optimistic expectations but inadequate management skills, it is also clear that a deterioration in the general economic climate is likely to bring about a rise in the rate of bankruptcy among small firms.

Finally, what are the real costs to the community of small business closures? This question has not been explored in any depth in Australia and it is too readily assumed that firm closures typically result in a loss of economic welfare. There is undoubtedly a real cost in economic resources involved in winding up the affairs of a defunct business and in the idle time of the proprietors and employees between the time of closure and finding alternative employment. However, against this has to be set the possible long-run gain in real output if the capital and labour resources are transferred to a more productive use. It is also worth mentioning that obstacles to the exit of small firms, arising, for example, through limitations on the sale or transfer of businesses,[23] tend to create a barrier to the entry of new firms into an industry. To be efficient in a dynamic sense an economy requires a regular turnover of businesses, with new firms replacing those which have not been able to meet the market test successfully.

5.3 The Role of Small Firms in Australia

The Bolton Committee of Inquiry on Small Firms in the United Kingdom drew attention to a variety of important functions that are performed by small firms in a developed economy. In particular, they noted that small firms have a role as

> a breeding ground for new industries and an important source of innovation in products, techniques and services
> a low-cost specialist supplier of parts and components to large companies

a source of actual and potential competition, thus contributing to
the efficient working of the economic system as a whole

a seedbed for new large and vigorous companies and an entry-
point for new entrepreneurial talent

a source of greater variety in consumer products and services by
virtue of their ability to flourish in limited or specialised
markets[24]

In this section we consider how well some of these functions are
performed by small firms in Australia. In particular, we consider
the role of small manufacturing firms in innovation and as specialist
suppliers to large companies. We also examine the competitive role
of small firms both in manufacturing and retailing.

A. Research and Innovation

In relation to their total employment, small manufacturing firms in
Australia maintain a relatively low research and development
effort. In 1978–9, for example, manufacturing firms employing
fewer than 100 persons were responsible for 28 per cent of industry
employment but only about 12 per cent of the man-years of R & D
effort. Nevertheless those small firms that do have an R & D
programme spend, on average, a higher proportion of their
turnover on this type of activity than do larger firms.

Small firms have introduced a few important innovations and
their record in this respect seems better when it is recognised that
Australia derives a great deal of its new technology from overseas
either through licensing agreements or through subsidiaries of
foreign companies.[25] After excluding innovations imported from
abroad and adapted for use in Australia, a survey by the Australian
Academy of Technological Sciences identified 66 Australian
innovations during the period 1970 to 1975.[26] About one half of
these arose originally from inventions made in government
research laboratories and universities, and the remainder were
industry inventions. Small firms were responsible for the initial
invention in a few instances, and in another case a small firm
collaborated with a government research organisation (CSIRO) in
the production and commercial development of the atomic
absorption spectrophotometer – a scientific instrument now used
world-wide.

It is interesting to note that the small firm in question was
subsequently taken over by a large United States scientific

instrument manufacturer. This case is not unique, as other small high-technology enterprises in Australia have also been acquired by overseas interests. At first sight, such takeovers do not appear to be in the best interests of Australians, particularly if the overseas purchaser decides to curtail the research and development programme of the local firm after it has been acquired. However, there is another side to this question. The price paid to Australian residents for the firm will normally exceed the value of the enterprise under its present ownership and in that sense Australians can gain from the sale. Moreover, a small local innovative firm may often find its growth prospects limited by lack of access to an international distribution network and perhaps by a shortage of capital. An equity link with a large multinational company is one way of overcoming such difficulties, and may eventually lead to additional Australian exports.

In practice, most foreign takeovers require specific approval under the provisions of the Foreign Takeovers Act. In considering whether to recommend approval, the Foreign Investment Review Board examines the likely net economic benefit to Australia, taking into account such factors as the effect on competition, efficiency, Australian involvement in research and development and in the supply of components. Thus there are safeguards in place to ensure that takeovers of local enterprises are in the best interests of Australians. A possible source of concern to small firms, however, is that the government will not normally intervene to prevent a foreign takeover if the total assets of the target company are less than A$2 million (approximately US$2 million).

B. Suppliers to Large Companies

Many small manufacturing firms in Australia are principally engaged in supplying parts or components for a few large manufacturing companies. General Motors-Holden's, Australia's largest manufacturer of motor vehicles, obtains supplies from about 4,000 separate firms, most of them small, even though it also manufactures some components in-house. Many small manufacturers of consumer goods, particularly clothing, are also dependent on a few large customers. The goods are often produced to specifications laid down by one or more of the major distributors and then sold exclusively through that particular chain of retail outlets.

A survey undertaken by the Small Firms Research Group at the

University of Newcastle, NSW, in 1973 revealed the extent to which small manufacturing firms in Australia sell their output to only a few large customers.[27] It was found that one-quarter of all the firms surveyed sold at least half of their output to one or two customers. In the case of the textiles, clothing and footwear industry, 36 per cent of the respondent firms sold at least half their output to just one or two purchasers.

Large firms are likely to enjoy lower costs as a result of their purchasing arrangements with small suppliers, as the Bolton Committee recognised. Yet the small suppliers probably increase their risks as a result of their dependence on only a small number of customers. The risk is not so much that a large customer will fail but that such a customer could suddenly shift his orders to another small supplier if there is seen to be any price advantage in doing so. The University of Newcastle survey showed that, compared with other small manufacturing firms, those firms with only a few customers emphasised that low prices were an important source of their competitive advantage. Firms with a wider spread of customers laid relatively more stress on the non-price features of their products, such as quality, good design and after-sales services.[28]

Finally, another interesting result from this survey can be mentioned. It was found that the majority of the small firms with a limited number of customers had not made any significant additions to their product range during the preceding five years.[29] By contrast, most of the other firms had added some important new products. This result suggests that small firms producing to specifications laid down by their major customers can be in danger of focusing too much on the reduction of costs in the manufacture of existing products, and paying too little attention to the need to keep up with new product developments.

C. *Small Firms as a Source of Actual and Potential Competition*

According to the Bolton Committee, one of the most important roles for small firms in a developed economy is to provide a seedbed from which new small firms develop. They act as a source of actual and potential competition which could impose a check on monopoly profits and act as a spur to greater efficiency by large companies. Important as these functions are, it is not easy to judge how successfully they are carried out by the small firm sector in a particular economy. Changes in the share of small firms in total employment or output are clearly not a reliable indicator. For example, even if the percentage of employment contributed by small firms has fallen over time, many individual small firms may have grown rapidly to the point where they can now challenge the leading industrial enterprises. Conversely, an increase in the employment share of small firms may largely reflect the relative growth of those industrial and commercial activities in which small firms are already dominant, rather than representing additional competition for the established giant firms.

In Australia, as in other developed countries, many small firms are operating in limited or specialised markets where it is not economic for large firms to compete. It is only in certain industries that there is actual or potential competition between small firms and large. These industries include, for example, the manufacture of soft drinks, bread, cakes and pastries, men's suits, architectural aluminium products, paper stationery and some plastic products. It appears that in most of these industries the larger firms, employing one hundred persons or more, have increased their share of industry output during the past decade, while very few firms which were small at the beginning of the period have moved up into the ranks of the large enterprises. This apparent lack of competitive success by small firms could be related to the characteristics of the industries concerned. Most of the industries just mentioned are mature slowly-growing industries in which there is limited scope for new firms to enter by introducing radically different products.

However, this description cannot be applied to the plastic products industry where employment grew by 35 per cent between June 1969 and June 1979, accompanied by a significant extension of the product range. It is interesting to note therefore that in a major part of this industry, plastic products not elsewhere classified (nec), the number of small firms more than doubled during the decade, while the share of employment contributed by small firms increased slightly. Moreover, several firms which commenced operations in the late 1960s or early 1970s have since increased their employment to more than one hundred, with one or two achieving Stock Exchange listing within a few years of starting up.

This example points to the growth opportunities for small firms in new industries and in industries where rapid technological change is taking place. However, some of the newer high-technology industries which have been exhibiting rapid growth in the United States and other major industrialised countries have yet to develop in Australia. For example, local production of semiconductors is negligible, the microelectronics industry is very small, biotechnology ventures have scarcely begun and almost all computers are imported. Thus, in manufacturing industry, at least, instances of spectacular growth by small innovative firms have been rare. How far this can be attributed to problems of availability of finance and how far it is a function of the small size of the economy and Australia's comparative advantage in exporting primary products, is not clear. However, it is worth noting that in the service sector, particularly in road transport, construction and the computer service industry, there have been many more cases of spectacular growth by small firms, even to the point where they have been able to challenge the industry leaders.

5.4 Difficulties Confronting Small Firms

The economic difficulties that small firms encounter are not identical to those faced by large firms. For a small firm, problems such as the availability of long-term finance, short-term liquidity, the costs of tax compliance and the burden of form-filling tend to be of much greater significance than they are for a long-established large enterprise. Thus it may be argued that specific government policies are needed to address the particular problems of the small business sector. However, this argument would not be universally accepted in Australia. While there is some evidence of a recent shift in attitudes government initiatives to assist small firms have so far been quite modest in comparison with those introduced in many other developed countries.

Whether there is a need for additional policy initiatives depends of course on the nature and extent of the problems facing small firms, and whether there are powerful non-economic reasons for supporting the small business sector. The purpose of this section is to identify the particular problems that are of most concern to small business proprietors in Australia and to examine the reasons for their concern. The problems attracting most attention are in the areas of taxation, availability of finance, and the market power of large firms. Each of these areas will be considered in turn.

A. Taxation

In general, the tax rates levied on business income do not discriminate between small companies and large. The profits of a small private company are subject at present to a company income tax rate of 46 per cent, equal to the rate charged on the profits of a large public company. A concessional rate of tax is not available on the first tranche of profits, as it is in some developed countries.

Changes in the tax system since 1972–3 have in fact removed certain income tax concessions which small companies previously enjoyed.[30] Prior to that year private companies paid a lower rate of tax on their profits than resident public companies. In addition, a reduced rate of tax applied to the first A\$10,000 of profits. While this last concession was equally available to public companies and private companies, it was relatively more important to small companies.

While small companies are no longer favoured by the present system of company income tax, they can be subject to an additional undistributed profits tax (commonly known as Division 7 tax) which is not levied on public companies. The undistributed profits tax is payable only if the private company fails to distribute at least 20 per cent of its post-tax trading profits as dividends to shareholders.[31] In that event, the tax is levied at the rate of 50 per cent on the amount by which the dividend distribution falls short of the required minimum.

In the past, the Division 7 tax arrangements have been criticised by small businessmen mainly on the grounds that they limit the small company's ability to retain adequate profits to finance expansion. A further line of criticism sometimes expressed is that the very existence of the tax implies an element of discrimination against small companies compared with large. Pressures from small business groups have in fact led to a considerable easing of the Division 7 tax provisions in recent years. Prior to 1976–7, private companies were required to distribute 50 per cent of their after-tax profits in order to escape liability for the additional undistributed profits tax. But this proportion has been progressively reduced to 20 per cent, with the latest reduction being announced in the 1982–3 Federal Budget in August 1982.

Despite the criticisms that have been made, the principle behind Division 7 can be defended on equity grounds. The tax is intended to prevent high-income shareholders from controlling the dividend policy of a private company so as to escape part of their own income tax liabilities. In the absence of such a tax, some private company shareholders would be able to pay less tax on a given gross income than public company shareholders with an identical income.[32]

However, if equity considerations are regarded as less important than the need for small business growth and development, a different view of the Division 7 provisions tends to emerge. By limiting the volume of internal funds available to a profitable private company, the tax may have the effect of restricting the growth of some efficient and vigorous small firms. Yet it is doubtful whether the total abolition of this undistributed profits tax would be the most cost-effective way of encouraging the growth of viable small firms, even if equity considerations were set on one side. Abolition of the tax would not assist unincorporated businesses or small private companies which do not require additional internal finance for expansion. Therefore it would seem more sensible to exempt from Division 7 tax only those companies which do need extra internal funds for their growth and development. Moreover, a number of alternative policy measures might be more cost-effective in encouraging small business development. To take one example, improved institutional arrangements for the supply of long-term finance to small firms would tend to have a wider impact. Such measures could assist unincorporated enterprises as well as private companies, new firms and not merely profitable established companies.

Another aspect of taxation which is of particular concern to small firms is the cost of complying with taxation requirements. These costs include the accounting and clerical costs associated with furnishing tax returns, making Pay as You Earn (PAYE) income tax deductions from the wages and salaries of employees, collecting payroll taxes on behalf of the state governments, and collecting and remitting sales taxes. In addition, small wholesalers are sometimes obliged to remit sales taxes to the Taxation Department before they have received payment for the goods in question. This implies of course that they are bearing interest charges on the advance sales tax remittances.

A survey conducted in 1979 as part of a government inquiry into the paper burden faced by small firms, established that more than three-quarters of the costs of government paperwork arose from taxation requirements. Wholesalers, in particular appear to incur higher costs in form-filling than retailers or manufacturers and this probably reflects the additional clerical costs associated with sales tax collections and remittances.[33]

An earlier survey of the effects of taxation on small firms[34] provided a comparison between the magnitude of compliance costs and the size of the firm's wages and salary bill. This study showed that the relative importance of tax compliance costs declines sharply as the size of the firm increases, as indicated in Table 5.4.

This finding lends support to the view that small firms are disadvantaged by having to bear relatively higher compliance costs than large firms. At the same time, however, the absolute amount of these costs is not very great, amounting in 1979 to an average of A\$600 per firm. Most of these costs are probably deductions from the firm's taxable income. It is also probable that the financial statements prepared by an accountant or tax agent during the course of preparing a small firm's annual tax return are directly useful for the internal control of the business. In other words, even if no income tax returns were required, part of the clerical costs nominally included as tax compliance costs would still have to be incurred. For these reasons and because of the administrative complexity of compensating firms for their net compliance costs, government action to remove this problem seems unlikely.

A third difficulty facing small firms in the taxation area is potentially the most serious. It has been found that compared with larger firms, small firms are less able to take advantage of generally available tax concessions, partly because of the way in which the eligibility conditions have been framed. For example, an investment allowance, currently at a rate of 18 per cent, applies to new plant and equipment purchases costing more than A\$975 per item. Small firms tend to have less capital-intensive operations than

Table 5.4: Costs of Tax Compliance of Respondent Firms by Employment Size, Australia, June 1973

Number of persons employed[a]		Percentage of firms estimating compliance costs to exceed 2.5% of wages and salaries	
Manufacturing	Non-manufacturing	Manufacturing	Non-manufacturing
1–9	1–4	79.0	88.6
10–29	5–9	49.4	71.3
30–49	10–19	31.9	69.7
50–69	20 and over	29.4	46.0
70 and over		11.6	

Note: a. Including working proprietors.

large firms and to that extent are less likely to benefit from the allowance. Moreover, small firms are likely to buy less-expensive items of equipment with relatively more of the items having a value less than the lower limit for eligibility. Small firms are also more inclined to buy second-hand equipment, which does not qualify for the allowance. Finally, the investment allowance is of less immediate value to new or recently-established firms, most of them small, since they are not yet earning profits.

A recent survey by the Bureau of Industry Economics[35] found that among small manufacturing firms which had undertaken a major expansion between 1976 and 1978, the investment allowance was of benefit to less than one half of the firms employing fewer than ten persons. Yet 94 per cent of the firms employing 20 to 99 had benefited from the allowance. These and other data obtained in the course of the survey suggest that very small firms are particularly handicapped in their access to business taxation allowances and concessions.

While several aspects of the Australian taxation system appear to disadvantage small firms compared with large, small business proprietors and their families are probably favourably treated by the tax system in comparison with wage and salary earners with similar pre-tax incomes.

This favourable tax investment could have some implications for the size and growth of the small business sector, since it may induce a greater number of wage and salary earners to set up in business on their own account than would otherwise have done so.

The major income tax advantages of small business ownership in Australia lie in the opportunities for income-splitting among members of a family and the deductibility of business expenses for tax purposes. Neither of these avenues of tax avoidance is normally available to a household consisting only of wage and salary earners. Income-splitting can be achieved if the small business owner admits his wife and children into the business as partners or shareholders or by the formation of a family trust. Although there are safeguards to prevent undue loss of income tax revenue through artificial income-splitting devices, these rules are not aimed at the small firm run by a single family.

Finally, in comparison with the tax systems of some other developed countries the Australian tax system has some features contributing to a more favourable environment for the growth and development of small firms. In particular, estate and gift duties have been virtually abolished both in the Commonwealth and the States during the past five years. The abolition of these taxes is likely to assist in maintaining the continuity and development of small firms whose existence could have been threatened by the death of a principal partner or shareholder. Secondly, capital gains taxes are not levied as such in Australia. If a small business proprietor realised a real capital gain on the sale of his business he would not normally incur any income tax liability on the gain, provided that he had owned the business for at least twelve months. Since the monetary rewards from small business ownership may often be reflected in capital appreciation rather than in current income, there are obvious advantages in the absence of capital gains taxation.

B. *Availability of Finance*

A number of recent research investigations and official reports[36] have drawn attention to an apparent shortage of risk capital for fast-growing and innovative small firms in Australia. In seeking additional finance for growth and development more than 80 per cent of small firms approach a trading bank.[37] More than half of these firms succeed in obtaining from this source at least part of the finance they require. However, the trading banks are secured lenders, usually requiring as collateral security assets with a value equal to two or three times the amount of the loan. Land and buildings are by far the most acceptable forms of collateral and it is rare for the banks to take account of the value of plant and machinery, stocks, shop fittings or goodwill in assessing the amount of security provided. The banks are of course concerned with the business prospects of the small firms to which they lend, but favourable business prospects and an expected cash flow sufficient to repay the loan with interest are not sufficient to gain bank finance unless there is also adequate collateral. Hence, new and fast-growing small firms find it relatively difficult to obtain a trading bank loan.

This problem is further exacerbated by existing government regulations which prescribe the maximum interest rate that can be charged from time to time on bank loans and overdrafts of less than A$100,000. Since this ceiling interest rate is artificially low, it encourages additional demands for small bank loans from small businesses and other bank customers. At the same time, the banks have an inducement to divert more of their funds towards loans of

A$100,000 or more, since these are not subject to interest rate controls. The net effect is to create a shortage of bank loans and advances for small businesses. Consequently, the banks are obliged to ration loans to their small business customers, normally using as the criteria for allocation, the collateral offered and the past track record of the firms concerned. Thus, new and fast-growing small firms, are further disadvantaged by their short history and relatively small collateral. It may be noted that the Committee of Inquiry into the Australian Financial System, which reported in 1981, recommended that this and other interest rate controls be abolished.[38] The government has not yet decided whether to accept this recommendation.

Apart from the trading banks, other financial institutions providing medium and long-term finance for small firms include finance companies and the Commonwealth Development Bank (CDB). The finance companies provide leasing and hire purchase finance and term loans. They do not provide risk capital. The Commonwealth Development Bank, part of the publicly-owned Commonwealth Banking Corporation, has a particular responsibility to provide medium-term and long-term finance for small businesses. The Act under which it was established in 1959 includes the statement that 'in determining whether or not finance shall be provided . . . the Development Bank shall have regard primarily to the prospects [of the enterprise] becoming or continuing to be, successful and shall not necessarily have regard to the value of the security available in respect of the finance.'[39] Yet the Development Bank provides only debt finance and not equity capital and its loans are subject to the interest rate ceiling applying to trading bank loans of less than A$100,000. These constraints oblige the CDB to adopt a more cautious approach to financing small firms than might seem desirable in view of its charter. A recent survey found that recently-established and rapidly growing small firms tended to be less successful in obtaining finance from the CDB than other small firms. While this result can be partly explained by the fact that the CDB acts as 'a lender of last resort', it would seem that the Bank makes a smaller contribution to financing small high-risk ventures than many would judge to be appropriate.

A number of private venture capital companies have been established in Australia during the past thirty years but almost all of these have either ceased operations entirely or are not seeking new business. Thus there is now virtually a complete absence of institutional sources of equity capital for small firms, although occasionally individual investors can be found to take a minority interest in a small private company with outstanding prospects.

This dearth of risk capital sources may reflect to some extent a low level of demand for equity capital by small firms. Small business proprietors are reluctant to accept an injection of equity capital from an external source, for fear that this may diminish their control. Yet these fears are exaggerated, partly because Australia has had little or no experience of financial institutions subscribing equity and then seeking to influence management decisions.

A rather different financial problem facing small firms concerns the changes in their net trade credit position during the course of the business cycle. A relatively severe credit squeeze took place in Australia in 1973–4 and the effects of this on the availability of trade credit to a sample of small firms have been documented in a study commissioned by the National Small Business Bureau.[40] It was found that small firms with little bargaining power in relation to their (larger) customers and suppliers were pressed for prompt payment while being obliged to extend the period of credit granted to major customers. This deterioration in the net trade credit position had a more serious effect on the liquidity of small firms than the reduction in bank overdraft limits. A solution to this problem is not easy to find since it reflects a basic imbalance between the bargaining strength of small and large firms which is more evident in a period of tight credit. However, even if fluctuations in the net trade credit position of small firms cannot be avoided, the impact on their liquidity can be minimised by more careful cash flow budgeting and better debt collection procedures.

C. The Market Power of Large Firms

Trade practices legislation in Australia is designed to preserve and encourage competition by curbing abuses of market power which is usually present when small and large firms are on opposite sides of a business deal. In this respect two areas of particular concern for small retail firms have been the conditions of some franchising agreements and some shopping centre leases.

Franchising is quite widespread in Australia and recent estimates suggest that about 19 per cent of small non-manufacturing firms are engaged in some kind of franchised operation.[41] In the motor trades, comprising motor vehicle and parts dealers as well as service stations and other petrol retailers, 57 per cent of small firms have some franchised activities. In recent years the independent service station proprietors have criticised the major oil companies for allegedly practising price discrimination between their company-owned retail outlets and the franchised petrol retailers. Other criticisms have focused on what is claimed to be inadequate security of tenure for franchisees and lack of compensation when a franchise agreement is terminated. In this industry these problems have probably been alleviated to some degree by the Petroleum Retail Marketing Franchise Act, 1981 which addressed most of these matters. At present, however, there is no corresponding federal legislation to protect franchisees in other industries.

In the case of shopping centre leases, problems have sometimes arisen because of the way in which joint costs have been allocated between large retailers and small. In its examination of the conditions contained in shopping centre lease agreements the Trade Practices Commission has found instances in which small retailers have been asked to bear a disproportionate share of advertising costs or of contributions to a local merchants' association. Moreover, problems can arise if the lessor reserves the right to ban a lessee from displaying advertising signs or extending the range of goods he sells. These conditions are likely to be inimical to small business developments.

5.5 Government Initiatives to Assist Small Firms

As mentioned previously, government initiatives to assist small firms in Australia have been quite modest in comparison with the initiatives taken in some other developed countries. The broad thrust of recent Commonwealth government measures has been to reduce or eliminate certain obvious disadvantages of small firms rather than to discriminate in their favour. The state governments have adopted a slightly different stance, seeking to assist small firms by the provision of counselling services, loan guarantees and some payroll tax exemptions.[42] However, the monetary value of this assistance has not been large. In this section, the principal elements in the policies towards small business will be outlined.

A. Finance
Earlier in this chapter, reference was made to the role of the Commonwealth Development Bank as a source of finance for small

firms. Prior to June 1978, the Bank provided finance only to rural industries, small industrial undertakings, fishing and tourist ventures. For the most part small firms in the service sector were not eligible for loans from the Bank. In 1978, the charter of the CDB was broadened to allow it to lend to small enterprises in all business sectors, including wholesale and retail trade, the professions, entertainment and service undertakings generally. This change has had some effect on the composition of the Bank's lending. For example, outstanding loans to retail and wholesale firms represent over 10 per cent of non-rural business loans or about 2.5 per cent of total rural and other loans. Nevertheless, the Bank's loan portfolio is still dominated by the rural sector which accounted for almost three-quarters of the outstanding loans at 30 June 1981.

Although the CDB lends at interest rates which correspond closely to those charged by the major private trading banks, the loans can be regarded as concessional having regard to the risks involved and the terms of the loans. The ability to offer loans at concessional interest rates arises from the public ownership of the Bank and its exemption from tax liabilities and dividend commitments. The Australian Financial System Inquiry concluded that concessional finance from the CDB was not the most cost-effective way of providing assistance to primary producers and other small businesses, and recommended that any subsidies needed should be 'by way of direct grants or tax concessions or be channelled through existing commercial institutions'.[43] The government's decision on this recommendation has also not yet been made.

Some state governments have introduced loan guarantee schemes in recent years with the object of assisting viable small firms which lack collateral to obtain finance from the banks or other financial institutions. A loan guarantee scheme was introduced in New South Wales in 1977 and this was followed in 1979 by a similar but less restrictive scheme in Victoria. So far a relatively small number of guarantees have been approved. About twenty firms in Victoria and a smaller number in New South Wales had been assisted up to the end of 1981. It has been suggested that the present conditions of a state government loan guarantee do not make the scheme attractive to the major lending institutions. This is because the lender cannot ask the government agency to honour its guarantee unless it has already endeavoured to recoup its bad debt by foreclosing on the small firm concerned. There are also some broader economic questions about loan guarantees which need to be explored. It is possible that if the guarantees were extended widely they would have the effect of diverting scarce capital to marginally viable small firms and away from other small firms with better security and prospects. It is not clear whether the existence of loan guarantee schemes does serve to augment the total amount of finance going to the small business sector.

B. *Small Businesses Counselling and Management Advice*

One of the most significant aspects of state government support for small firms lies in the counselling and information services they provide. In most cases counselling is free and can cover such issues as starting a new business, availability of finance, financial management and marketing.

Following an agreement with the state governments in 1976, the Commonwealth Government has discontinued its own counselling service for small enterprises. However, it is responsible for preparing films, publications, and management training packages directed at improving the quality of small business management. It also runs training courses for small business counsellors in the various states.

C. *Taxation*

Earlier in this chapter the principal problems that small firms encounter in the taxation field were discussed and some of the recent changes that have occurred, particularly in the area of business income taxation were mentioned. Recent initiatives by the Commonwealth Government have included the abolition of Commonwealth estate and gift duties from 1 July 1979; easing of the undistributed profit tax arrangements as discussed previously; an increase in the exemption limit for sales tax payments; and greater tax deductibility for superannuation contributions by self-employed persons. Small firms have been eligible also for the investment allowances and accelerated depreciation provisions which have been granted to industry generally. These various measures may be viewed as part of a neutral policy towards small firms not as a policy to stimulate the growth and development of the small business sector.

Apart from the measures just described the state governments exempt from payroll tax firms with a very small wage and salary bill. The exemption limits have been raised several times in recent years but the changes have corresponded broadly with the general upward movement in domestic prices and wages. After allowing for the effects of inflation, the exemption limits have not risen in real terms.

D. Research and Development

The Industrial Research and Development Incentives Act, 1976 provides for the payment of grants to firms engaged in approved research and development programmes. There are two main types of grant, commencement grants and project grants. Commencement grants are aimed at firms which have not previously been involved in R & D or whose activities in this area are in their infancy. These grants are therefore of particular interest to the large number of small firms without previous R & D experience but which have innovative potential. Experience with the new R & D incentives scheme has shown that small independent firms have also received a significant fraction of the project grants approved. Unlike commencement grants, project grants are only awarded to projects which are thought to have technical and commercial merit and where the applicant firm has demonstrated a successful R & D performance in the past. Thus small firms with a demonstrated capability for innovation are also benefiting from the R & D incentive arrangements. However, the success of these innovative firms in the long-run will depend not only on their technical capacity and research support but also on the availability of venture capital, their marketing and production skills and a good distribution network.

5.6 Conclusion

Small firms play an important role in the Australian economy. Their significance has not diminished during the past decade despite increasing economies of scale in manufacturing industry, slow economic growth, and a dearth of major new government initiatives specifically designed to assist them. As far as can be judged, the rate of formation of new firms remains high, reflecting a desire for independence on the part of many individuals, an adequate supply of enthusiastic entrepreneurs and, perhaps, the perceived tax advantages of operating a small business.

Despite the current recession and the uncertain economic

outlook, the future prospects for the small business sector seem reasonably satisfactory, in part because of the anticipated continuation of growth in the service sector. Technological changes, notably in the microelectronics field, no longer point inexorably to a further increase in the minimum efficient scale of business operations.

But in view of the high level of public expenditure and the breadth of government intervention in the economy, there is a particular need to ensure that government actions do not inadvertently stunt the growth and development of the small firm sector. The great diversity of small business activity and the very large number of small firms means that the effects of government policy changes on the small firm sector are not easy to monitor. Yet the future health and vitality of the sector will depend on how well this task can be carried out.

Notes

1. Report of the Committee on Small Business (Chairman, F.M. Wiltshire), *Parliamentary Paper No. 82*, June 1971.
2. Ibid., p. 7.
3. That is, from single-establishment enterprises employing less than four persons, including the working proprietors.
4. For details of the coverage of this industry see the footnote to Table 5.2.
5. Including banks, finance and insurance companies, stockbrokers, real estate agents and developers, technical legal, accounting, data processing and advertising services.
6. Including medical practitioners, dentists, opticians, veterinary services, hospitals and nursing homes.
7. Information is available from the integrated economic censuses conducted by the Australian Bureau of Statistics about two of these industries – wholesaling and construction. In wholesaling, firms employing fewer than twenty persons accounted for about 30 per cent of total employment in 1969. In the construction industry, excluding general government construction, firms of this size accounted for about 63 per cent of employment in 1979.
8. This percentage was derived from the small firms' share of each industry's employment in June 1979 (as shown in Table 5.3) and the industry's share of total manufacturing employment in June 1969.
9. Obtained from $(32.0-30.2)/(32.0-29.4)$.
10. That is for industry i,

$$\frac{E_{SPi}}{N_{SPi}} \Big/ \frac{E_i}{N_i} \times \frac{N_{SPi}}{F_{Si}} \Big/ \frac{N_i}{F_i} \times \frac{F_{Si}}{F_i} = \frac{E_{SPi}}{E_i}$$

where E_i = employment
N_i = number of plants
F_i = number of firms

and the subscripts $_{SP}$ and $_S$ refer to the plants operated by small firms and the number of small firms respectively. Industry totals are identified by subscript $_i$ only.

11. The two industries in which there was a fall in average employment in the plants operated by large firms were textiles and non-metallic mineral products. In this context, all manufacturing firms with an employment of one hundred or more are regarded as large firms.

12. It should not be overlooked, however, that some large and medium-sized firms may have reduced their employment to fewer than one hundred during this period. This would have tended to boost the number of small firms.

13. Total employment in the clothing and footwear industries declined by 35 per cent between 1969 and 1979 with small firms more severely affected than large.

14. R.A. Price 'Business Closures through the Recession' paper given to Sixth Conference of Economists Hobart, May 1977 p. 24.

15. An increase in 'the stock' of small firms could also occur if a large number of medium-sized firms were to cut back their employment levels to the point where they fell within the scope of the small firm definition. However, given the relatively small number of medium-sized firms, this factor alone cannot explain the observed net growth in the number of small enterprises in this period.

16. B.L. Johns, W.C. Dunlop and W.J. Sheehan, *Small Business in Australia – Problems and Prospects* (George Allen and Unwin, Sydney, 1978), pp. 39–40; Bureau of Industry Economics, *Finance for Small Business Growth and Development, Research Report No. 10* (Australian Government Publishing Service, Canberra, 1981).

17. *Reports to the Minister for Business and Consumer Affairs on the operation of the Bankruptcy Act 1966–70* (Australian Government Publishing Service, Canberra).

18. R.A. Price, 'Business Closures through the Recession'.

19. K.M. Renfrew, W.J. Sheehan and W.C. Dunlop, *Financing and Growth of Small Businesses in Australia*, a report prepared for the Bureau of Industry Economics (Australian Government Publishing Service, Canberra, forthcoming 1983).

20. The most pessimistic estimate is based on the assumption that the small firms which could not be traced have all closed.

21. Assuming that the number of new firms being established each year is approximately equal to the number of closures. On this assumption the 'stock' of small firms remain constant.

22. A.J. Williams, *A Study of the Characteristics and Performance of Small Business Owner/Managers in Western Australia*, unpublished PhD thesis, the University of Western Australia, 1975.

23. Such limitations or restrictions may arise in the form of stamp duties levied on the sale or transfer of a business or the conditions in some franchise agreements giving the franchisor the right to terminate the franchise without compensating the franchisee for any improvements for which he is responsible.

24. *Report of the Committee of Inquiry on Small Firms* (HMSO, London, 1971).

25. Over 90 per cent of patents granted in Australia are taken out by foreign residents.

26. Sir Ian McLennan, 'Innovation in Australian Industry 1970–1975' in Department of Industry and Commerce, Bulletin 21 (Australian Government Publishing Service, Canberra, March 1977).

27. Johns, Dunlop and Sheehan, *Small Business in Australia*, pp. 48–50.

28. Ibid., pp. 54–5.

29. Ibid., p. 49.

30. However, there have been some offsetting improvements in the tax treatment of private companies as will be described later.

31. In practice, the shareholders may choose to reinvest their dividends in the company. But the required nominal distribution ensures that they do not escape personal income tax on the dividends.

32. The gross income of the shareholder is taken to include his share of the retained profits of the company as well as the dividends received.

33. In Australia, all sales taxes are collected at the wholesale level.

34. B.L. Johns, W.C. Dunlop and W.J. Sheehan, *Taxation and the Small Firm in Australia* (University of Newcastle, NSW, 1974), reproduced in a slightly edited form in Taxation Review Committee, *Commissioned Papers* (Canberra, Australian Government Publishing Service, 1975). See also Johns, Dunlop and Sheehan, *Small Business in Australia*, p. 181.

35. Bureau of Industry Economics, *Finance for Small Business Growth and Development* (1981).

36. Bureau of Industry Economics (1981), Study Group on Structural Adjustment, *Report*, March 1979, vol. 1 (Canberra, Australian Government Publishing Service, 1979).

37. The data in this and the following sentences are as reported in Bureau of Industry Economics (1981).

38. Australian Financial System, *Final Report of the Committee of Inquiry September 1981* (Canberra, Australian Government Publishing Service, 1981).

39. Commonwealth Bank Act 1959, s. 73(1).

40. B.L. Johns, W.C. Dunlop and K.M. Lamb, *Finance for Small Business in Australia: An Assessment of Adequacy* (Canberra, Australian Government Publishing Service, 1978).

41. Bureau of Industry Economics (1981), pp. 30–1.

42. It should be noted that this reflects agreement between the State and Commonwealth Governments in 1976 on their relative responsibilities in the small business area.

43. Australian Financial System Inquiry (1981), *Final Report*, p. 481.

6 FEDERAL REPUBLIC OF GERMANY

6.1 Introduction: The Definition of the Small Firm

West Germany's small firms are its *mittelständische Unternehmen*. That they are labelled with reference to the social order (*'mittelständisch'*) rather than to size ('small') should indicate that we are dealing here with a category which in Germany is as much a social and political (even ideological) as an economic one.[1] The essential characteristics of these firms are generally agreed to be legal and financial independence (and, on a more stringent definition, even basic functional independence, e.g. as sub-contractors) with active participation by the owner(s) in the management of the firm, which holds a limited share of its market.

The operational definition of the small firm needed for practical purposes of policy or research invariably requires the abandonment of these criteria, with the possible exception of that of legal independence, in favour of more readily operationalised criteria of size based on turnover and/or employment.[2] Definitions based on employment size predominate in practice, but there is little agreement as to where the cutoff between 'small' and 'large' should fall.[3] No doubt in tacit acknowledgement of the absence of agreed definitions the West German Federal Government, in its most recent report on the small firm sector (*Mittelstandsbericht*), preferred to baulk the issue of definition by remarking laconically in a footnote to the opening sentence: 'the Federal Government does not consider useful any general and schematic definition of 'small and medium-sized' firms'.[4] Being a review of previous research this chapter cannot allow itself any too restricted definition of the small firm; the approach adopted has generally been to describe West Germany's *total* population of firms in terms of (usually employment-related) criteria of size.

Three basic definitions of 'the firm' are current in West German statistics. The 'site' (*Arbeitsstätte*) is, broadly, the lowest spatial level of business organisation (a set of self-contained premises); the 'establishment' (*Betrieb*) is the lowest technical level of organisation, being still a local unit but possibly comprising two or more functionally interdependent sites; the 'company'

(*Unternehmen*), finally, is the lowest general managerial and legally independent level of organisation, being usually the lowest-level unit required by law to maintain books. It should be stressed, however, that the *Unternehmen* is on a lower level than the 'enterprise' in the Anglo-Saxon sense of unit of ultimate control, which in Germany would be the *Muttergesellschaft* or *Konzern*. In practice, the vast majority of sites are simultaneously establishments and companies: as many as 83.4 per cent of the sites recorded in the 1970 Census of Sites (*Arbeitsstättenzählung*) were simultaneously establishments and companies, i.e. that is, they were single-site, single-establishment companies.[5]

Table 6.1 provides some sense of the statistical difference which different definitions of the firm make by comparing the size distribution of the total of 'sites' (*Arbeitsstätten*) and 'companies' (*Unternehmen*) and of the employment in them in 1970. The distributions of the total number of firms vary only to a relatively minor extent. The distributions of employment differ more significantly. When firms are defined as *companies* there is a pronounced concentration of employment in the 500-plus category relative to when they are defined as *sites*. The tables of this chapter employ varying definitions of the firm; the definition used on each occasion is indicated.

Table 6.1: Percentage Distribution of Firms and Employment by Firm Size in 1970 with the Firm defined as 'Site/*Arbeitsstätte*' and 'Company/*Unternehmen*'

Definition of firm	1–9	10–49	50–99	100–199	200–499	500+	Totals (000's)
				A. Firms			
'Sites'	87.5	10.0	1.3	0.7	0.4	0.2	2,140
'Companies'	88.5	9.3	1.1	0.6	0.4	0.2	1,908
				B. Employment			
'Sites'	24.6	19.7	9.1	9.2	12.0	25.4	21,259
'Companies'	22.0	15.9	7.1	7.3	9.9	37.8	21,264

(Number of employees)

Source: *Statistisches Bundesamt* (1981)[41] and PROGNOS (1979).[38]

6.2 The Size Distribution of Firms and Employment

Table 6.2 reproduces an attempt by Dahm *et al.*[6] to construct a long time-series of the distribution of total employment by firm size since 1882 within the boundaries of contemporary West Germany. Notwithstanding certain inconsistencies in definition and coverage over time the table documents a sharp decline in the employment share of the smallest firms (employing fewer than five persons). From over 60 per cent in 1882 this share had declined to under 30 per cent by 1925. That it rose again almost to 40 per cent in 1933 is explained by Dahm *et al.* primarily as a consequence of a 'flight into self-employment' during the Depression, coupled with the statistical effect of the mass redundancies of the period having been principally among the employees of large firms. In 1950 the firm-size distribution of employment was broadly similar to that in 1925.

Table 6.2: Percentage Distribution of Total Employment by Firm Size, 1882–1950

Number of employees	1882	1895	1907	1925	1933	1950
1,000 plus	2.9	4.4	6.6	13.2	8.4	12.1
200–999	9.0	11.3	13.8	17.0	15.2	14.8
50–199	10.1	14.0	16.8	16.6	14.4	16.2
10–49	12.1	15.8	17.9	16.6	14.4	20.0
5–9	4.7	8.1	7.7	7.4	7.9	11.7
1–4	61.2	46.5	37.3	29.3	39.7	25.1

Note: Firm is variously defined by Dahm *et al.* as site (*Arbeitsstätte*) or establishment (*Betrieb*).
Source: Dahm, Stockmann and Zeifang, 1981, p. 29.

There have been three Censuses of Sites (*Arbeitsstättenzählungen*), which provide the only comprehensive and reliable estimate of the firm population, since the foundation of the Federal Republic in 1949. The most recent was held in 1970; the date of the next, already overdue, is still uncertain. Table 6.3 provides data from the three censuses.

The table's marginals show that between 1950 and 1961 the number of firms (sites) grew considerably (+20.1%), the number of persons employed in them massively (+66.3%). This major growth in employment was due in particular to the arrival of German refugees from Eastern Europe. During the 1960s total employment in firms grew further by a modest 2.6 per cent, while the number of firms themselves dropped back by 12.1 per cent. As a consequence of these different movements, the average size of the firm has increased markedly during the two decades covered by the table – from roughly six persons in 1950 to some 10 in 1970.

Table 6.3: Percentage Distribution of Firms (Sites) and Employment by Firm Size in 1950, 1961, 1970

Year	1–9	10–49	Number of employees 50–99	100–199	200–499	500+	Totals (000's)
			A. Firms (*Arbeitsstätten*)				
1950	92.4	6.3	0.7	0.3	0.2	0.1	2,029
1961	89.6	8.2	1.1	0.5	0.3	0.1	2,436
1970	87.5	10.0	1.3	0.7	0.4	0.2	2,140
			B. Employment				
1950	36.1	19.4	8.3	7.9	9.5	18.7	12,459
1961	27.0	19.1	9.1	8.9	11.5	24.1	20,720
1970	24.6	19.7	9.1	9.2	12.0	25.4	21,259

Note: The data cover all employers excluding the public and voluntary sectors, agriculture and private householders in their capacity as employers.
Source: Decennial Censuses of Sites (*Arbeitsstättenzählungen*) as published in *Statistisches Bundesamt* (1952), (1963) and (1981) and own calculations.

The lower half of Table 6.3, showing the size distribution of total employment, is strongly characterised by change at the extremes: the share of firms employing fewer than 10 persons dropped from over 36 per cent in 1950 to under 25 per cent in 1970, during which time the share of firms employing 500 persons or more rose from under 19 per cent to over 25 per cent. The 1970 figures show that 87 per cent of West Germany's firms employed fewer than 10 persons (and almost 25 per cent of the total workforce), 97 per cent of them fewer than 50 persons (and some 45 per cent of the workforce). It is certain that the employment share of small firms declined further during the 1970s.[7]

There is, of course, growing awareness in West Germany, as elsewhere, that a not insignificant and perhaps increasing proportion of economic activity escapes the net of official statistics.

A recent estimate by Huber[8] suggests that West Germany's 'alternative' economy involves between 6,000 and 15,000 'projects' and 30,000 to 135,000 individuals. The range in the proferred values speaks amply of the difficulties of estimation. Huber arrives at a personal best guess of some 11,500 projects, each involving some five to nine persons or roughly 80,000 people overall. Some of these individuals probably also hold 'straight' employment, while others are registered as unemployed.

6.3 Small Firms and the Manufacturing and Service Sectors

Between 1950 and 1961 the total number of firms (sites) increased by 20.1 per cent, and declined by 12.1 per cent in the following decade. Table 6.4 shows that the manufacturing and service sectors contributed quite differently to this overall development.

The number of manufacturing firms declined steadily, at a rate of approximately 1.9 per cent per annum, during the two decades to 1970. The service sector, by contrast, experienced net growth over the same twenty years, the number of firms increasing by some 40 per cent. Service growth occurred especially during the 1950s, when the number of service firms increased at a rate of almost 5 per cent per annum, followed by a decline of some 1 per cent per annum during the 1960s. Overall during the twenty years between 1950 and 1970 the number of manufacturing firms declined by approximately the same proportion (38.4 per cent) as the number of service firms increased (40.4 per cent). The percentage of firms in manufacturing declined from 40.6 in 1950 to 23.0 in 1970.[9]

The continuing decline in the number of manufacturing firms has been accompanied by a declining share of small firms (1–9 employees) among all manufacturing firms. Whereas in 1950 over 90 per cent of all manufacturing firms fell into this size class, by 1970 the percentage had dropped to almost 78. All of the other size groups of firms have gained at the expense of the smallest; the group of firms with 10–49 employees has grown to become a sizeable segment of the manufacturing economy, increasing its share of total manufacturing firms from 7.2 in 1950 to 19.7 per cent in 1978.

In the service sector, too, there has been a trend away from the smallest firms, but the development has been more muted. Thus between 1950 and 1970 the number of service firms in the smallest-firm category declined by just four percentage points from 95.8 to

91.8 per cent of all service firms (manufacturing: from 90.6 to 78.1 per cent). The most striking size-related difference between the manufacturing and service sectors will be evident from the lower part of Table 6.4, which shows a marked degree of sectoral polarisation in as much as almost 80 per cent of the smallest firms (1–9 employees) in 1970 were to be found in the service sector, and an almost equal percentage (77.3 per cent) of the largest firms in the manufacturing sector. As the figures for the earlier years show, the manufacturing percentage among small firms has decreased since

Table 6.4: Percentage Distribution of Manufacturing and Service Firms (Sites) and Employment by Firm Size in 1950, 1961, 1970

	1–9	10–49	50–99	100–199	200–499	500+	Totals
				Number of employees			
			A. Manufacturing[a]				
1950	90.6	7.2	1.1	0.6	0.4	0.2	730,885
1961	83.0	12.2	2.2	1.2	0.8	0.4	580,392
1970	78.1	15.7	2.8	1.6	1.1	0.6	450,050
1977[b]	72.8	19.7	3.3	2.0	1.4	0.8	314,008
			B. Services[c]				
1950	95.8	3.8	0.2	0.1	0.0	0.0	1,068,849
1961	93.4	5.6	0.6	0.2	0.1	0.0	1,651,823
1970	91.8	7.0	0.7	0.3	0.1	0.1	1,500,552

	1950		1961		1970	
	1–9	500+	1–9	500+	1–9	500+
Manufacturing	39.2	91.2	23.8	79.5	20.3	77.3
Services	60.8	8.8	76.2	20.5	79.6	22.7

Notes: a. Manufacturing is here defined as manufacturing industry in the sense of sector 2 of the eight-fold *Systematik der Wirtschaftszweige*; it excludes construction and utilities.
b. Author's own estimate calculated from the '*Industriebericht*' and the '*Kleinbetriebserhebung*' in September 1977 (*Statistisches Bundesamt*, 1979) in conjunction with the *Handwerkszählung* of March 1977 (*Statistisches Bundesamt*, 1979: 208). The marginal total at right underestimates the true figure; the percentage figures may, however, be assumed to be broadly accurate.
c. Services are here defined as sectors 4–7 (wholesaling, retailing and other trading activities; transport and communications; banking and insurance; other services supplied by firms or the professions) of the eight-fold *Systematik der Wirtschaftszweige*.
Source: Own calculations from *Statistisches Bundesamt* (1952)[41] and Fiebig and Kammertöns (1979, Tables 1 to 6).[42] See also note b above.

Table 6.5: Percentage Distribution of Employment in Manufacturing and Service Firms (Sites) by Firm Size in 1950, 1961, 1970

	1–9	10–49	Number of employees 50–99	100–199	200–499	500+	Totals
			A. Manufacturing[a]				
1950	25.9	16.6	8.9	9.8	13.1	25.6	6,318,149
1961	13.2	14.7	8.9	10.1	14.9	38.2	10,016,448
1970	10.6	14.3	8.6	10.1	15.2	41.1	10,245,944
1977[b]	8.4	13.4	8.1	9.8	15.4	44.9	8,921,592
			B. Services[c]				
1950	65.0	20.3	5.1	3.6	3.5	2.6	3,540,887
1961	48.7	22.3	8.0	6.2	7.1	7.7	7,721,554
1970	43.8	23.6	8.5	7.3	7.9	8.9	8,303,121

	1950		1961		1970	
	1–9	500+	1–9	500+	1–9	500+
Manufacturing	41.6	94.6	26.0	86.5	23.0	85.1
Services	58.4	5.4	74.0	13.5	77.0	14.9

Notes: a, b and c: see Table 6.4.
Source: See Table 6.4.

1950 while the service share among large firms has increased markedly.

The distribution of employment by firm size in the manufacturing and service sectors is shown in Table 6.5. Relating the totals of this table to those of Table 6.4 further highlights the size differences between the two sectors. Thus whereas the average manufacturing firm in 1970 employed some 23 persons, its service counterpart employed between five and six persons. The average size of the firm has grown in both sectors since 1950, but growth in the maufacturing average has outstripped that in services. Thus the average size of the manufacturing firm grew from some 9 persons in 1950 to 23 in 1970 (and probably to 28 by 1977), while the service firm averages increased much more modestly, from over 3 to over 5 persons during the two decades.

The distribution of employment by size-class of firm tells a familiar story of decline among the smallest firms. In the manufacturing sector in 1950 as many people were employed in firms with fewer than 10 employees (25.9 per cent) as in firms with

500 and more (25.6 per cent); by 1977 the share of the smallest firms had declined to 8.4 per cent of all manufacturing employment whereas that of the largest firms had increased to almost 45 per cent. The service sector exhibits, once again, a trend in the same direction but on a smaller scale. Small firm employment still predominated in 1970 (almost 44 per cent of service employment was in firms with fewer than 10 employees) but markedly less so than twenty years earlier (1950: 65 per cent). The proportion of service workers in firms with 100 or more employees has been steadily increasing from 9.7 per cent in 1950 to 24.1 per cent in 1970.

The lower half of Table 6.5 once again demonstrates the predominance of services among the smallest firms and of manufacturing among the largest ones. The most dramatic changes in the sectoral distribution of employment among the largest and the smallest firms came during the 1950s when service firms made significant inroads into the relative employment shares of both the smallest and largest manufacturing firms. In 1970 some 77 per cent of small firm (fewer than 10 employees) employment was in the service sector, while over 85 per cent of large firm (500 and more employees) employment was in manufacturing.

6.4 Birth and Death Rates of Firms

The 1950s was the decade of the new firm; the number of firms increased by over two hundred thousand (+9.3 per cent) between 1950 and 1961 (see Table 6.2). Between 1961 and 1970, by contrast, the number of firms declined from 2.4 million to 2.1 million (−12.1 per cent). It is noted by Steiner[10] that the number of self-employed persons in West Germany declined by some 27 per cent between 1960 and 1977 (from 3.3 to 2.4 million persons). Figures such as these have prompted worries about a 'new firm deficit' (*Gründungsdefizit*).

Measurement of the birth and death rates underlying the net changes noted in the previous paragraph is exceedingly difficult because of statistical inadequacies.[11] The most reliable data have been assembled by Clemens *et al.*[12] for the state of Northrhine-Westfalia for the ten years 1966–75.[13] It can be estimated from their figures that on average some 45,200 new firms were established in Northrhine-Westfalia in each year during the period (the annual values ranging between 42,800 and 49,400), as compared to a figure of 53,400 for deaths (ranging annually between 49,100 and 56,400).[14] The 1970 Census of Workplaces estimated the number of firms (companies) in Northrhine-Westfalia at some 481,500. Thus, as a rough estimate, some 11 per cent of firms die each year, and are replaced by a number of new firms close to 9 per cent of the stock. Over the ten-year period the replacement rate of old firms by new was 84.7 per cent, that is, 533,900 deceased firms were replaced by 452,400 new ones. The annual replacement rates range between 76.9 and 94.1 per cent; thus in no year was there a surplus of new firms over old. Clemens *et al.* were unable to undertake any rigorous analysis of the relationship between birth/death rates and the business cycle, but do suggest that the *primae facie* evidence is against any unambiguous relationship (pp. 8–9).

Bankruptcy is one of the more extreme forms of death for a firm, and one which is rare. Probably fewer than five per cent of firms which die do so as declared bankrupts,[15] and figures for the five years 1976–80 show that less than one firm per thousand went bankrupt each year.[16] The average annual insolvency rate in this period was, in fact, 0.57 per thousand (the annual values ranging between 0.46 and 0.69 per thousand). Insolvency was most frequent in the construction industry (five-year annual average 1.63 per thousand) and least probable in the service sector excluding wholesaling and retailing (0.25). The manufacturing rate was somewhat above average at 0.77.

Table 6.6 shows that there has been a steady and marked increase in the relative number of bankruptcies among young firms (less than five years old) coupled with a marked decrease in the percentage for older firms (above 20 years of age – and especially those above 50 years of age). These figures almost certainly imply a rising insolvency rate among young firms, but should not be taken to imply that young firms have a particularly high insolvency rate. Direct evidence is not available; indirect evidence is provided in Table 6.7, which shows the distribution of insolvencies and insolvency rates by firm size.

While the smallest firms (1–5 employees) account for the highest percentage of insolvencies (31.4 per cent), they have – perhaps surprisingly – the lowest insolvency rate. The relationship between firm size and probability of insolvency appears curvilinear and probability of insolvency is highest among firms with 101–200 employees.[17]

Table 6.6: Percentage Distribution of Bankruptcies by Age of
Firm, 1976–80[a]

Age of firm (years)	1976/7	1978/9	1980
0–4	26.6	35.7	47.1
5–10	22.2	21.7	24.9
11–20	16.5	13.3	11.0
21–50	18.7	16.0	12.4
51+	15.9	13.3	4.5

Note: a. For the first two periods, from 1 April of the first year to 31 March of
the second in each case; for the third period, the twelve calendar months of
1980.
Source: *Creditreform* (annual).

Table 6.7: Percentage Distribution of Total Insolvencies by
Employment Size Class and Insolvency Rate per 1,000 Firms in
each Size Class, 1976–80

Employment size class	Percentage distribution	Insolvency rate
1–5	31.4	0.22
6–10	17.1	0.57
11–20	16.8	1.48
21–50	17.0	2.99
51–100	9.0	4.22
101–200	5.2	4.58
201–500	2.8	4.17
501+	0.6	1.94
All firms	100.0	0.57

Source: *Creditreform* (annual).

6.5 The Role of the Small Firm

The refound enthusiasm in recent years for the small firm is often
associated with claims for them which are difficult to sustain
empirically. This section limits itself to aspects of their role for
which empirical evidence is available.

A. Firm Size and Job Creation

The recent findings by David Birch[18] in the United States have clearly contributed much to the rekindling of interest in the small firm. The German evidence on the relationship between firm size and job creation is fragmented but tends to confirm an important role for the smaller firm. Friedrich and Spitznagel[19] undertook a study to typologise firms in relation to patterns of growth. The study used survey material covering 844 manufacturing firms (representing some 9 per cent of total manufacturing employment in West Germany). The authors concluded that they could reject the hypothesis that larger firms are the motors of growth (measured by them as a mix of output, turnover and slack capacity). The growing firms were predominantly firms with fewer than 200 employees. Employment was found to be strongly and positively correlated with growth. Thus indirectly Friedrich and Spitznagel confirmed an important role for smaller firms in job creation.

A survey by Infratest[20] of 598 firms in existence between 1973 and 1980 (in selected West German labour market regions with high unemployment) showed an almost unbroken trend of employment growth in firms employing fewer than 10 persons and an overall positive trend among firms with between 10 and 99 employees. Larger firms exhibited employment decline. Firms with fewer than 10 employees had increased their employment by 50 per cent in the seven years, firms with 10 to 99 employees by 13 per cent; firms in the 100 to 999 category had reduced employment to 94 per cent of its 1973 value, those with over 1,000 employees to 88 per cent of the starting value.

In 1979 at least, when an economic upturn was being forecast, West Germany's small firms were more buoyant about their employment prospects than were larger firms. Schwarting[21] found through a postal survey (in the Cologne area) that whereas between 70 and 80 per cent of firms with fewer than 200 employees expected to increase employment in the coming three to five years, this was true of only slightly over half of firms in the 200 to 999 employee range and of only 11 per cent of firms employing 1,000 and more people. Moreover, firms in the first category expected overall to generate between four and six jobs for each one destroyed, while in the second category the ratio fell to almost 2:1. The largest firms expected to manage only two new jobs for every ten lost.

One difficulty in interpreting the results of the above studies is any business cycle effect. Gruhler[22] in 1979 undertook an aggregate data analysis of employment change among West German manufacturing firms, comparing the growth years of 1968–71 with the slack years of 1972–75. He believes there to be a clear relationship between firm size, employment change and the business cycle. In the growth period firms with 500 or more employees expanded their employment greater than statistically expected, whereas firms below 50 employees performed well below expectation. In the slack period, fortunes were reversed, the small firms (with up to 49 employees) shed just 49 per cent of the statistically expected 70,000 jobs; the largest firms (1,000 and more employees), by contrast, shed 106 per cent of the expected 514,000 jobs.

B. Firm Size and Apprenticeship Training

Small firms account for a disproportionately large share of apprentice traineeships in West Germany. The 1970 Census of Workplaces showed that some 57 per cent of all apprentices were to be found in firms employing fewer than 50 people (such firms accounting for 36 per cent of total employment excluding apprentices). Large firms with 500 or more employees accounted for 16 per cent of apprentices but 28 per cent of total employment (excluding apprentices) according to von Henninges and Otto.[23] Furthermore Schmidt[24] estimates that the percentage of apprentices in firms employing fewer than 50 people today exceeds 60 per cent and emphasises their role in providing traineeships for 'problem groups'; thus he estimates that over 70 per cent of handicapped apprentices and over 60 per cent of foreign workers' children in apprenticeships are to be found in these small firms.

C. Firm Size and Innovation

Analysis of the relationships between firm size and innovation is still bedevilled by inadequate data. The following remarks draw primarily upon the two most recent empirical studies in West Germany. May's[25] analysis is principally concerned with the relationship between research and development inputs and activity, on the one hand, and firm size, on the other. She shows that the average absolute amount spent by firms on R & D increases markedly with increasing firm size. However, when small firms engage in R & D (their engagement tends to be sporadic; that of larger firms continuing) they tend to spend *relatively* more than large firms. May's data suggest (pp. 39–41) that small firms employing fewer than 100 persons tend to spend almost 3 times more per employee and almost 2½ times more in relation to turnover than do all firms on average. May notes (p. 40) that the explanation may be the 'lumpiness' of R & D investment (that is, the need to cross a relatively high initial investment threshold in order to engage in R & D).

In an analysis of the patents issued to mechanical engineering firms in West Germany in 1977 Kleine[26] found that firms employing up to 200 employees accounted for 20 per cent of total employment in the sector but only 7 per cent of the patents issued; firms with 1,000 or more employees accounted for 47 per cent of employment and 58 per cent of patents. The interpretation of these figures must recognise, however, that larger firms tend to underutilise their patents to a greater extent than do small ones, as shown by Grefermann and Röthlingshöfer.[27] Smaller firms tend to implement their own innovations faster than do larger ones: the share of implemented, unprotected own innovations is higher among smaller firms than among larger ones – an explanation for which is the cost and delay attached to patent registration.[28]

In a further study of the diffusion of two new technologies in the West German textile industry Kleine's data suggest in one case that the uptake of new technology is higher among larger firms than among smaller ones and, in the second case, that larger firms tend to adopt new technology more rapidly than smaller ones.

6.6 Difficulties Confronting Small Firms

The most recent comprehensive study of the difficultues confronting small firms is an investigation by Geiser[29] who examines the factors constraining the development of small industrial firms.[30] Table 6.8 relates to the eight problem areas and five firm size classes employed by Geiser. The upper value of each pair of entries in the table is the percentage of firms naming the particular problem area; the lower value is a measure of the intensity with which the particular problem constrains development.[31]

Difficulties in the areas of sales and personnel were each mentioned by 83.2 per cent of all firms; the third-ranking problem area, 'general environment', also scored relatively highly (79.1 per

Table 6.8: Frequency and Intensity of Factors in Eight Problem Areas Which Constrain the Growth of Industrial Firms

Problem area	Number of employees					All firms
	1–19	20–49	50–199	200–499	500–999	
Sales	80.7	78.6	83.8	87.5	93.5	83.2
	3.8	3.4	3.3	3.2	3.2	3.4
Personnel	75.0	82.1	83.8	92.9	90.3	83.2
	3.5	3.7	3.2	3.2	3.0	3.3
General	70.5	76.2	81.8	87.5	87.1	79.1
environment	3.4	3.3	3.1	3.1	2.8	3.2
Finance	68.2	67.9	73.7	73.2	67.7	70.4
	3.9	3.6	2.8	2.9	3.0	3.3
Management	65.9	71.4	68.7	64.3	64.5	67.6
	3.2	2.7	2.5	2.3	2.0	2.6
Production	55.7	65.5	68.7	76.8	71.0	66.2
	3.1	3.1	2.6	2.5	2.6	2.8
Purchases	62.5	60.7	55.6	66.1	61.3	60.6
	3.7	3.4	2.8	2.6	2.1	3.1
Location	51.1	53.6	56.6	50.0	58.1	53.6
	4.4	3.9	3.1	3.0	2.9	3.6

Source: Geiser (1981, p. 121).[29]

cent). The lowest-ranking problem area was location (53.6 per cent), which however achieved the highest overall intensity rating (3.6). The problem areas of sales, personnel and general environment not only achieved a high overall rate of mention, their frequency of mention displays a positive correlation with increasing firm size (which is also evident for the problem areas of production and – to a lesser extent – location). A more intriguing finding, however, is that the intensity of constraint tends to decrease with increasing firm size. This correlation tends to hold for all problem areas; thus although smaller firms need not necessarily experience the same scale of problems as larger ones, they tend to experience those problems with greater intensity. Why this should be is not clear: it may be that the ambition to grow is greater among smaller firms, so that problems tend to be more of a constraint; it may be that smaller firms are exposed to objectively greater constraints; it may also be that larger firms are better managed in the sense of being more adept at resolving difficulties as they occur, so that constraints tend to be less intense.

Table 6.9 shows the ten most important factors constraining firms' growth according to Geiser's study. These are the ten most

Table 6.9: The Ten Factors Most Constraining the Growth of Industrial Firms

Problem area	Constraint on growth	Number of employees					All firms	Importance
		1–19	20–49	50–199	200–499	500–999		
Personnel	Difficulties in acquiring skilled workers	56.8	69.0	71.7	83.9	87.1	70.7	304
		4.0	4.4	4.3	4.1	3.6	4.3	
General environment	Cost burden due to compliance with legislation and performance of administrative functions for the state	59.1	57.1	62.6	75.0	80.6	64.0	237
		4.2	3.8	3.5	3.7	3.1	3.7	
Personnel	High direct and indirect labour costs	53.4	54.8	56.4	71.4	51.6	57.3	223
		4.2	4.0	3.9	3.7	3.4	3.9	
Sales	Difficulties in increasing sales to existing customers	53.4	44.0	50.5	58.9	67.7	52.5	204
		4.5	3.6	3.8	3.9	3.6	3.9	
Location	Lack of space for expansion	44.3	44.0	43.4	37.5	58.1	44.1	194
		5.1	4.8	4.1	3.7	3.4	4.4	
General environment	Restrictions on entrepreneurial independence by the state	46.6	50.0	54.5	66.1	61.3	53.9	189
		4.0	3.6	3.5	3.4	2.9	3.5	
Sales	Difficulties in finding new foreign markets/ export problems	39.8	39.3	41.4	55.4	58.1	44.1	185
		5.0	3.9	4.0	4.1	3.7	4.2	
Sales	Difficulties in finding new domestic markets	55.7	44.0	43.4	55.4	71.0	50.8	183
		3.8	3.6	3.4	3.5	3.4	3.6	
Sales	Competition from large firms	50.0	35.7	53.5	50.0	64.5	48.9	181
		4.1	3.3	3.8	3.7	3.3	3.7	
Management	Overburdened management	52.3	56.0	44.4	51.8	51.6	50.8	178
		3.9	3.9	3.1	3.2	3.0	3.5	

Source: Adapted from Geiser (1981).

important factors in the sense that when, for all firms, the frequency of mention is multiplied by the intensity of constraint these ten factors have the highest products (which are shown in the right-hand column labelled 'Importance'). Difficulties in acquiring skilled workers stand out as the major constraint because of both a high frequency of mention and a high intensity of constraint. There is a clear positive relationship between frequency of mention and increasing firm size, which is equally true of the second-ranking difficulty, the costs on firms of compliance with all manner of governmental legislation (including the costs of making compulsory statistical returns and of performing other administrative tasks required by the government). Here the familiar pattern of decreasing intensity with increasing firm size is evident (whereas there is some suggestion in the case of difficulties in acquiring skilled workers that the very smallest firms experience less constraint than firms in the intermediate size classes). The problem of lack of space for expansion enters the table not least because of its relatively high overall intensity score of 4.4. This constraint also shows the highest intensity score for any single size-class: although relatively few firms employing fewer than 20 people experience this constraint (44.3 per cent), it is a very intense constraint (intensity score of 5.1).

6.7 Public Policy and the Small Firm

To provide a survey of public financial and non-financial assistance to small firms in West Germany within the space of a few pages is no easy task. A basic complication is the federal character of the constitution of state, on the basis of which the ten (including West Berlin) federal states (*Bundesländer*) would claim for themselves the predominant if not exclusive competence for providing direct assistance to small firms (and, indeed, to firms in general). In practice, however, probably the greater role financially is played by the federal government (*Bundesregierung*). Thus there are both federal and state government programmes of aid available to small firms. An added complication, however, is that much assistance available to small firms is not exclusively available to them. For reasons of data availability this brief review is biased towards federal assistance.[32]

It is a measure of the political significance attached to small firms policy in West Germany that a *Mittelstandspolitik* ranges alongside sectoral policy and regional development policy as a third element in the government's overall economic structural policy. The broad objectives of this structural policy for small firms are three: (i) to ensure the competitiveness and hence continued existence of the small firm sector; (ii) to improve the performance of small firms; (iii) to assist small firms to adapt successfully to economic structural change. The justification for a small firms policy are structural disadvantages associated with firm size. These structural disadvantages are deduced from economic theory, and are held to be evidenced by the rapid decline in recent years of the number of small firms in certain sectors (e.g. retailing). It is intended, however, that policy shall never do more than 'help firms help themselves', that is, policy should not compromise the market principle. The specific measures taken within this general policy framework may be broadly classified under four headings: providing and lowering the cost of capital; improving competitiveness; creating a more favourable general operating climate for small firms, and measures relating to public purchasing.

Two financial characteristics of small firms are held to justify measures to provide and lower the cost of capital. Analysis by the *Kreditanstalt für Wiederaufbau*, a public bank which administers many federal government loan programmes targetted at (not only small) firms, has shown that small firms' capital investment tends to be irregular and lumpy, often requiring large sums relative to own capital and available securities. In addition, the own capital reserves of small firms tend to be low and hence to put them at particular risk whenever there is a down-turn in demand (see below).

A range of loan programmes is available to small firms out of the ERP Special Fund (*ERP-Sondervermögen*), a 'pot' of finance constituted out of residual Marshall Plan funds at the expiry of the European Recovery Programme in Germany. Of these various loan programmes, all administered via the commercial banking system in conjunction with the *Kreditanstalt für Wiederaufbau*, the two major ones are, first, for the setting-up, extension and reorganisation of establishments in the designated regional development areas and, second, for first-time set-ups and for relocation occasioned by legislative or planning requirements, including investment to combat noise, emissions and other environmental nuisance. To the first of these programmes some 870 million DM were devoted in 1980, to the second roughly 820 million DM.[33] Between 1970 and 1978 it is estimated that the regional development programme provided assistance for almost 35,000 investment projects. During the same period the other major programme provided aid to roughly 28,000 individuals setting up in business for the first time and some 7,500 awards for relocation and environmental improvement measures.

ERP loans typically have a duration of 10 to 15 years (according to asset type) and offer rates of interest one or two percentage points below market rates at the time the loan is signed and fixed for the loan duration (although with a right of cancellation if market rates move down). One attraction of the loans is undoubtedly their fixed rate of interest. Another is that a two-year initial principal repayment holiday is typically granted (but no interest-free period).

In order to facilitate bank borrowing by small firms when the usual securities for a loan are not available, there exists a network of *Kreditgarantiegemeinschaften*. These are present in every state and are organised as mutual societies, usually sector by sector and with employers' associations taking a leading role. Both the federal and state governments provide assistance to them, by themselves guaranteeing risks assumed by the *Gemeinschaften* and by providing liquidity with which to meet cases of default. Arrangements vary, but guarantees are usually limited to a maximum value varying sectorally between some 300,000 DM for the professions (lawyers, accountants, and so on) to up to 1 million DM for manufacturing industry. Guarantees may normally not exceed 80 per cent of the value of a loan and may usually not exceed a duration of 23 years in relation to buildings and 15 years otherwise.

The major innovation of recent years in the category of capital-related programmes of assistance has been the introduction in 1979 of a federal government programme designed to lower the share of own capital necessary for a first-time set-up. The programme effectively involves a heavily-subsidised twenty-year loan, providing 3 DM for every 2 DM provided by the individual (the ratio is 2:1 in certain regions) up to a maximum award of 100,000 DM (110,000 DM in certain regions), which together with the actual own capital of the applicant may not exceed one-third of the total investment. Most of the subsidy value lies in two initial interest-free years and ten initial years of principal repayment holiday. This programme attracted some 5,000 successful applicants in the first 18 months of its existence. It involves relatively little cost to the federal exchequer, since the loan finance is provided by the banking sector. In its first full year of operation (1980) it involved federal expenditure of less than 5 million DM in interest subsidies; in 1982 expenditure is expected to have risen to some 20 million DM.

The second class of measures to assist small firms are those intended to improve firms' competitiveness; they include measures of assistance for consultancy, training of managers and employees, and, of particular importance, research and development in products and processes. It is estimated that in 1979 the federal government budget provided some 640 million DM for measures of these kinds, representing an almost ten-fold increase since 1970. Over 80 per cent of this total was for various programmes assisting research and development. The major programme is a direct labour subsidy for R & D personnel (*Personalkostenzuschüsse für Forschung und Entwicklung*), which in 1980 (with 390 million DM) accounted for virtually half of the federal budget devoted to these schemes.

The outstanding characteristic of this programme is that it provides a direct subsidy on wages and salaries. The programme is specificially intended for small firms, and the upper size limits for eligibility are generously defined – turnover of less than 150 million DM, or fewer than 1,000 persons employed on average during the previous three years. It applies only to firms not directly or indirectly under the majority ownership of one or more other firms. Awards are calculated (on the basis of expenditure in the previous year) on the total of taxable wages and salaries paid by the firm to personnel engaged in R & D. The latter is generously defined and is certainly not related to, for example, formal organisational criteria such as an equipped laboratory or separately organised R & D departments within the firm. Indeed one of the attractive features of the programme is intended to be its minimum of bureaucracy. In the first year of operation (1979) over 4,500 firms were assisted. Awards amount to 40 per cent on the first 300,000 DM of R & D labour costs, thereafter 25 per cent. The maximum award is 400,000 DM per firm and year (rates are higher in Berlin).

The final two categories of assistance to small firms are, to recapitulate, measures to improve the general operating climate of small firms and arrangements relating to public purchasing. In the first of these two categories fall various legislative and administrative measures which directly or indirectly favour smaller firms against larger ones although the effect is sometimes incidental to the original purpose of legislation. It would certainly be misleading to suggest that new firm-related legislation is systematically scrutinised and modified with respect to its firm-size implications. But a number of specific measures have been taken, two of which are noted here. Particular importance attaches to the laws relating to competition, particularly the regulation of cartel behaviour. Two relevant principles of German law are the general concern to constrain large firms' exercise of market power, but also a specific dispensation to facilitate cooperation between small firms. The second example involves the state retirement pension scheme, access to which was originally denied to the self-employed. The removal of restrictions has, however, resulted in an estimated 110,000 self-employed persons taking advantage of the provisions.

In the area of public purchasing, a number of measures favouring small firms are contained in a federal government directive of 1976. These include the requirements that: (i) large contracts be segmented in order to facilitate tendering by small firms; (ii) small firms be invited to tender, whether tender be open or closed; (iii) consortia of small firms be permitted to take on larger contracts; (iv) where large firms sub-contract, they include, whenever appropriate, small firms among the sub-contractors.

6.8. Conclusion and Prospects

The immediate outlook for small firms in West Germany is not good. In 1981 a postwar record 11,500 insolvency proceedings were recorded involving the estimated loss of some 320,000 jobs. The present year is expected to see a new record of almost 13,000 insolvencies and 450,000 jobs lost.[34] Insolvent firms are invariably small firms (Table 6.7).

Many factors, of course, have contributed to the growing number of business failures. One has attracted particular comment. As profit margins have narrowed, firms' gearing and under-capitalisation have increased. It is estimated that from the middle sixties to the late seventies post-tax profits of West German firms expressed as a percentage of turnover declined from an average 3.3 to 2.4 per cent.[35] During the same period the capitalisation ratio (own capital as a percentage of book value) of the average West

German firm fell from 30 to 21 per cent. The latter figure compares with estimates of 58 per cent for US and 48 per cent for UK firms.[36] Smaller firms in West Germany are even more under-capitalised than large so that firms with a turnover of less than DM 10 million had an average capitalisation ratio of just 15 per cent.[37] Shrinking markets and high and uncertain interest rates are a severe threat to the under-capitalised firm.

Table 6.10: Percentage Distribution of Total Employment by Firm (*Unternehmen*) Size, 1970, 1985

	Number of employees						
Year	1–9	10–49	50–99	100–199	200–499	500+	Total (000's)
1970	22.0	15.9	7.1	7.3	9.9	37.8	21,260
1985	22.7	16.1	7.6	7.0	10.1	36.5	19,100

Source: PROGNOS, 1979, p. 53.

On a more positive note for small firms, the consultancy firm PROGNOS forecasts (Table 6.10) their share of total employment in firms to increase in West Germany by 1985 relative to 1970 – although not dramatically.[38] The increased share of small firms will largely be due to a structural shift in the distribution of employment in favour of the service sector, in which small firms predominate (Tables 6.4 and 6.5). PROGNOS expects the service share of total employment in firms to have increased from 28 per cent in 1970 to 41.4 per cent by 1985. Interestingly, the sectors in which small firms are expected to increase their share of employment most are those expected to show (often considerable) employment decline by 1985. Conversely, in the sectors of anticipated growth, the general trend is expected to be towards larger rather than small firms.[39] These counteracting trends emphasise that the predicted shift towards smaller firms will be an artefact of a structural change towards services rather than of a secular shift towards small firms.

At the time of writing registered unemployment in West Germany has reached an all-time high since the foundation of the Federal Republic in 1949 and is poised to cross the two million threshold by the end of the year. If West Germany had fewer small firms than it does, registered unemployment would be higher than it is. That is one implication of the findings discussed in the earlier section on firm size and job creation. Another implication is that small firms will be likely to contribute disproportionately to new jobs creation in the difficult years which lie ahead.

In the discussion of difficulties confronting small firms the study by Geiser was cited, which shows that while small firms tend, perhaps surprisingly, to experience fewer problems overall than do larger ones, these problems tend to be a more powerful constraint upon their development. This finding may be related to another which is quite widespread in the literature, namely that small firms tend to be poorly managed compared to larger ones. The combination of a disproportionate contribution to job creation and poor management suggests that the job generation potential of small firms is larger than their actual contribution. In other words, if small firms were better able to solve the problems which constrain their development they would expand and create more jobs.

It is almost certainly an illusion to think that training courses can be devised to bring the management of small firms up to the level of large ones. While there may be some scope for improved training in certain basic management skills, a more useful direction for policy might be improvements in the institutional environment in which small firms operate.

There are probably few problems hindering small firms' growth which are not in principle resolvable – if not with internal resources then through the application of external resources of commercially supplied business services or public assistance. External resources are, however, often ignored by firms, partly because of genuine ignorance as to their availability or applicability and not infrequently because of distrust of outside 'interference'. In a favourable institutional environment resources are made better known and there is more trust than distrust.

First results from the German component of a four-country study conducted by Hull and Hjern[40] strongly suggests that local institutional arrangements can make a significant difference to how firms perceive their problems and to how successful they are in mobilising all manner of external resources. In the most impressive local instance examined in the German study the results had been achieved in large measure through the efforts of a single individual who, in the course of ten years' steady application as 'intermediary', had developed a trusting relationship with his local population of firms and with the public and private organisations capable of providing the resources which 'his' firms might need to resolve their problems. The evidence points to a markedly above-average rate of new job creation in the locality as a consequence of this favourable institutional climate.

The institutional climate within which small firms best flourish is a subject which has attracted little attention. The reason may be that concepts from neo-classical economics tend to dominate our thinking about firms. Thus we tend to think of them as 'lonely organisations' struggling to survive in a hostile market environment. The image is appropriate, but it is only part of the story; it ignores the many institutions upon which (small) firms draw in order better to survive in the market. The institutional climate which best serves small firms is a worthwhile object of research and embodies considerable potential for the policy innovator.

Notes

1. W. Abel, and H-G. Schlotter, 'Mittelstandspolitik' in E. von Beckerath *et al.* (eds.) *Handwörterbuch der Sozialwissenschaften*, vol.'7, Gustav Fischer, J.C.B. Mohr (Paul Siebeck) and Vandenhoeck & Ruprecht, Stuttgart, Tübingen and Göttingen, 1961 pp. 395–402.

Naujoks, W. *Unternehmensgrößenbezogene Strukturpolitik und gewerblicher Mittelstand*, Verlag Otto Schartz & Co., Göttingen, 1975.

2. The authoritative text on the theoretical and operational difficulties of defining 'the small firm' in the West German context is N. Gantzel, *Wesen und Begriff der mittelständischen Unternehmung*, Cologne and Opladen, 1962.

3. In three recent instances the divide between large and small in West German manufacturing industry was set at 200 in Berliner Senator für Wirtschaft *Kleine und mittlere Unternehmen in Berlin*, Senator für Wirtschaft, Berlin, 1977. In other cases it was set at 500: Hamburger Staatliche Pressestelle *Hamburger Mittelstandsbericht 1981*, Staatliche Pressestelle, Hamburg. It has also been set at 1000: IFO 'Promotion of Research in the EEC' *IFO-Digest*, no. 2, 1980, pp. 41–7.

4. Bundesregierung *Bericht der Bundesregierung über Lage und Entwicklung der kleinen und mittleren Unternehmen* (Mittelstandsbericht), Drucksache 7/5248, Deutscher Bundestag, 1976.

5. Own calculation from Statistisches Bundesamt *Betriebe, Beschäftigte und Umsatz im Bergbau und im Verarbeitenden Gewerbe nach Beschäftigtengrößen-klassen 1977*, Fachserie 4 Produzierendes Gewerbe, Reihe 4.1.2, Verlag W. Kohlhammer, Stuttgart and Mainz, 1979.

6. G. Dahm, R. Stockmann and K. Zeifang, *Die Entwicklung der Struktur von nichtlandwirtschaftlichen Arbeitsstätten und Unternehmen von 1875 bis 1970*, Conference Paper, University of Mannheim, 1981.

7. In a cross-time series analysis of inflation-adjusted tax return data filed by firms it has been estimated that the share of firms classified as 'small' fell from 65.9 per cent of all firms in 1970 to 62.1 per cent in 1976.

176   Federal Republic of Germany

J. Steiner, B. Börstler and W. Reske, *Die Entwicklung von Unternehmen und Umsätzen in der Bundesrepublik Deutschland von 1970–1976 auf der Basis nominaler und realer Daten*, Verlag Otto Schwartz & Co., Göttingen, 1979.

8. J. Huber, *Wer soll das alles ändern – Die Alternativen der Alternativbewegung*, Rotbuch Verlag, Berlin, 1980.

9. The denominator is the sum of the totals of manufacturing and service firms reported in Table 6.4.

10. J. Steiner, 'Deutschland braucht neue Gründerjahre' in *Der Arbeitgeber*, no. 12, 1979, pp. 714–716.

11. Figures for the numbers of new and old firms are collected by the individual states (*Länder*) of the Federal Republic, which do not follow common conventions of definition, classification and publication. A common set of data is not available. Moreover, the data which are collected relate to administrative transactions in the statutory 'registers of trades' (*Gewerberegister*) and tend significantly to overestimate, when taken at face value, the true numbers of new and old firms. See note 13.

12. R. Clemens, W. Langen and W. Naujoks, *Sektorale und regionale Gewerbeanmeldungen und Gewerbeabmeldungen in Nordrhein-Westfalen 1966–1975*, Verlag Otto Schwartz & Co., Göttingen, 1978.

13. Northrhine-Westfalia is the most populous state. At the 1970 Census of Sites (*Arbeitsstättenzählung*) Northrhine-Westfalia accounted for some 25 per cent of all sites in the Federal Republic and 28 per cent of the employed population.

14. The figures are estimates for real births and deaths. Clemens *et al.* were able, through a detailed analysis of the original data for the years 1973–75, to estimate the true number of new firms (first time set-ups and similarly new branch establishments) at some 66 per cent of all new registrations and of deceased firms at some 79 per cent of all deletions.

15. Estimated by relating the 2,340 insolvencies in the Northrhine-Westfalia in 1975 (Creditreform (annual) Jahresbericht (year), Verband der Vereine Creditreform e.V. Neuss, Neuss.) to the figure of 47,710 deletions of firms in that region and year reported by Clemens *et al*.

16. All figures in this section and in Tables 6.6 and 6.7 are taken or calculated from the Annual Reports of the *Verband der Vereine Creditreform e.V.*, a leading credit information service in West Germany. The *Creditreform* insolvency analyses are based on 15–20 per cent samples of all insolvencies in West Germany in the respective time period.

17. The reader is reminded that reference is to insolvencies in their (German) legal definition. The correlation between firm failures in general and size (age, etc.) may, of course, be different.

18. D.L. Birch, *The Job Generation Process*, Massachusetts Institute of Technology, Cambridge, Mass., 1979.

D.L. Birch, 'Who Creates Jobs?' *The Public Interest*, no. 65, Fall 1981, p. 3ff.

19. W. Friedrich and E. Spitznagel, 'Wachstum, Beschäftigung und Investitionstätigkeit im Verarbeiten Gewerbe' in *Mitteilungen aus der Arbeitsmarkt- und Berufsforschung*, vol. 13, no. 4, 1980, pp. 514–520.

20. Infratest *Begleitforschung zum Arbeitsmarktpolitischen Programm der Bundesregierung für Regionen mit besonderen Beschäftigungsproblemen*, Band 4 (Betriebserhebung), Infratest, Munich, 1980.

21. U. Schwarting, 'Das zukünftige Arbeitsplatzangebot' *Der Arbeitgeber*, no. 16–17, 1979, pp. 887–889.

22. W. Gruhler, *Unternehmensgröße und Beschäftigung in der Industrie*, Deutscher Instituts-Verlag GmbH., Cologne, 1979.

23. H. v. Henninges and M. Otto, *Entwicklungstendenzen des Ausbildungsumfanges von Klein-, Mittel- und Großbetrieben in der Bundesrepublik*

Deutschland, Bundesinstitut für Berufsbildung, Berlin, 1978.

24. H. Schmidt, 'Klein- und Mittelbetriebe entscheiden über die Zukunft der beruflichen Bildung' *Informations-bulletin des Europäischen Zentrums für die Förderung der Berufsbildung*, 1981, no. 7, pp. 6–8.

25. E. May, *Forschungs- und Entwicklungsaktivitäten kleiner und mittlerer Unternehmen*, Institute für Mittelstandsforschung, Bonn, 1980.

26. J. Klein, *Innovation und Unternehmensgröße*, discussion paper no. IIM/dp 80–9, International Institute of Management, Wissenschaftszentrum Berlin, Berlin, 1980.

27. K. Grefermann and K. Röthlingshöfer, *Patentwesen und technischer Fortschritt*, Teil II, Schriften der Kommission für wirtschaftlichen und sozialen Wandel, vol. 10, Göttingen, 1974.

28. I.H.K. Koblenz, "*Kein Technischer Fortschritt ohne Mittelstand*", Industrie – Und Handelskammer zu Koblenz, Koblenz, 1975.

29. J. Geiser, *Unternehmensgrößenbezogene Wachstumshemmnisse mittelständischer Industriebetriebe*, Verlag Otto Schwartz & Co., Göttingen, 1981.

30. Geiser's analysis relates to 358 firms nation-wide in manufacturing having up to 500 employees. Firms with over 500 employees could elect themselves into the sample if they considered themselves '*mittelständisch*' (which 31 – 8.7 per cent of the sample – did).

31. The intensity index is a weighted average based on individual firms' rankings of the intensity of constraint ('small', 'large', 'very large') posed by each factor. The index ranges in value from +2.0 to +8.0.

32. There is no recent good-quality overview, in English, of small firm policy in West Germany. The best available remains G. Bannock, *The Smaller Business in Britain and Germany*, Wilton House Publications, London, 1976. German studies tend to be stronger on the federal dimension and ignorant of the states' role. The interested reader is advised to consult Bundesregierung *Mittelstand – Leistung und Wettbewerb*, Bonn, Bundesministerium für Wirtschaft, 1979.

E. Dichtl, H. Raffée and H. Wellenreuther, 'Mittelstandspolitik' in *Wirtschaftswissenschaftliches Studium*, no. 11, 1981, pp. 533–539.

Zeitschrift für das gesamte Kreditwesen, *Die Finanzierungshilfen des Bundes und der Länder an die gewerbliche Wirtschaft*, Fritz Knapp Verlag, Frankfurt, 1982.

33. Deutscher Bundestag *Bericht der Bundesregierung über die Entwicklung der Finanzhilfen und Steuervergünstigungen . . . (achter Subventionsbericht)*, Drucksache 9/986, 1981.

34. *Handelsblatt* 'Arbeitslosigkeit trifft alle Industriezweige gleich', October 8/9, 1982.

35. Cited in *Der Tagesspiegel* 'Insolvenzen schaffen Arbeitslage', February 7, 1982.

36. *Der Tagesspiegel* 'Eigenkapitalmangel ist die wichtigste Konkursursache', October 10, 1981.

37. Deutsche Bundesbank 'Ertragslage und Finanzierungsverhältnisse der Unternehmen im Jahre 1980' in *Monatsberichte der Deutschen Bundesbank*, vol. 33, no. 11, 1981, pp. 17–26.

38. PROGNOS, *Analyse und Prognose der Unternehmensgrößenstruktur*, Basel, 1979.

39. In construction, for example, small firms employing up to 50 persons are expected to increase their share of employment from 50.8 to 59.8 per cent of total employment in the sector – but the sector is expected to have shrunk by 21.7 per cent over these fifteen years. Conversely, in the 'boom' sector of banking and insurance (+19.0%) the share of employment in firms employing up to 100 persons is expected to have declined from 25.9 to 23.1 per cent.

40. C. Hull and B. Hjern, 'Helping Small Firms Grow: An Implementation

Analysis of Small Firm Assistance Structures' in *European Journal of Political Research* 10, 1982, p. 187–198. C. Hull and B. Hjern, *Förderung kleiner und mittlerer Industriebetriebe als Mittel der Beschäftigungspolitik vor Ort*, Manuscript, Wissenschaftszentrum Berlin, 1982.

41. Statistiches Bundesamt (1952, 1963, 1979, 1981) *Statistisches Jarbuch (year) für die Bundesrepublik Deutschland*, Verlag, W. Kohlhammer, Stuttgart and Mainz.

42. K-H. Fiebig and M. Kammertöns, *Daten zur Entwicklung Kleiner und Mittlerer Betriebe aus Bund, Ländern und Städten (Materialsammlung)*, Deutsches Institut für Urbanistik, 1979, Berlin and Cologne.

7 SWEDEN

7.1. Introduction

The Swedish economy has experienced considerable structural changes during the 1970s. Industries such as iron ore, steel and wood-processing, which have traditionally been very strong, have now plunged into crisis. Major problems have also been encountered in other parts of the economy and one company crisis has succeeded another. The difficulties of industry – and not least those of large-scale companies – in adjusting to new conditions can be seen in the reductions in productive capacity and the reductions in staff which have taken place. The effect of the industrial crisis on unemployment has however been limited, due to the massive efforts of society to reduce the negative effects of these structural changes.

Concurrently with this industrial crisis the growth potential of small firms has been given increasing attention. Political efforts have been made to bring about the birth of new business and to support expansion in existing small firms. Besides general efforts to change the framework for business, governments have also specifically eased the access to finance for small firms and created an organisation for the provision of business services.

Despite the importance of small firms in the Swedish economy, knowledge of the problems and the conditions of small business is inadequate. Furthermore, there is no satisfactory theory to depict the economic reality of todays small firm. Whilst classical and neo-classical economic theory have taken the small firm as their starting point, both assume conditions which are significantly different from those prevailing in developed industrial countries such as Sweden. Seen against this background, efforts in the theoretical field are urgent in small business research.

In the theoretical development advocated here it is necessary to take into consideration that the majority of the markets in the modern industrial state are dominated by large-scale companies. As a result, small firms should be seen in relation to large firms and be regarded as complementary to, rather than competitive with, large-scale companies. The concept of the market also needs to be revised. Instead of regarding it as a meeting place for buyers and sellers where new relationships constantly arise, small firms should be seen as components in relatively stable systems of production and distribution.

Thirdly, changes in the spatial distribution of small firms' markets can be seen. The focus of the small firms' marketing remains primarily local, but developments in transportation and communications have widened the horizon of many small firms and even forced others into international markets in order to survive.

Fourthly, the creation of new types of business organizations should be noted. One example is the linking of small firms into ownership groups and the establishment of various forms of co-operation between firms, so as to take advantage of scale economies and to meet the demands of the market.

Another matter that should be taken into consideration in a theoretical development is the increase in political measures to assist small firms. In recent years the economy has become markedly more politicised, and the 1970s can be described as the decade of selective politics in Sweden. Numerous measures have been introduced and organisations have been created to implement new small business legislation. According to supporters of a free-market system, the mixed economy has become a 'negotiation' economy, where successful dealings with government authorities and officials has become more important than competence in manufacturing and marketing.

This coupling of politics and economics has also meant that small firms have been, during the past few years, increasingly seen as a means of mobilising local/regional resources for development in areas badly affected by unemployment. Confidence that central political bodies and government authorities will/can do something for these places has evaporated and local initiatives are currently fashionable. Small business has a central role in these local development strategies.

These issues are developed in the remainder of this chapter but to appreciate the significance of small firms the reader should be aware of the historical and statistical context of small firm development in Sweden.

7.2. The Small Business Concept

In analysing the scope and development of small firms three different business concepts are used: the technical, the legal, and the economic business unit. The distinction between the three can most clearly be seen if they are applied to the 'large-scale companies' which dominate manufacturing industry in the modern industrial state. These large companies – i.e. economic entities – normally comprise several subsidiary companies – legal entities – which in turn can have many production units – technical entities. For a majority of firms, the three concepts coincide. The economic entity is simultaneously a legal entity and a technical entity, but the distinction has to be clearly appreciated when interpreting the statistical material.

The technical entity – the production unit – is the most suitable business concept if tendencies towards concentration at the production level are of interest. Alternatively if interest is focused on concentration in the economy as a whole, and the development of legally independent small firms, then the economic business concept is the most appropriate.

Swedish business statistics, which from an international point of view are comparatively good, are based partly on the technical entity and partly on the legal entity as a business concept. In addition, there is a Group Register (Koncernregister) which provides a list of all subsidiary firms within the Group but there are no statistical series covering the development of economic entities over time.[1] The following account of the scope and the development of the Swedish small firm population over a period of time will therefore be based on the legal business entity definitions.

There is no generally accepted distinction between, on the one hand, small and medium-sized firms, and on the other hand, large firms. The number of persons employed is generally used as a measure of size in Sweden, and the official dividing line for small and medium-sized firms is set at 200 employees. Within this group, small firms (fewer than 50 employees) and medium-sized firms (50–199 employees) can be distinguished.

In this chapter the number of persons employed is used as the measure of size. No distinction is made between small and medium-sized firms. Small firms will be defined to be those with up to 200 employees.

7.3. The Development of the Business Population

Swedish business statistics are not very pleasant reading for a supporter of small firms, since it is clear that the latter have continuously lost ground compared with large firms during the whole postwar period. The tendencies toward concentration within the Swedish economy were especially obvious during the 1950s and 1960s. The information available for the 1970s shows a continued domination by large scale companies, even if it is not as marked as during previous decades.

In spite of the increase in economic concentration over time there are still a large number of small firms in the Swedish economy and the tendencies toward concentration have weakened markedly during the past few years. Small firms are needed in a modern industrial society as a complement to large-scale companies. The extent of this complementarity can be debated, but there is no doubt that small firms will continue to be of importance within the Swedish economy for many decades.

In Table 7.1 the development of the Swedish business population since 1970 is shown for those sectors of the economy dominated by private firms – mining and manufacturing industry (ISIC 2 and 3), construction industry (ISIC 5), wholesale and retail trade, restaurants and hotels (ISIC 6), transportation and storage (ISIC 71) and business services (ISIC 832). During the 1970s the number of firms in all sectors decreased except in business services, which showed an increase of slightly more than 2,300 in the decade. The period 1978–80 however saw an increase in the number of firms in wholesale and retail trades etc, as well as in transportation and business services. The decrease in the manufacturing sector is also less than the average for the decade but the contraction within construction continued unabated. The latter must be seen in the light of a massive building programme of flats and small houses which was undertaken during the 1960s. More than 100,000 flats and small houses were built each year to overcome a shortage in the market. In the 1970s demand declined dramatically and in 1981 less than half of the number of flats and small houses were built, compared with the peak years of the 1960s. There is little sign of change in the immediate future. New flats and small houses in the past have been heavily subsidised by the government to keep down the costs to the occupier, but because of current high budget deficits

Table 7.1: The Development of the Business Population During the 1970s Within Principal Sectors (Legal Entities)

Sector	Size of Firm (number of employees) Year	1–4 Number	%	5–49 Number	%	50–199 Number	%	200+ Number	%	Total Number	%
Mining and manufacturing (ISIC 2 and 3)	1970	13,718	51.0	10,828	40.3	1,726	6.4	612	2.3	26,884	100
	1978	12,092	50.5	9,766	40.7	1,512	6.3	600	2.5	23,970	100
	1980	12,085	50.9	9,540	40.2	1,514	6.4	611	2.5	23,750	100
Construction (ISIC 5)	1970	23,585	78.6	5,861	19.5	472	1.6	95	0.3	30,013	100
	1978	19,163	75.8	5,739	22.7	325	1.3	63	0.2	25,290	100
	1980	17,457	74.5	5,629	24.0	298	1.3	59	0.3	23,443	100
Wholesale and retail trade, restaurants and hotels (ISIC 6)	1970	36,336	72.4	12,713	25.4	897	1.8	208	0.4	50,154	100
	1978	33,798	69.0	14,149	28.9	854	1.7	206	0.4	49,007	100
	1980	34,756	69.6	14,161	28.4	803	1.6	211	0.4	49,931	100
Transport and storage (ISIC 71)	1970	13,666	80.4	3,066	18.0	214	1.3	55	0.3	17,001	100
	1978	11,328	76.1	3,291	22.1	220	1.5	55	0.4	14,894	100
	1980	11,517	76.0	3,359	22.2	218	1.4	60	0.4	15,154	100
Businesses and services (ISIC 832)	1970	6,686	74.6	2,120	23.6	126	1.4	36	0.4	8,968	100
	1978	8,077	74.8	2,520	23.4	148	1.4	44	0.4	10,789	100
	1980	8,373	74.2	2,690	23.8	167	1.5	51	0.5	11,281	100

Source: Centrala företagsregistret, Statistiska centralbyrån.

the level is now gradually being reduced, pushing up costs and hence reducing demand.

Changes in the number of firms are also reflected in the employment trends of small firms during the 1970s, shown in Table 7.2. The increased employment in small firms within the business services sector reflects the specialisation that has taken place in the Swedish economy during the 1970s. A number of functions have been hived-off to specialist firms. For example, accounting in many small firms is undertaken by auditing bureaus which have computing capacity at their disposal. Another example of greater specialisation is the increased number of advertising companies and legal firms.

A. The Development of Manufacturing Industry

Underlying the overall decline of small firms in the mining and manufacturing industries during the 1970s are significant differences between industries. There was a net decline in the number of small firms in the textile and clothing industries, whereas numbers in the engineering and chemical industries increased. The number of persons employed in small firms also increased in the latter industries.

Table 7.3 shows that over the 1969–79 period in 5 out of 10 industries small firms have lost ground in comparison with large firms, while in three industries the reverse has occurred. Two of these three industries are typical industries in crisis, (mining, textiles) where total employment is declining, and even the third (other manufacturing) shows signs of decline. Thus, the relatively greater importance of small firms in these industries is because small firms have been relatively more successful in coping with a contracting market than have large companies.

It is interesting to note that small firms have maintained their position within the chemical and the expanding engineering industries. Whilst only 30 per cent of employment within the latter industry is in small firms, this represents more than 125,000 jobs, or more than 40 per cent of the total employment in small firms in mining and manufacturing industries as a whole.

B. Mergers and Closures

The net changes in the stock of firms, discussed above, illustrates one aspect of the development of the Swedish economy over time, yet underlying even these relatively modest net changes from one

Table 7.2: Numbers Employed in Small Firms by Sector, 1969–79

Sector	Mining and manufacturing		Construction		Wholesale and retail trades, restaurants and hotels		Transportation and storage		Business services	
Year	Number	%	Number	%	Number	%	Number	%	Number	%
1969	344,119	35.3	137,209	54.2	291,835	60.8	75,372	a	44,985	69.7
1977	308,103	33.3	119,072	59.6	296,413	63.7	74,768	43.2	54,912	66.1
1979	302,871	32.5	117,521	59.3	292,606	63.6	75,608	41.9	58,944	62.8

Notes: % indicates employment in small firms divided by total employment in each sector.
    a. Presentation of statistics changed.

Source: Centrala företagsregistret, Statistika centralbyrån.

Table 7.3: Employment in Small Firms in Mining and Manufacturing, 1969–79

Industry	Year 1969		1977		1979	
	Man-years	%	Man-years	%	Man-years	%
Mining	4,953	27.6	3,630	34.7	3,266	33.5
Food production, etc	34,101	42.4	23,625	31.3	23,218	30.9
Textile and clothing	45,788	61.6	30,837	65.5	28,409	68.3
Wood	54,835	74.3	49,933	73.1	48,792	71.9
Pulp, paper and paper products	38,774	27.7	35,401	26.4	34,814	25.2
Chemicals	19,119	31.4	19,231	32.9	19,341	31.2
Earth and quarrying	16,589	40.4	12,051	37.5	10,547	32.8
Iron-, steel- and metal-works	6,830	9.4	3,930	5.3	3,769	5.7
Engineering	116,454	28.8	124,281	29.7	125,748	29.0
Other forms of manufacturing industry	6,676	76.2	5,184	80.1	4,937	78.9
Total	344,119	35.3	308,103	33.3	302,871	32.5

Note: The figures show the number of persons employed in small firms and employment in small firms compared with the total figure for employment in each industry.
Source: Centrala företagsregistret. Statistika central byrån.

year to another, is a considerable in- and outflow of firms. In this section the data available on in- and outflows will be presented, with the important caveat that there is no reliable information on the number of closures. There is, however, relatively reliable data on the number of mergers and bankruptcies in the Swedish economy. Finally, considerable efforts are made to provide satisfactory statistics on new establishments, although experience suggests the number of establishments is systematically underestimated.

Table 7.4: Number of Company Take-overs in the 1970s

Year	Number of companies taken over	Year	Number of companies taken over
1970	328	1976	611
1971	309	1977	598
1972	404	1978	582
1973	495	1979	590
1974	728	1980	674
1975	828		

Source: Statens Pris-och Kartellnämnd

Data shown in Table 7.4 on company acquisitions show a considerable number of firms change ownership each year. During the first half of the 1970s a marked increase in mergers were recorded. At the beginning of the decade the number of company take-overs was about 300 annually but by 1975 this figure had almost tripled. After this date numbers fell again and at the end of the decade had stabilised at about 600 annually.

Company acquisitions have occurred principally in manufacturing and in the wholesale and retail trades. Of the company acquisitions in 1979, 215 were industrial firms and 185 were wholesale and retail firms. The data also show that larger firms acquire smaller ones, with two out of three acquirers having more than 200 employees and four out of five acquired firms having fewer than 50 employees.

Pettersson[2] has analysed mergers in the Swedish economy. He found that approximately 80 per cent of the firms acquired in one way or another, had economic difficulties, either because they found themselves in a contracting market whereby they became less solvent, or else they had expanded too quickly under favourable market conditions. In the latter case the company had become too highly geared, causing serious liquidity problems to arise.

Pettersson's study also showed that small, independent firms were the prime acquirers of contracting firms. The large firms, on the other hand, were more likely to acquire expanding firms and were virtually the exclusive purchasers of expanding firms with a record of success.[3]

The relative decline of small firms must be seen in the light of the relatively high frequency of acquisition of firms in the Swedish economy. Merely to replace firms 'lost' in mergers requires a modest birth rate. Furthermore, the number of closures appear to have increased over time, though the data are less reliable on this matter. In the last few years the number of closures in the manufacturing industry have, according to estimates made, fluctuated between 1,100 and 1,500 firms.[4] A considerable, and increasing, proportion of these have disappeared from the market due to bankruptcy, as shown in Figure 7.1.

Figure 7.1: Bankruptcies Within the Manufacturing Industry, 1971–81[5]

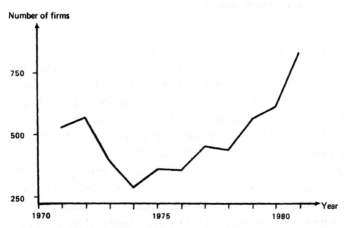

Source: Accordcentralen

C. New Establishments

During the 1970s there was much discussion on the role and importance of new establishments in the economy. Several empirical studies have been conducted in Sweden but the lack of reliable statistics has hindered comparisons over time and the conclusions from the different studies have been contradictory. Although efforts have been made to overcome the problem of underestimation of new establishments in official statistics, data for recent years continue to be less reliable than that for the earlier periods.

Studies of new establishments have, almost without exception, concentrated upon manufacturing industry. A current study from the National Industrial Board (Statens industriverk) shows

Figure 7.2: New Establishments in Swedish Manufacturing Industry, 1965–80

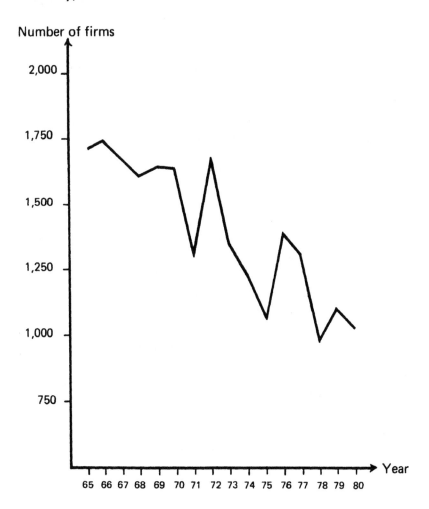

there was a reduction in the number of new establishments in manufacturing industry during the years 1965–80 (Figure 7.2). The numbers of new businesses established has almost halved during the fifteen years under study. Due to the time-lag in the statistics it is likely, however, that the graph for new establishments in recent years will be adjusted upwards after revision. Nevertheless, even after such an adjustment the formation of new establishments, as we enter the 1980s, is still much lower than it was during the 1960s.

There are no reliable statistics of current new establishments in any other sector of the Swedish economy, although it is clear that many new businesses are being formed. This is especially true of the business-service sector, where the stock of firms increased by 26 per cent during the 1970s. The creation of new establishments is also thought to have been high in the wholesale and retail trade, and so on, and in transportation and storage.

The number of firms without employees has also increased markedly during recent years.[6] The reason for this increase is unclear but it is likely to be due partly to a significant number of sole proprietorships – firms which have no employees – and partly to a large number of non-working firms. It is not possible to determine whether the number of sole proprietorships has increased over time, but this seems to be a likely explanation.

D. New Types of Business

During the 1970s interest in alternative forms of ownership management and business control has increased. An expression of this was the appointment of a Commission in 1977 to investigate co-operatives and their place in society. Within the scope of this investigation a separate study was made of employee-owned firms.[7] The survey shows that in 1979 there were 60 employee-owned firms in the manufacturing and construction industries. All except five were established after 1965 with a peak year of 1977, after which the number of establishments has stabilised just below the level of 1977. About one half of the firms trading in 1979 became employee-owned between 1977 and 1979 – see Figure 7.3.

The increased number of employee-owned firms, especially during the latter part of the 1970s, could be interpreted as a manifestation of the greater consciousness of employees of the importance of work-place control. Gabrielsson's study however showed that within employee-owned firms this is not a primary driving force since relatively few employee-owned firms are

Figure 7.3: Year of Establishment for Employee-owned Firms[8]

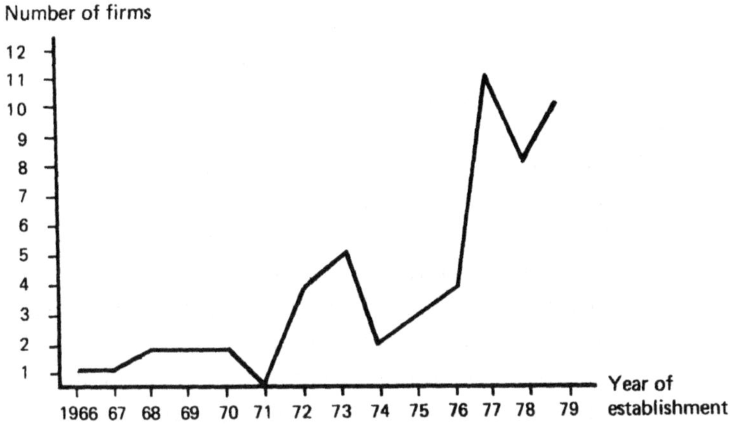

Number of firms

Source: Å. Gabrielsson, 1980.[7]

genuine new establishments. The most common occurrence is for the employees to take over a firm facing either economic difficulties or a succession problem. Employee ownership is therefore more likely to be a defensive action by the employees to save jobs, rather than being motivated by an eagerness to create new businesses.

Only five of the firms studied were positive attempts to create employee-owned firms. Two of these were established already in the 1920s and had a sindicalist background. In the remaining three cases a small number of employees left their former employer and established competing firms. In one of the cases the motivation was the employees' discontent with the company management, whilst in another there were risks of redundancy.

According to Gabrielson, the fact that positively motivated attempts at worker owned firms are rare must be seen in the light of the obstacles to be overcome in the establishment of such firms. The government has recently attempted to reduce these obstacles. For example, consulting grants can be given during a trial period to cover 50 per cent of the costs for consultation in realising either a company take-over or a new establishment, but many difficulties still remain.

Another development in the economy is increased co-operation between independent firms. Co-operation can in theory be of mutual benefit for many small firms, which can achieve the advantages of large-scale production whilst retaining most of the advantages of small-scale business.

During the 1970s these ideals were a powerful influence upon the government's industrial policy. Unfortunately, in many cases, co-operation was not a success. Even if it could be achieved with the assistance of the authorities, basic problems still existed, manifested by continually receding markets, increasing losses, and reductions in the work force.

It has also proved to be very difficult and time consuming to induce far-reaching co-operation agreements between small firms. Organisational changes, either within a firm or between different firms, normally encounter inherent resistance by the established structures. A study by Lindmark and Ekman[9] shows that the idea of co-operation clashes with deeply-rooted ideas and growth patterns in small firms. Co-operation requires some modification in the business ideas of the presumptive co-operation partners and thus requires changes in both the physical system as well as the social and value systems of the firms. In the projects studied clashes in all three subsystems partly explained why co-operation was never realised.

Other studies also show that the majority of co-operation projects fail in the establishment phase, but even the projects that de facto lead to a regular co-operation often ceased within a few years. In a study by Edström[10] it is shown that almost one half of the established co-operations were broken off within five years.

It is clear that co-operation between small firms can be a proper and necessary 'solution' in certain situations,[11] but it should not be taken as a general prescription for firms with problems. Recognition of the many problems and difficulties which must be overcome is essential before a co-operation project of a far-reaching nature can be changed from theory into practice.

7.4. The Role of Small Firms in the Swedish Economy

The starting point for classical and neo-classical economic theory is the perfectly competitive market where firms are small in relation to the market which they serve. Even though formal theories also exist of oligopoly and monopoly, economists continue to be influenced by a model of perfect competition, which in essential matters lacks ties with reality. As previously mentioned, within the Swedish manufacturing industry, no fewer than two-thirds of the employees are found in large companies.

Galbraith[12] asserts that large business is a prerequisite for a well-developed industrial society aiming at technical renewal. The technological imperatives – such as, the increasing period of time between the product idea and its implementation on the market, the increased capital intensity of production, increased specialisation and thus great dependence between production stages and functions within the company – lead dominant firms to attempt to obtain the maximum possible control of the market. Small firms are peripheral to the modern economy according to this approach.

Small business researchers have asserted however, that small firms are responsible for much of the dynamic in business development. Small firms are seen as a source of renewal through which antiquated production forms are eliminated.[13] This suggestion does not however seem to have much empirical support, with surveys showing there are only a limited number of small firms with essentially creative business ideas or products, and with the ability to develop a market niche of their own.[14] Studies of the motives for the establishment of new firms also show that professional experience is a prerequisite for persons who have started their own businesses and this indicates that new firms are started primarily in trades with which the entrepreneur is already familiar – i.e. business establishments through "spin-off".

Explanations of the continued existence of small firms can therefore be found in the fact that the small firm complements large-scale companies. Business on a large scale is, as noted above, based on a high capital intensity, standardisation, large markets, and long planning time from idea to finished product. Due to these technological conditions a number of 'niches' are created for small firms in the market system. This applies to the market for final goods and perhaps most importantly to the market for input goods.

The idea that small firms are a complement to large-scale companies by supplying components and semi-manufactured goods is not new. Baumback *et al.*,[15] for example, maintain that it is in this area that the specific competence of small business lies. 'Thus it is in the manufacture of producer's goods (products made for other manufacturers) wherein most of the opportunities exist for the small, independent enterprises. As big business grows, so does small business'.

Empirical support for this assertion is provided in a study by the Swedish Association of Metalworking Industries (Sveriges Mekanförbund)[16] which found that a majority of the small engineering firms conformed to the role of sub-contractors. The Association found that 57 per cent of firms having fewer than 25 employees, sold more than half of their turnover to other manufacturing firms. This corresponds with the results shown in two papers by Fredriksson and Lindmark,[17] who demonstrated that the role of sub-contractor is characteristic of firms in the metal and engineering industries. In fact, no fewer than two out of three small firms operate as sub-contractors. An analysis of the sales by the firms to the 30 largest manufacturing companies in the country showed that half of the firms sold a substantial part of their output to these large companies. Moreover, for one in eight of the juridically independent sub-contractors, these supplies make up the dominant element, since more than 50 per cent of their production is apportioned to the 30 largest manufacturing companies.

The car industry in particular bases its production on sub-contracting. The significance of the expression, 'To build a car the Volvo way', is shown in that 64 per cent of production value is made up of components which are bought from outside. For the production of passenger cars Volvo utilises more than 1,300 sub-contractors of which more than 700 are Swedish. Thus, a rough estimate indicates that Volvo alone – the biggest manufacturing firm in the country – 'covers' nearly 5 per cent of all small firms in Sweden in its extensive system of sub-contractors.[18]

Production in the modern industrial society is to a great extent carried out in hierarchically-built production systems, having at their head the giant firm, with many small manufacturing firms having established connections as sub-contractors or suppliers of production and engineering services.

A. Production and Distribution Systems

In the perfect competition model the individual firm, by its own actions, cannot affect the price of the product which is manufactured, since this is set exogenously. The theory also assumes the firm is a profit maximiser having perfect knowledge of factor and product prices, as well as of its own production function.

In a market economy with these characteristics, the relationships between firms might be thought to be unstable, yet empirical observation suggests the opposite. Production and distribution systems exist in the sense that long-term relations have been built up between firms. In a case study by Fredriksson and Lindmark[19] it was found that the firms examined had engaged the same subcontractors for many years. For the majority of contractors the co-operation had lasted during the major part of the life of the buying companies, amounting in some cases to more than 30 years. Outright changes of suppliers were exceptional. In the majority of cases the transactions between buying companies and contractors were designed so that flows of material were largely regulated by the turnover of the buying companies. Production was not 'taken home'* to any great extent even during recessions, since the buying company was anxious to remain in contact with its contractors pending an economic upswing. In other cases 'taking production home' was not possible, since the organisation was unable to provide these products and services 'in-house'.

Similar conclusions are presented by Håkansson and Wootz[20] in their study of the purchasing behaviour of firms. They state that the relationships between buyers and sellers in industrial markets are usually very stable, and that stability tends to increase in relation to the extent of previous contacts.[21]

This picture of stability in the relations between purchaser and supplier is emphasised in a recent study made by the Ministry of Industry (industridepartementet) with the Swedish Metal Workers' Union (svenska metallindustriarbetarförbundet) and the Swedish Association of Metalworking Industries (Sveriges Mekanförbund).[22] The study comprised 22 large and medium-sized firms which bought parts and intermediate goods on the Swedish market. It showed that for 14 of the 22 buying firms, less than 5 per cent of the suppliers are replaced or added per year. This share amounted to between 5 and 10 per cent in the remaining firms. These results were confirmed by the sub-contracting firms included in the study.

Analyses of the efficiency and development of the smaller sub-contracting firms show furthermore that they are as efficient, and dynamic as firms with other lines of business.[23] This is particularly true of firms incorporated in the production systems of large-scale companies. For example, sub-contractors operating in the manufacture of metal products and machinery that orientate themselves towards large companies show a capital intensity which

---

* This phrase means that during recessions sub-contracting firms reduced orders more than in proportion to the reduced output of the dominant firm.

is clearly above average for small firms in the sector. Likewise, management within these firms has higher levels of educational attainment than for the average small firm.

Sub-contractors, as a group, also seem to be in an equally good or better financial position than most small firms. These results indicate that the role of sub-contractor has not been chosen in the absence of alternative activities.

Several explanations may be provided for the stability of the sub-contracting relationships. The first derives from the decision-making of the large firms. The choice of suppliers is not made according to the strict rationality principles prescribed in economic theory. Knowledge of potential suppliers is limited and satisficing-thinking is characteristic of the purchasing procedure. Organisational conditions in the purchasing firm – for example the separation of the purchasing function from the production function – may also lead to existing suppliers being preferred to new ones.

Another factor leading to stability is that the large firm seeks to obtain control of its environment and as far as possible tries to avoid uncertainty. Changes of supplier entail an increased uncertainty in an introductory stage. The buying firm cannot be sure the new supplier will meet delivery dates or reach the specified quality. The problem of delivery dates can be overcome by increased stock but this is expensive, so it is important for firms to maintain continuity in material flows to minimise inventory costs.

By changing suppliers, transaction costs also increase. Obtaining components and intermediate goods on the open market involves costs in addition to the price of the product and the increased inventory costs. Search costs to find potential suppliers, and costs to evaluate the identified suppliers are examples.

Within marketing research there is an approach which studies sales on the industrial markets. Several interesting contributions have been published by Swedish researchers within this area which are relevant to this discussion. In this research firms are seen as components in networks having relations with customers, suppliers, banks, and so on. A significant characteristic of these relations is that they function as bonds between the firms. Hammarkvist *et al.*, distinguishes five types of bond: technical bonds; time bonds; knowledge bonds; social bonds; economic and legal bonds. The network of firms becomes more or less tightly structured depending upon the nature of the bonds. For example, the high technical and capital intensity of industry is leading to tightly-structured networks. The stability in this type of network is high, with the implication that it is difficult for new firms to enter into these markets.

The limited empirical data available concerning the organisation and the structure of the wholesale and retail sectors indicates that the comments on the relations between various manufacturing firms are also applicable to these sectors. Common marketing activities are utilised by the purchaser and the supplier, and the products of the manufacturing firms become a part of the image that the wholesale and retail firms try to give their customers. As with manufacturing firms, these relations have a tendency to become stronger over time.

B. The Geographical Dimension of the Production and Distribution Systems

Another aspect of current production and distribution systems is their geographical compositions. Fredriksson and Lindmark for example argue that production systems are distinguished by considerable geographical distribution, but that around both the large-scale companies and their production units and the small firms, local systems of sub-contractors develop. In the national/international systems local clusterings can be identified in which small firms are the suppliers.

Empirical results support this thesis. It was found that small firms which concentrate on sub-contracting, on average sell more than one-third of their output to local customers. For approximately every tenth sub-contracting firm, the local manufacturing industry is the dominant market, as more than 50 per cent of the firms' production is sold locally. The local market orientation is especially pronounced within the metal-working and engineering industries.

A closer analysis of local material flows shows that on the whole they consist of special supplies. They contrast with the moneywise 'heavy' – but for a smaller number of comparatively large contractors proportionally less extensive – flows of material consisting of more standardised parts and intermediate goods conveyed across long distances. In other words, standard supplies are chiefly provided by large firms, sometimes via wholesalers, which because of their relative insensitivity to distance form national or international patterns. On the other hand more distance-sensitive special supplies are largely taken from local firms.

A gradual break-up of local production systems can be seen over time, with national and international business relations becoming more common. This is taking place concurrently with improved communications and transportation, facilitating close contact even with remotely-situated suppliers. Another cause of the gradual loosening of the couplings with local suppliers is greater specialisation within the economy. Because of the reduced number of suppliers, firms are forced to procure more specialised products outside the locality.

In recent years the Swedish economic debate has increasingly focused upon competition from low-income countries in East Europe and South East Asia. Misgivings have been voiced that Swedish sub-contracting firms are being driven out of markets by firms from these areas and that production systems are thus radically changing character.

Table 7.5: Purchases under Sub-contracts by the Purchasing Firms[24] from Various Markets (per cent)

Sweden	55	France	2
Norway	3	Italy	1
Finland	3	The rest of Western Europe	7
Denmark	3	The Far East, Japan	1
Great Britain	6	North America	3
West Germany	15	Eastern Europe	1

Source: Industridepartmentet *et al.*, 1981.[14]

The empirical data available offer little support for such misgivings. An internationalisation of the production systems can certainly be observed, but this process is slow and does not indicate any dramatic changes in this respect during the past few years. In the previously quoted survey from the Ministry of Industry (industridepartementet) an analysis of the firms' purchases of input goods from various markets has been carried out. This is reproduced as Table 7.5 and it shows more than half of the purchases of input goods were from firms in Sweden. Otherwise the purchases were made from Western Europe, and then especially from West Germany and Great Britain. Only 1 per cent of the purchases of input goods in the firms investigated were from countries in South East Asia or Eastern Europe. According to the firms, these purchases have increased somewhat in the past few years, but they remain marginal. It is also worth noting that Great Britain is the country that has diminished most in importance while the opposite is true for sub-contracts from West Germany.

Swedish wholesalers and retailers are dominated by large-scale companies and individual small firms which have merged into chain stores in order to meet competition from large firms. The indications which are available concerning these firms' purchasing patterns suggest that they are similar to those of the large industrial firms.

C. Small Firms and the Export Market

The increasing internationalisation of the Swedish economy has also altered the sales made by small firms. It is true that small manufacturing firms are not as internationally oriented in their business as are large firms, but the former are becoming increasingly involved in foreign markets. From an ongoing study by Lindmark and Lundmark, Table 7.6 shows that approximately one half of the small manufacturing firms have export sales to some extent,[25] and 15 per cent of the firms export more than 25 per cent of their goods. Principally wood, metal and engineering small firms are the most internationally oriented in their business activities, but the textile and clothing industries also have large shares of exports.

Classification according to size of firm shows that export orientation, as expected, increases with size, although export sales are also found in the smallest firms.

Table 7.6: Export Sales in 1980 for Manufacturing Firms

Size of firm (employees)	Percentage of output exported						Total
	0	1–10	11–25	26–50	51–75	76+	
< 19	68.7	20.0	4.2	5.0	0.8	1.3	100.0
20–49	42.6	27.4	10.5	13.7	4.2	1.6	100.0
50–199	17.4	35.0	18.8	15.0	8.8	5.0	100.0
Total	51.0	25.1	8.8	9.8	3.3	2.0	100.0

Source: Lindmark and Lundmark (forthcoming): preliminary results.

7.5. Problems in Small Firms

Lindmark and Lundmark are currently studying how small firms
within the manufacturing industry mobilise local, regional and
national resources to solve problems and meet greater challenges.
Data on the firms' views of the problems it faces have been obtained
for these analyses. They were obtained partly in the form of a postal
questionnaire which included all the independent manufacturing
firms with 10–199 employees in four counties (län),[26] and partly in
the form of a field survey with 25 randomly-chosen firms in each
region. Some of the results from the postal questionnaire study are
presented below.

There are two questions in the postal questionnaire concerning
problems and challenges encountered during the past three-year
period. The first asked the firms to state the problem areas in their
own businesses and they were given six fixed answers from which to
choose. There was also the alternative of a write-in answer. The
answers received to this question can be summarised thus:

Only a small number of firms said they have not had any
problems or encountered any greater challenges during the past
three-year period.
The responses show a considerable variety in the types of
problems mentioned.
The arithmetic mean number of problems identified was two.

Table 7.7: Problems and Challenges in Small Firms

Types of problem	Firms with problems (%)
Finance	39.3
Purchasing	8.5
Product and production development	30.2
Personnel	35.7
Sales	30.2
Management	16.1
Other	8.7

Source: Lindmark and Lundmark (forthcoming): preliminary results.

As Table 7.7 shows it is not unexpected that the most common problem, as perceived by the firms themselves, is that of finance. At least two different types of problem are concealed within this reply. Some firms are expanding rapidly and require finance for fixed and working capital, whilst others have poor profitability leading to liquidity and insolvency problems. The most serious types of problem are, after those dealing with finance, in descending order of importance, personnel, sales and product and production development.[27] The increased efforts on the part of society to support the marketing and product developing activities of small firms, thus seem to be essential components in an active small business policy.

The firm's personnel problems are, like its financing problems, multivariate. There are firms with difficulties in recruiting staff – particularly skilled workers – and firms with superfluous staff due to a fall in orders. Swedish labour market legislation requires the employer to negotiate with the trade unions before labour can be laid off. The employer must be able to prove that acceptable grounds for the laying off exist – for example, scarcity of work – after which negotiations are held over a priority list of employees who must leave the firm. The principal rule is that the last employed person must be the first to leave, but there are often exceptions in small firms, because if the firm applied this rule strictly, it could lose key persons from the business, which could jeopardise its survival. Many small firms find this negotiation procedure laborious and difficult and the employer is often uncertain of the administrative procedures involved.

Product and production development problems, as well as sales problems, become more common as the firm grows in size. This is partly because the owner becomes more aware of problems as the firm grows, but primarily because demands on the business increase with growth. The firm outgrows the local market and has to seek customers outside its own region. The question of export ventures can also arise. For firms with products of their own, product development becomes of paramount importance, and the firms which are sub-contractors in national production systems must continuously improve production methods in order to meet the demands of the customer.

Another interesting result is that many respondents stated that they faced complex problems – problems which affect several functions. This is emphasised by the answers to the second question in the postal questionnaire concerning problems and challenges. Here the firms were asked to state in their own words what they had experienced as being the most difficult problem or the greatest challenge during the past three years. The answer was clearly that the bigger the firm, the more complex the problems which it faced.

One conclusion that can be drawn from these results is that government assistance, if it is to be effective must be varied and flexible. The results also suggest that the formal programs for different functions or areas in a firm are not enough, and that tailor-made, or firm specific solutions may, in many cases be more appropriate. It is noteworthy that land and premises problems cause difficulty only in exceptional cases. Usually firms can expand and develop within the area where their business is conducted and when this is not possible, new suitable land can usually be obtained in the locality.

Regional differences occurred in the views held by small firms of their own problems, particularly on the question of finance. The data show that manufacturers in Västerbotten find financing considerably less difficult than comparable firms in the other three counties. This could be because manufacturers in Västerbotten have a lower investment propensity than other manufacturers but other responses show this is not the case. A more likely explanation is that the supply of capital varies between regions, with investment capital being easier to obtain in Västerbotten, which is part of the regional development area. Loans and grants which are a part of the regional policy package of economic aid are more easily available. Risk capital can also be obtained from the Norrland Fund (Norrlandsfonden), an organisation not directly coupled to regional policy, but which has the duty of supporting firms in the country's four most northerly counties, of which Västerbotten is one.

7.6. Swedish Small Business Policy

In various government documents small firms are depicted as the foundation of a decentralised market economy. They are also viewed as an important prerequisite for the attainment of a widely-spread economic and settlement structure in the country. In line with these attitudes it is emphasised that measures to improve the business opportunities for small firms are of vital importance for economic development.[28]

The step from rhetoric to practical politics is however, considerable. Despite this view of small firms, big-business measures continue to dominate legislation, even though interest in promoting the development of small firms has increased appreciably during the past few years.

A historical reflection upon Swedish small business politics shows this development is of a relatively recent origin. Whilst some functions of today's small business organisations date from the 1930s, the majority of current initiatives have come into existence during the past 10–15 years. It is above all during the later 1970s that a more clearly formulated small business policy has been discernible. The first proposal unifying the small business issues was introduced in Parliament (the Riksdag) in 1977 and this was followed in the spring of 1982 by a new government bill of measures to improve the conditions and development opportunities for small firms. Government expenditure directed towards assisting small firms grew by 90 per cent in real terms during the 1970s. Loans and grants amounted to a total of 1.6 billion Swedish crowns in 1970 (in 1980 prices) while the corresponding amount for 1979 was 2.7 billion Swedish crowns. This expenditure is however relatively modest in comparison with total industrial policy expenditure in the 1970–9 period, as is shown in Table 7.8.

During the 1970s, 106 billion Swedish crowns were according to calculations paid to the corporate sector in the form of grants, loans, and credit guarantees. Seen in fixed prices, the contributions of the government to the economy have increased by 200 per cent during the period. This great increase brought Sweden to the level of those OECD-countries which make the greatest investment in industrial policy assistance measures.

The largest sum in the government assistance policy is directed business contributions. Measures in the form of loans, grants, and guarantees which have been paid to large-scale companies are included in this group. Research and development contributions and export promoting contributions have also gone primarily to large-scale enterprises. Small firms obtain a higher proportion of grants and loans to industrial sectors and of the regional assistance measures, but on balance large-scale companies have been the predominant recipients of industrial policy expenditure in Sweden. This is underlined by noting that measures directed towards small

Table 7.8: Industrial Policy Expenditure, 1970–9 (billions of Swedish crowns)

	70 70/71	71 71/72	72 72/73	73 73/74	74 74/75	75 75/76	76 76/77	77 77/78	78 78/79	79 79/80	Sum	%
Industrial location aid and transportation grant	0.8	1.1	0.8	1.2	1.5	1.1	1.1	1.1	0.8	1.1	10.5	10
Small firms contributions (mainly loans from the Industrial Credit Bank, The Swedish Business Credit Association, Ltd; the Development Foundations)	1.6	1.6	1.5	2.0	1.8	2.0	2.4	2.5	3.1	2.7	21.1	20
Firm and industry contributions through the Investment Bank and the National Industrial Board	1.4	1.4	1.1	1.0	1.5	1.9	1.4	2.6	1.5	1.3	15.0	14
R & D contributions through the National Board for Technical Development and the Nordic Industrial Foundation, R & D deductions at company taxation and contributions to energy research and energy savings	0.4	0.4	0.5	0.5	1.2	1.2	1.3	1.4	1.4	2.1	10.3	10
Export Credit Financing through the Swedish Export Credit Corporation and the Investment Bank Ltd	1.0	1.4	2.3	1.2	1.9	2.1	2.2	2.2	1.1	1.6	16.9	16
Non-permanent industrial grant	0.3	0.9	0.5	0.5	0.9	1.9	5.1	5.0	8.8	8.1	31.9	30
Sum of grants	5.5	6.8	6.8	6.3	8.7	10.2	13.4	14.8	16.6	16.9	105.8	100

Note: Recalculations to 1980-year's prices have been made using the industrial price index.

Source: Sou, 1981:72. Att avveckla en kortsiktig stödpolitik, Stockholm.

firms to a great extent have been in the form of loans, while the contribution to large-scale enterprises have been mainly grants.

This emphasis on large-scale companies in government assistance policy is partly historical, with political interest in small firms being relatively recent. It is also true that economic reality has forced the government to incur high levels of expenditure in order to save large-scale companies in a crisis. Yet these explanations are incomplete. For example, the strong over-representation of support for export contributions and research and development in large-scale companies is probably to a great extent institutionally conditioned. Large-scale companies are better organised to claim these forms of support whilst the government bureaucracy has found it difficult to reach small firms. To rectify this, organisational changes have been made in the formulation of the assistance programmes.

The central organisation in Sweden for promoting export activities (Sveriges Exportråd), which has its office located in Stockholm is now using regional organisations as the Regional Development Funds as intermediaries for its measures. Special regional campaigns are also being launched to encourage small firms to export.

Finally, it is considerably easier for large-scale companies to voice their need for assistance than it is for small firms. They can – unlike small firms – virtually demand assistance because of their commanding position in the economy. Their regular contact with government officials, in a variety of contexts, also gives them a better understanding of where pressure on government is likely to be effective.

A. *The Design of Small Business Policy*

Swedish small business policy is difficult to separate from other forms of political assistance programme which can be of use to small firms. In monetary terms the regional and industry policies, for example, are as important as the direct contributions to small business. Selectivity in the measures intended for small firms is generally lower than those targeted towards large companies, although in comparison with many other countries, selectivity in the Swedish small business policy is quite pronounced.

The organisation of Swedish assistance policy is complex. At the central level there are some fifteen authorities, organisations, and firms which administer the assistance programmes from which small firms can benefit. If those at the regional and local level are included, this figure is more than doubled. The assistance measures can broadly be categorised into two – financial aid and company services. In Swedish small business policy the latter type of contribution has increased in importance over time. In short, assistance policy is a question not only of money but also of knowledge and information.

A further development is that greater importance is now being placed on efforts to create new firms and new products, and on encouraging small firms to export. This is evident in the government proposal on measures for small firms, which it presented in the spring of 1982. Points of departure for a united innovation policy are discussed, measures are presented to stimulate the purchasing of technology from small firms, and additional funds are earmarked for promoting exports.[29]

Contributions have also been made to improve the general framework for the business community with some tax changes having been implemented and others being planned. For example, in the late 1970s taxation in small family firms was lowered and there are plans to end double taxation of profits given to shareholders. Measures to reduce the firm's reporting to various authorities can also be counted to this category, since many business leaders consider this to be a heavy burden.

B. Financial Aid

Within the framework of Swedish small business policy, special credit institutions have been established by government to complement the functions of the mainstream capital market, so as to enable small firms to obtain loans on favourable terms. The granting of credits for these institutions is made possible by borrowing in areas such as the bond loan market which normally are closed for small firms. For example, the Industrial Credit Bank (AB Industrikredit) – a bank owned jointly by the government and the Swedish commerical banks – provides small firms with loans for investments in buildings, plant and machinery as well as for working capital. Loans may also be provided for marketing and product development.

Besides direct lending activities, government organizations support the small firm by granting credit guarantees which facilitate borrowing in the banking system, despite limited securities. Credit guarantees exist, for example, for the financing of credits for export sales and to financially facilitate structural change in certain industries.

A third form of financial aid comprises additional contributions to the capital of small firms. The capital base of the small firm is frequently inadequate and there remain considerable difficulties for small firms in trying to attract external risk capital. For most small firms this is a greater problem than obtaining loans for investment and working capital. A number of investment and development companies have been established to correct this problem and further measures are planned, such as creating a market for the stocks of unlisted corporations. The investment and development companies have been established in depressed regions and in places where a large proportion of employment is in 'crisis' industries such as steel and shipbuilding, so as to create new job opportunities. There is a variety of ownership structures in these companies, but in all cases the majority of the capital comes from the government. Other owners are local and regional authorities, private banks, firms and individuals.

The record of the investment and development companies has not, however, been wholly satisfactory. Instead of investing capital in new firms which are expanding, several companies have been forced to serve as rapid-deployment forces in order to save firms in crisis. Certainly many jobs have been saved in the short term, but the measures have not had their intended long-term effects, because of the sensitivity of the investment and development companies to local/regional pressure in times of crisis.

There are no direct grants to small firms within the framework of small business policy, although there are grants in the regional policy package, and for research and development, export activities, and so on. The conditional loans are a special form of grants which can be obtained for product development. The loans are designed so that the borrower has to repay the loan only if the product for which the loan was provided proves a commercial success.[30] If this is not the case, then the loan is written off.

C. Company Services

The majority of information and service assistance to small firms in Sweden comes from private firms and organizations, with government measures being complementary. During the past few years, however, government has markedly strengthened its position, with one result being to regionalize the assistance which it provides for companies.

The principal expression of these regionalization efforts is the founding of regional development funds (utvecklingsfonder) – one in every county. Their purpose is to stimulate the development of small, primarily manufacturing firms, through the provision of credit and company services. Some service firms serving manufacturers can also be considered as belonging to this target group. The credit facilities comprise loans for working capital, and the above-mentioned conditional loans for product development.[31] The funds can also act as guarantor for bank loans.

The company service activities of the development funds, which are undergoing considerable expansion, are manifold – information provision, general advice and company analyses, educational service and contact activities. The service activities are aimed mainly at product renewal, and development, marketing and export-promoting activities. Efforts are also being made to stimulate the establishment of new firms in the various regions. In the next few years the company services of the development funds will be extended, while the credit operations of the funds will remain at the present level.

D. Local Mobilisation of Resources

Whilst the employment situation in Sweden is better than many other West European countries, labour market problems exist in many places. National political initiatives have made insufficient impact in certain areas and so local/regional initiatives are now being tried. Concepts such as self-reliance have become honourable words in these local development strategies.

It is inappropriate to discuss these new developments in the Swedish economy, except to note the increasingly important role for local goverment units in economic policy. The municipalities often have an important role in self-reliant development strategies, although there is also a strong municipal economic commitment even in places not engaged in these types of initiatives.

The traditional economic policy of local government has been to provide land and infrastructure, but this has gradually changed during the past two decades with more municipalities being forced to assist firms in their own locality. During the 1960s some municipalities with large unemployment problems offered building-sites at subsidised prices, but today this seems to be the rule rather than the exception. In small municipalities local government also builds industrial premises which are then let at subsidised rents. Alternatively premises may be taken over by the authority from firms and then rented back. This makes capital available to the firms which can be used for investment in plant and machinery and as working capital.

Those municipalities which have taken over firms to save jobs illustrate the escalation of local government's economic involvement. There are also examples of local governments having technique (selective) purchasing policies in order to support local firms. Finally, many have taken initiatives in creating various activities to market the attractions of their own municipalities and its firms.

Many aspects of economic development are outside what the municipalities may legally undertake. Voices have been heard urging that the municipal law should be changed so that it accords with practice whilst others feel that the present developments should be stopped.[32] The question is whether there is any turning back. In the serious employment situation currently affecting many municipalities, the pressure for action from voters is great but competition between municipalities and regions is now increasing to such an extent that it could significantly affect the competitive position of many firms.

7.7. Conclusion

The evidence presented in this chapter illustrates that in a sophisticated developed economy such as the Swedish the neo-classical view of perfect competition does not accurately describe the trading conditions under which most firms operate. For example, two-thirds of Swedish employment in manufacturing industry is in large-scale companies, and there is every sign that industrial concentration is increasing, though less rapidly than in previous decades. Within manufacturing there has been a fall in the opening rates of new establishments, an increase in bankruptcies and a high rate of acquisition by large companies of smaller enterprises.

The role of small firms in the economy has also changed. In the modern industrial state small firms should be seen in relation to large firms and be regarded as complementary to, rather than competitive with, large-scale companies. One such role is as sub-contractor in production systems dominated by large companies. In many respects the small firm, in this role, can immunise itself from competition since there is demonstrable reluctance on the part of large firms to change suppliers.

The importance of large firms in the Swedish economy is also illustrated by their receipt of government assistance, but these matters are starting to change. Increasingly, the relatively poor performance of large enterprises has encouraged governments to reassess the opportunities for wealth creation and new jobs in smaller enterprises and a complex package of assistance is now available from national, regional and local agencies. A great variety of types of small business has been spawned with worker co-operatives becoming more frequent. Swedish small business policy, however, is difficult to separate from other forms of political assistance programmes which may assist small firms. In monetary terms the regional and industrial policies, for example, are as important to small firms as are more direct contributions.

Swedish experience has also demonstrated that the problems faced by small firms vary between regions and between industries. It is also true that the firms themselves view these problems as primarily financial, although problems over personnel, sales and product development are frequently raised by Swedish firms. Consequently, most of the small business initiatives involve easing access to finance, together with the provision of information and in particular the stimulation of business services. Whilst it is, of course, essential to tailor the public provision of *assistance* to the *specific* needs of firms, the diversity of schemes can also lead to the problem that the small business owner cannot possibly be aware of all the incentives available. In Sweden, as elsewhere, the formulation of a policy for small business has to maintain a balance between tailoring schemes to the needs of the specific firm on the one hand, and minimising the number of bewildering and competing schemes on the other. The emphasis should be upon small business programmes that are less specific than those currently in operation, with the delivery organisations being able to adapt the measures to the requirements of the individual firm.

Notes

1. In 1979 there were 3373 group companies with private propriety interests in Sweden. Within these group formations there are 8441 firms in operation. A clear majority of these group companies (slightly less than 85%) had less than 200 employees. The small, economically independent, firms are thus somewhat fewer in number than appear from the statistics which now are based on the legal business concept. Nevertheless deviations should not be over emphasized.

2. C. Pettersson, *Familjeföretagsförsäljningar – Analys och förklaringar till utvecklingsförlopp och beteenden*, University of Umeå, Dpt of Business Adm. and Economics, Umeå, 1980.

3. Only 8% of the mergers in industry during the period 1946–1969 were characterised by vertical integration, while 80% were horizontal, i.e. amalgamations of companies with competing or supplementary activities. This is shown by B. Rydén, *Fusioner i svensk industri. En kartläggning och orsaksanalys av svenska industriföretags fusionsverksamhet 1946–69*, Industrins-utredningsinstitut, Stockholm, 1971.

4. The figures for closures probably include firms which have ceased to exist due to a change of name. The data should thus only be regarded as a rough indicator of closures within the Swedish manufacturing industry.

5. SIND 1982:2, Nya företag – villkor och möjligheter. Liber förlag. Stockholm.

6. Centrala företagsregistrer, Statistiska centralbyrån.

7. Å. Gabrielsson, Löntagarägda företag. Kartläggning av förekomst och några problem och deras lösningar. SOU 1980:36. Stockholm, 1980.

8. The figure includes only firms which traded in 1979. The number of establishments for the previous years were thus somewhat underestimated as the employee-owned firms which had been discontinued or had merged into other types of business during the 1970's were not included in the report. Eleven such firms have been identified in all. This means that the tendency which can be seen in the diagram would not appreciably be upset if these firms would have been included in the material.

9. L. Lindmark and B. Ekman, Selektiv ekonomisk politik och industrins strukturanpassning. En studie av branschproblem, myndighetsåtgärder, förändringströgheter. SIND PM 1981:22, Liber Förlag. Stockholm.

10. A. Edström, The Stability of Joint Ventures. FE-rapport 54. University of Gothenburg, Dpt of Business Adm. Gothenburg, 1975.

11. K. Nilsson and P. Nilsson, Småföretag i samverkan – effekter och erfarenheter av samverkan mellan femton småföretag under två decennier. SIND PM 1981:6, Liber förlag. Stockholm.

12. J.K. Galbraith, *The New Industrial State,* Hamish Hamilton, London, 1967.

13. D. Ramström, Små företag – stora problem. Norstedts, Stockholm, 1975.

14. Industridepartementet, Svenska Metallindustriarbetareförbundet & Sveriges Mekanförbund, 1981. Svenska underleverantöreridag. Sveriges Mekanförbund. Stockholm.

15. C.M. Baumback, K. Lawyer and P. Kelley. How to Organize and Operate a Small Business. Prentice-Hall, Englewood Cliffs, New Jersey, 1973.

16. Sveriges Mekanförbund, Samarbetet mellan huvudleverantör och underleverantör – En form av strukturrationalisering inom verkstadsindustrin. Sveriges Mekanförbund, 1967.

17. C. Fredriksson and L. Lindmark, Nationella och lokala produktionssystem. En strukturstudie av svenskt näringsliv, University of Umeå, Dpt of Business Adm. and Economics, Umeå, 1976.

C. Fredriksson and L. Lindmark, From Firms to Systems of Firms – A Study of Inter-regional Dependence in a Dynamic Society. In Hamilton, F.E.I. & Linge,

212 Sweden

G.J.R., Spatial Analysis, Industry and the Industrial Environment. Volume 1 –
Industrial Systems. John Wiley & Son. Chichester 1979.

18. ibid.

19. C. Fredriksson and L. Lindmark, Några mindre och medel stora
verkstadsföretags inköp från underleverantörer – en praktikfallsstudie. University
of Umeå, Dpt of Business Adm. and Economics, Umeå, 1973.

20. H. Håkansson and B. Wootz, Företagsbeteende. Studentlitteratur. Lund,
1975.

21. *See also* I. Hägg and J. Johansson, (eds.), Företag i nätverk – ny syn på
konkurrenskraft. SNS. Stockholm, 1982.

K.O. Hammarkvist, H. Håkansson and L-G. Mattsson, Marknadsföringens roll
för internationellt verksamma industriföretags utveckling. Working paper IVA/
MTC. Stockholm, 1981.

E. Sundin, Företag i perifera regioner, Fallstudier av företagartradition,
företagsmiljö och företags framväxt i Norrbottens inland. University of Umeå, Dpt
of Business adm. and Economics. Umeå, 1980.

22. Industridepartementet, Sveriges Mettalindustriabetareförbund & Sveriges
Mekanförbund, 1981.

23. C. Fredriksson and L. Lindmark, 'From Firms to Systems of Firms.'

24. The results of the survey are based on information from 22 Swedish buying
firms. It contains all the large Swedish firms and a selection of medium-sized buying
firms. The figures given in the table are mean values. A large firm is thus as important
as a small one.

25. The reply percentage for the investigation was approximately 60%, which
means that the results are based on answers from more than 500 firms.

26. The counties (lan) which are included in the survey are Göteborgsand
Bohuslän, Västmanland, Östergötland, and Västerbotten. The counties can be said
to represent industrial Sweden in miniature. See also note 25.

27. There are certain differences for each industry in the problem images of the
firms, but these differences are relatively limited.

28. Regeringens proposition 1981/82:118 Småföretag. Åtgärder för de små och
medelstora företagen samt innovationspolitikens inriktning. Norstedts, Stockholm.

29. Ibid.

30. The conditional loans for product development in small firms have proved to
fill a great demand. During a two-year period starting in mid-1978, 443 product
development loans were granted totalling 77.4 million Swedish crowns. The concept
of a product development loan is somewhat inappropriate as these can be obtained
for development and marketing of new products, processes or systems for industrial
production. Loans can also be granted for marketing of old products in new
markets. Loans are normally granted for up to 50% of the estimated project costs.
An upper limit is set on the loan amount at 3 million crowns per project (applicable in
April 1982).

31. The highest loan amount for business loans is at present (April 1982)
1,000,000 Swedish crowns. The maturity is normally at the most 10 years.

32. G. Alsén, L. Melin and A. Nilsson. Från central stödpolitik till lokal
krispolitik – Ett fall av betydelse. Paper presented at the Conference 'Regional
organisation and strategies', Sunne, 1981.

PART TWO

8 INTRODUCTION: NEWLY-DEVELOPED AND LESS-DEVELOPED AREAS

The two chapters in this Part are a contrast with earlier contributions on small firms in developed economies. Here Tan Thiam Soon and Philip Neck examine the role of small firms in South East Asia and in Africa respectively.

The first contrast between these and the preceding contributions is that both Tan and Neck cover several countries. Tan covers small firms in Indonesia, Malaysia, Singapore, Philippines and Thailand, whilst Neck surveys small firms on the whole of the African continent. The reasons for the wider coverage were partly because of the shortage of data on trends in the small firm sector in a single country, but also to provide an effective but not lengthy counterweight to the studies of small firms in the developed countries in Part I.

The contrasts between the two chapters themselves will also be clear. In the case of South East Asia, whilst the Philippines and Thailand are not developed, Singapore is a highly-developed economy with 'over-full' employment. Indeed the main problem of small firms in Singapore is coping with the high-wage policy introduced by the government in 1979, which makes it difficult for them to recruit workers in this tight labour market. In many respects the small firm in Singapore has more in common with small firms in the earlier chapters than those described elsewhere in Part II.

If Singapore, in a spectrum of development, is at one end then many of the areas described by Philip Neck are at the other. In particular the problems of shortages of raw materials, of being landlocked or being politically unstable have prevented many Central African countries from taking more than the first tottering steps towards industrialisation.

Given these contrasts in the level and expected future economic development of the countries discussed, there remain several common themes which distinguish Part II from Part I. The first is the shortage of capital in LDC's, leading to a need to investigate the use of more labour-intensive production methods, and the second is a disenchantment with prestige development projects (again perhaps Singapore should be excluded here). This implies a recognition that small-scale industries, since they derive from the informal sector, are more culturally suited to providing the basis for prosperity in less-developed areas.

The interest in small and medium-sized enterprises in the newly and less-developed countries stems primarily from the inability of agriculture to provide employment for the increased population. The shortages of capital mean that those non-farm jobs which are created need to maximise their use of labour, subject to the criterion of economic efficiency.

This point is clearly made by Tan Thiam Soon in Chapter 9 where he notes that in Indonesia large-scale capital-intensive industries require an investment of US $50,000 per worker whereas small-scale industries require an investment of US $500 per worker. The exception is in Singapore where full employment has already been reached. The low cost of job creation in small-scale enterprises is also noted by Neck in Chapter 10.

The current interest in small-scale enterprises in developing countries contrasts with the attempts at stimulating industrialisation in the 1960s by siting of 'modern' prestigious establishments in these areas. In addition to the high capital costs of creating employment by such methods many developing countries lack the physical and cultural infrastructure to facilitate the effective development of such enterprises. Instead of attempting to attract large-scale enterprises, many LDC's are embarking upon policies which give greater emphasis to indigenous small-scale development. The prime beneficiaries of such policies are those employed, rather than the owners of capital. It is also argued that small-scale enterprise develops more naturally from the informal sector which predominates in many less-developed countries and places less demands upon the provision of costly infrastructure. Furthermore, many large enterprises have received positive discrimination from the governments of LDC's, often to the detriment of local firms. For example, they have received access to credit on a scale which has significantly reduced its availability to small local firms and they have benefited from tariff restrictions and licensing agreements. Instead of stimulating their development, in several cases these advantages have insulated the firm from external competition which has encouraged technical inefficiency.

The main problem in the African context, as Neck shows vividly, is the low base from which such countries begin their development process. The low levels of income and hence demand, the absence of infrastructure to facilitate the transport of goods, the poor communications, the low levels of literacy, all constrain the development of all sizes of enterprise. Nevertheless it is important to recognise that in such economies the informal sector provides incomes which, although not high, would not otherwise exist. The informal sector does then provide an entry into entrepreneurship upon which it is possible to build.

It is also important to recognise the difference which exists between what may be called the modern small-scale industries and those in more traditional industries. Whilst it is clear that the traditional small-scale industry provides employment and incomes that would otherwise not exist it is not clear that these represent a real basis for the leap to industrialisation which, for example, Singapore has achieved.

Finally, the two chapters provide a stark contrast in terms of the number and sophistication of state initiatives to assist small firms, not simply in terms of finance but also with respect to managerial training. All the countries described in South East Asia appear to provide positive discrimination in favour of small firms enabling loans to be made at below market prices. In all cases there are also extension services, training programmes and a variety of other forms of assistance. In the African case although there is a wide range of assistance many schemes are hampered by the absence of experienced personnel and by shortages of funding. Neck points to the absence of qualified officers capable of preparing, or assisting entrepreneurs to prepare, feasible proposals. He also points to an absence of technical development appropriate for the small firm sector, whilst management training for small enterprises has, Neck feels, suffered from a mismatch of supply and demand, and a lack of harmonisation.

Despite these diversities between the two chapters both chapters conclude on a generally optimistic note, and it is perhaps worth while to emphasise the conclusions of the Prime Minister of Malaysia in 1978 which Tan quotes with clear approval. Dr Mahathir Bin Mohamed stresses the interdependence of all sizes and scales of enterprise in the process of economic development. As Neck shows, development of the small firm sector depends upon the existence of physical and social infrastructure and upon the growth of the agricultural sector. In short, as Tan says, small-scale industries must be regarded as a complementary part of the whole industrial development programme.

9 SOUTH EAST ASIA

9.1. Introduction

Promotion of small enterprise development is a recent phenomenon in South East Asia which for the purposes of this
chapter is defined as Indonesia, Malaysia, Singapore, Philippines
and Thailand. It was almost non-existent until industrialisation
took place around the 1960s in most of the countries. Almost
without exception, one of the main objectives of industrialisation
was to solve the unemployment problem in the countries. An
alternative solution to the unemployment problem is to encourage
the development of small enterprises, especially in the less-
developed areas. Among the South East Asian countries, because
of their political, social, geographical and cultural differences, the
pace of economic development is different in each country, and so
are the policies toward the promotion of small enterprise
development as well as the assistance programmes.

9.2. Definitions

There is no consensus on the definition of a small firm. Definition of
a small firm or enterprise varies from one country to another, and
depends on the phase of a country's economic development and its
prevailing social condition. Even within one country, there may be
more than one definition of a small firm adopted by different
institutions or agencies which are involved in helping small
enterprises, to suit their purposes or functions.

In Indonesia, according to the Central Bureau of Statistics,
before 1973 industries were classified according to employment size
as well as whether power was utilised. Small industries were defined
as those enterprises employing between 1 and 9 workers if no power
was utilised, or those enterprises employing between 1 and 4
workers if power was utilised. Those enterprises employing only
family labour were classified as handicraft industries. After 1973,
such distinction on the basis of power-utilisation has been abolished
and small industries are now defined as those establishments

employing between 5 and 19 workers while those employing fewer than 5 workers are classified as handicraft industries. Establishments with between 20 and 99 workers are defined as medium industries and those with more than 99 workers are large industries.

There are, however, various other definitions of small and medium-scale industries, depending upon the type of industry or purposes for which statistics were compiled. For example, in the textile industry, those manufacturing units with up to 100 powerlooms are considered as small industries, while those having between 101 to 400 powerlooms are considered as medium industries. The large industries are those manufacturing units with more than 400 powerlooms. If only handlooms are used, they are classified as handicraft industries. Operating capital is also used to define a small industry. Indigenous Indonesian firms with operating capital of less than Rp 500,000 and a work force of fewer than 10 persons are considered as small industries.

In Malaysia, the Advisory Council for Consulting and Advisory Services for Small-Scale Industries and Business defines small industries as those enterprises with fixed assets of less than M$ 250,000. A more widely-accepted definition of a small industry is any industrial unit with a total capital investment of not more than M$ 250,000 in land, building, plant, machinery and equipment or with employment of fewer than 25 paid full-time employees. One researcher, however, defines a small enterprise in Malaysia as a manufacturing or commercial enterprise employing less than 50 full-time paid workers.[1]

The Philippine Commission on Small and Medium Industries defines small industry as any manufacturing or industrial service enterprise with total assets of not more than ₽ 1 million. The University of Philippines Institute of Small Scale Industries (UP–ISSI) defines a small-scale industry as a manufacturing or industrial enterprise in which the owner-manager is not actively engaged in production but performs the varied range of tasks involved in guidance and leadership without the help of specialised staff officers. However, for statistical analysis, UP–ISSI also defines small-scale industries as enterprises employing 5 to 99 workers and having total assets of ₽ 100,000 to ₽ 1 million.

When the ILO expert made the first study on small industries in Thailand, it was recommended that a small industry be defined as an industrial establishment with 50 or fewer employees. The Small

Industry Finance Office (SIFO) however, for the purpose of providing loans, defines a small industry as any enterprise whose total fixed assets not including land do not exceed two million baht (about US$ 100,000). For research and analytical purposes, a small industry is defined as an industrial enterprise employing between 10 to 49 workers.[2]

In Singapore, when the Light Industries Services (LIS) unit was first established in 1963, the eligible small industries were restricted to those establishments employing fewer than 50 workers and with fixed assets of less than S$ 250,000. However, the LIS scheme was abolished later in 1973. In 1976, when the new Small Industrial Finance Scheme was set up to provide low-interest loans to small industries, the firms applying for the loan under the new scheme had to be in manufacturing and assembly operations or supporting services related to manufacturing, and the firm should not have more than S$ 2 million in fixed production assets. The political leaders and government ministers in Singapore, however, still refer in their speeches to small industries as those establishments employing fewer than 50 workers. On the other hand, most of the researchers prefer to define small industries as those establishments employing fewer than 100 workers.[3]

A summary of the different definitions of small firms in the five countries mentioned above is given in Table 9.1.

Table 9.1: Definitions of Small Firms/Industries

	Number of workers	Fixed assets
Indonesia	1) Fewer than 19	
	2) Fewer than 10	Less than Rp 500,000
Malaysia	1) Fewer than 25	Less than M$ 250,000
	2) Fewer than 50	
Philippines	1) 5 to 99	₱ 100,000 to ₱ 1 million
	2)	Less than ₱ 1 million
Singapore	1) Fewer than 50	
	2) Fewer than 100	—
	3)	Less than S$2 million
Thailand	1) Fewer than 50	
	2) 10 to 49	
	3)	Less than 2 million baht

9.3. Trends in the Small Firm Sector

When industrialisation was introduced in this region, attractive incentives were offered by the governments to woo local as well as foreign investments. In most cases, the smaller establishments are not able to benefit from such incentive schemes as either minimum capital investment or legal status of corporation is required for eligibility. Where there is no such requirement, many small enterprises by virtue of their size and scale of operation find themselves unable to take advantage of incentives such as the Research and Development grants. Hence although there is no government policy which discriminates against the small firms, the design and implementation of various government policies undoubtedly favour the larger firms.

In Indonesia between 1974 and 1978, total manufacturing growth averaged about 12 per cent per annum while the growth of the small industry sector was only 5 per cent. According to the Industrial Census for 1974/5, 99.55 per cent of all manufacturing establishments in Indonesia are either small industries or handicraft industries. The distribution of manufacturing industries according to size of establishment is given in Table 9.2.

Table 9.2: Distribution of Manufacturing Industries in Indonesia

	Size (number of persons engaged)	Number of establishments	Total number of persons engaged
Handicraft industries	4 or fewer	1,234,511	3,899,856
Small industries	5 to 19	48,211	319,057
Medium industries	20 to 99	5,746	273,063
Large industries	100 and over	1,306	633,581

In terms of employment, the small industries and the handicraft industries together engaged more than 82 per cent of the total workforce in the manufacturing sector.

The New Economic Policy of Malaysia which was first incorporated in the Second Malaysia Plan (1971–5) and reinforced in the Third Malaysia Plan (1976–80) aimed at eradicating poverty through creation of employment and increasing the income of the lowest earning group, and at reducing economic imbalances between races and regions. As the Malays are considered economically less well off than the other races in Malaysia, special assistance and attractive incentives were offered to the bumiputras (the Malays and other indigenous natives in Malaysia) to encourage and increase their participation in commerce and industry. In the 1973 Census of Manufacturing Industries in Peninsular Malaysia, more than 80 per cent of the manufacturing establishments are small-scale industries (see Table 9.3).

Table 9.3: Distribution of Manufacturing Establishments in Malaysia

Number of Full-time paid employees	Number of establishments
0	3,148
1–4	3,270
5–9	1,352
10–19	1,079
20–29	565
30–49	590
50 and over	1,057
Total	11,061

Source: Census of Manufacturing Industries, 1973

In the Philippines the 1978–82 development plan of the government sets out a balanced growth strategy that includes the promotion of small-scale industries particularly in the less developed parts of the country. The rate of entry of new firms has been fairly high, especially in the low entry barrier industries because of the low requirements of capital and technology. According to one study made in 1979, about one-half of all enterprises in the Philippines at that time were found to have been established during the period between 1973 and 1979.[4] In the same study, it was found that between 1962 and 1968, the average growth rate of the smaller manufacturing firms employing 5 to 19 workers was more than twice the average growth rate of those manufacturing firms with 20 or more workers.

According to the Bureau of the Census and Statistics, during the period 1969 to 1971, about 80 per cent of the labour force in the manufacturing sector were employed by firms with fewer than 100 workers (see Table 9.4).

In Singapore, the proportion of small enterprises has continued at about 97 per cent of the total number of establishments for the past ten years. During the period from 1972 to 1980, the number of small enterprises employing fewer than 50 workers increased from 37,663 in 1972 to 67,414 in 1980, an overall increase of about 80 per cent. The number of establishments employing 50 or more workers during the same period increased from 1,281 to 1,960 or an overall growth of 53 per cent. Hence the small enterprise sector has a higher growth rate than the large enterprise sector (see Table 9.5).

Table 9.4: Share of Employment in the Philippines by Size of Firm, 1969–71

Size of firm (number of employees)	Percentage share in employment
1–4	70.0
5–19	5.2
20–49	2.2
50–99	2.3
100–199	2.8
200 and above	17.5

Source: Census of Manufacturing Industries

Table 9.5: Number of Establishments in Singapore by Size of Employment

Number of workers	1972	1976	1980
1–4	24,708	37,755	47,955
5–9	7,634	10,227	11,363
10–14	2,358	3,112	3,437
15–19	1,070	1,476	1,624
20–24	611	837	1,042
25–49	1,282	1,639	1,993
50 and over	1,281	1,588	1,960
Total	38,944	56,634	69,374

Source: Singapore Yearbook of Labour Statistics (1980)

In the manufacturing sector, the proportion of small industries employing between 10 and 99 workers has also been maintained at a steady, although slightly lower, level of around 85 per cent of the total number of manufacturing establishments. In terms of growth, during the period between 1972 and 1979 the number of small industries increased from 1,632 to 2,641 establishments, an overall increase of 62 per cent. The large industries during the same period increased from 299 to 481 establishments, an overall increase of 61 per cent. Hence the growth rates of small and large industries during the period are about the same.

In Thailand, a large majority of enterprises are small and family-owned. According to a survey conducted by the Department of Labour in 1973, about 95 per cent of the manufacturing enterprises employed fewer than 50 workers, and the share of employment in this sector was more than 40 per cent (see Table 9.6).

Table 9.6: Distribution of Enterprises in Thailand and Employment by Size of Enterprise

Size (number of workers)	Number of enterprises	Number of workers
1–4	16,765	45,596
5–9	8,786	63,237
10–19	3,757	52,553
20–49	2,249	68,148
50 and above	1,604	333,865
Total	33,161	563,399

Source: Department of Labour Survey (1973)

9.4. The Role of Small Firms

Small firms play a very important role in creating employment opportunities for the growing labour force, especially in the manufacturing industries. In Indonesia, large-scale capital-intensive industries require an investment of US$ 50,000 to employ one additional worker, and the medium-scale industries require an investment of US$ 5,000 for each additional worker employed. The small-scale industries, however, require an investment of only US$ 500 for each additional worker employed. Thus it is cheaper to create jobs in the small industries than in the medium and large industries. For the same reason, governments also encourage the promotion of labour-intensive industries with the view of generating more jobs, except in the case of Singapore where full employment has already been reached. Small enterprises require relatively little capital and low levels of technology. They can be easily established in the less-developed areas in the countries, and help in spreading economic activities from the urban to the rural areas. Hence promotion of small enterprises not only provides employment to those living in the countryside, but also help in reducing the flow of migration from the rural areas to the already crowded cities.

Small enterprises also provide a good training ground for entrepreneurship. The low cost of setting up a small business unit not only creates a new class of small capitalist, leading to wider distribution of income, but also offers employment to others.

The large industries are also important to the economy of a country. It is essential that sufficient and efficient supporting services are available in order to attract and retain large industries to invest and operate in the country. Sub-contracting is becoming increasingly important both to small industries for survival and to large industries for supporting services. To large industries the small enterprises can more economically provide essential goods and services. This enables the final products of the larger corporations to be more competitive in the export markets. Some products or components and accessories do not require high precision work and can be produced at the required standard by small industries, freeing resources for the large industries to concentrate upon more important areas, such as marketing, quality control and product design. This will also ensure that production in large industries will be uninterrupted, thus lowering the cost of manufacturing.

9.5. Difficulties Facing Small Firms

The problems of small firms are more or less universal, such as finance, marketing, technology and training. In Malaysia, one main reason for the low participation in commerce and industries by bumiputras (the Malays) is lack of capital. Of course this is also true with the other races, but more so for the bumiputras as the number of Malay-owned businesses is much smaller in proportion compared to the racial distribution of population in the country. The plight of small enterprises is aggravated by their difficulty in obtaining finance from the banks and financial institutions, as the latter normally insist on securities and collaterals. Small business owners are also frustrated by the necessity to fill in forms and to prepare lengthy working papers for loan application. Very often they lack the knowledge to supply all the information required for such an application.

Small industries generally employ traditional techniques of production, often use obsolete machinery and have poor plant layout. They also lack the knowledge of standards and quality, resulting in the production of substandard goods, wastage of raw material, manpower and productive resources. Hence there is a low demand and limited market for their production.

Lack of managerial competence is prevalent among small enterprises. This is not surprising since many small-scale entrepreneurs went into business without any basic knowledge of business management or accounting. It is a known fact that in many small business failures, poor managerial abilities of the entrepreneurs accounts for the highest quoted reasons.

The small enterprises in Singapore are faced with a problem different from the other countries. In Singapore, because of the high-wage policy introduced by the government in 1979 to restructure the economy and to encourage mechanisation and modernisation of industry, the labour cost increased by an average of 20 per cent per annum over the last three years. In addition, a new levy of 30 per cent was introduced recently on the payroll of foreign workers. An employer in Singapore has to contribute 20.5 per cent of employees' salaries towards a compulsory provident fund, 2 per cent of payroll tax, and 4 per cent of Skills Development Fund in addition to the monthly payroll. Small firms are finding it more expensive and difficult to recruit workers from an already tight labour market.

Small firms in Singapore are also more affected than those in other countries by urban renewal activities. Many small enterprises have been relocated away from their old premises where they enjoyed very low rental expenses and easy access by their regular customers from the neighbourhood. In the new premises, usually a flatted factory or a shop unit in a new housing estate, they have to pay a much higher rent. There are also other environmental control and health regulations to satisfy. It is understandable why champions of small enterprise development consider that the greatest help any government can give to the small businesses is to leave them alone, without any regulation or control, and then small businesses will survive and prosper on their own.

In Malaysia, in a sample survey of 239 enterprises,[5] the three major operational problems of small enterprises stated are, in descending order, capital, land and building and labour (see Table 9.7).

Table 9.7: Operational Problems of 239 Small Enterprises in Malaysia

	Percentage
Capital	28.1
Land/building	24.7
Labour	17.6
Marketing	6.6
Competition	5.7
Other	17.2
	100.0

9.6. Government Initiatives to Assist Small Firms

In general, governments in this region have recently recognised the important role of small enterprises in the industrialisation of the national economy, especially in providing employment opportunities and in increasing and upgrading indigenous enterprises in rural areas. Hence, small enterprise development has been included as part of the national development plans, and several programmes have been designed to assist the small firms in a number of ways.

A. Indonesia

The Second Five-Year Development Plan (Repelita II) of Indonesia set out to increase the role of the economically weak groups in the country. The economically weak groups refer mainly to the indigenous businesses. These groups are provided with credit facilities on softer terms than other groups. The P.T. BAHANA (Management of Indonesian Enterprises), a non-bank institution, has been established to promote the growth of the medium and small undertakings through the supply of several forms of technical and financial aid. P.T. BAHANA also provides capital and equity participation, and gives assistance in the field of management. It is involved in all fields of business activities of the private sector and in the management of the enterprises in which it has an interest. Once management quality has been upgraded and the trading prospects of the enterprise concerned have improved, P.T. BAHANA will withdraw participation by selling its shares to the public. The enterprises assisted by this institution are limited liability companies of the smaller and medium types. Another institution, P.T. ASKRINDO (Indonesian Credit Insurance) provides the guarantee and bears the risk resulting from non-repayment of bank credits supplied to the small and medium enterprises, while the Institute of Cooperative Credit Guarantees guarantees the credits granted by Bank Rakyat Indonesia to cooperatives.

To overcome the scarcity of credits (particularly working capital) for entrepreneurs in the economically weak groups such as retail traders, fishermen, producers of handicraft and other smaller undertakings in the villages and small towns in the regions, the Village Credit Agencies can provide petty loans with easy terms. These credits are implemented through a simple system and without stresses on guarantees. The obligation of self-financing to the amount of 25 per cent by the loan applicants is not an absolute condition, but rather the prospects of the undertakings are the determining factor in the applications for loans.

The Department of Industry also operates a special project called Industrial Extension Services for Small Industries which provides the following services:

general extension services
managerial and technical training
marketing assistance
material procurement assistance
mechanisation assistance
quality control and standardisation guidance
surveys

B. *Malaysia*

The New Economic Policy clearly stated that it aimed to eradicate poverty through creation of employment and by increasing the income of the lowest earning groups. It also proposed to reduce economic imbalances between races and regions. Hence it is not surprising that many of the assistance programmes are primarily designed to help the indigenous Malays or bumiputras, and that regional development is given high priority.

As early as 1951, the Rural Industries Development Authority (RIDA) was established and given the responsibility of promoting and developing rural small-scale industries. The organisation was later replaced by Majlis Amanah Rakyat (MARA) in 1966 to include the promotion of urban small-scale industries and businesses.

There are a number of agencies involved in providing assistance of one kind or another to small enterprises in Malaysia. To avoid duplication, a National Advisory Council on Consulting and Advisory Services for Small-Scale Industries and Business (referred to as the Advisory Council) was established in January 1973. The Advisory Council consisted of the following agencies:

(1) The Federal Industrial Development Authority (FIDA).
(2) The Majlis Amanah Rakyat (MARA).
(3) The National Productivity Centre.
(4) The Standard and Industrial Research Institute of Malaysia (SIRIM).
(All the above four institutions are government agencies.)
(5) The Malaysian Industrial Development Finance Industrial Consultants (MIDFIC), a private organisation.
(6) The Economic Planning Unit.
(7) The Federal Treasury.

The terms of reference of the Advisory Council were:
(1) To coordinate the activities of the institutions that provide advisory and consultancy services to small-scale business and industries with a view to avoiding duplication of efforts.
(2) To review from time to time the activities of these institutions and to advise on whether new activities should be undertaken and by which institution or institutions.
(3) To ensure that these institutions work together in

supplementing and complementing their services for small-scale business and industries against the background of the national objectives particularly relating to bumiputra enterprises.

(4) To review from time to time the criteria to be adopted for identifying small-scale business and industries.

In 1976, the Advisory Council was renamed the Co-ordinating Council for the Development of Small-scale Industries (CCDSI). The membership expanded to include the Credit Guarantee Corporation, Bank Pembangunan Malaysia (Development Bank of Malaysia), Bank Pertanian (Agricultural Bank) and the Implementation Coordination Unit in the Prime Minister's Department. The terms of reference were also extended to include coordination of activities relating to finance and training.

Financial Assistance. MARA was established in 1966 under the Ministry of National and Rural Development to motivate, guide, train and assist the Malays and other bumiputras with emphasis on the rural population to participate actively and progressively in commercial and industrial activities as a part of economic and social development. MARA Loan Division provides credit to small bumiputra commercial and industrial enterprises on the basis of the soundness, viability and growth potential of the enterprises. Loans can be used for working capital, purchase of property or vehicles, wholesale and construction work, or setting up a professional firm. Loans in excess of the amount paid by MARA will be forwarded to commercial banks for finance and MARA will guarantee the loan. The interest charged is well below the market rate. Most of MARA's loans are given out to the trade sector, followed by the building sector. In terms of size, more than 90 per cent of MARA'S loans are of M$ 5,000 or less. Nearly 60 per cent of the loans are given without any security. The large number of small loans and the high percentage of loans given without any security explains why MARA has problems supervising its loans and why a number of these loans cannot be recovered.

The Malaysia Industrial Development Finance Berhad (MIDF) was set up in 1960 to assist in a speedy and sound development of industries in Malaysia. MIDF provides loan and equity capital to new industrial ventures and for the modernisation and expansion of existing enterprises. There is no special division to process application for small-scale industries but a Special Bumiputra Unit has been set up to deal specifically with applications from bumiputra entrepreneurs. The majority of applications to this Special Unit are for small-scale ventures, and to this extent, the unit is directed toward encouraging small-scale business.

The Credit Guarantee Corporation Malaysia Limited was established in 1973 with 20 per cent of its shares owned by the Bank Negara Malaysia and the remaining 80 per cent subscribed by all the other commercial banks in Malaysia. The corporation provides guarantee cover for credit facilities made available by commercial banks to small entrepreneurs for financing their fixed capital and operational requirements. The borrowing company should not have a total paid-up capital and reserves exceeding M$ 200,000 in the case of a bumiputra company. In the case of a non-bumiputra company, the total capital should not exceed M$ 100,000. The maximum guarantee loan is M$ 100,000 for non-bumiputra borrowers and M$ 200,000 for bumiputra borrowers. If no security is provided, the maximum loan is M$ 30,000. The Corporation charges ½ per cent as guarantee fee, and covers 60 per cent of the amount of loan and advances in default and not recoverable by the commercial banks, provided that the banks have exhausted all means of recovering the loan. Prior to 1973, the commercial banks in Malaysia were generally reluctant to lend to small businesses. In March 1973, the Bank Negara issued a directive stating that all banks must lend out at least 3 per cent of their reserves to small businesses. In order to comply with this requirement, some banks were rather hasty in their loan appraisals and this resulted in some non-repayment of loans.

Bank Pembangunan Malaysia BPM (Development Bank of Malaysia) was established in 1973 with the objectives of developing, increasing and accelerating the active participation of the bumiputras in the economic activities of the country. BPM provides term loans on fixed assets for a period of up to 15 years. The limits to the amount of loans to be granted depend on the applicant's own capital and the security value of assets to be purchased. The bank may consider 100 per cent financing of fixed assets if the applicant can provide additional security. The bank is also prepared to finance on the basis of a capital gearing of more than 1:1 whenever the case merits it. The bank participates in equity (up to 30 per cent of the shares) and provides management and advisory services. The minimum loan amount is M$ 50,000. BPM loans are restricted to bumiputra-controlled businesses, defined as companies with at least 51 per cent share capital subscribed by bumiputras, employing a majority of bumiputra workers and managed actively by bumiputras.

The Bank Bumiputra Malaysia Berhad is a wholly government-owned commercial bank established in 1965 to meet the need for and remedy the lack of capital among bumiputras. A large proportion of the loans was used for small businesses and small-scale industries. In 1971, Bank Bumiputra introduced the Rural Banking Service (RBS) to meet the credit requirements of the rural sector. Following the establishment of the Credit Guarantee Corporation in 1973, a Special Bumiputra Participation Unit (Unit Khas Bumiputra) was created in 1974 to administer the loans given under the Rural Banking Service and the Credit Guarantee Corporation to bumiputra farmers and small businessmen.

Advisory Services. The Divisions of Advisory Services and Enterprise Development of MARA provide advisory and consultancy services to bumiputras. The type of advisory services cover the following fields:

Accounting
Company secretaryship
Marketing
Commercial design
Engineering/technical
Construction
Carpentry

Under the advisory and consultancy services to new entrepreneurs scheme, officials from the division search for and choose projects that are suitable for expansion and development. Once the projects are identified, suitable bumiputras are chosen and assisted. The Technical Information Branch publishes a technical guide pamphlet on matters relating to commerce and industry in addition to replying to queries from traders and entrepreneurs. The Division also provides subsidies to small enterprises enabling them to obtain expert services provided by other agencies such as MIDF Industrial Consultants and SIRIM.

The National Productivity Centre of Malaysia also provides consultancy and advisory services. The advisory services are provided free of charge while a nominal fee is charged for consultancy services.

Training Programmes. MARA conducts and sponsors courses for small-scale enterpreneurs to equip them with knowledge in marketing, management, accounting and other trade practices. The New Entrepreneurs Programme started in 1973 aims at increasing the number of bumiputras in commerce and industry by offering to them a 'package deal' assistance, which includes conducting feasibility studies, planning and preparation of projects, providing training and advisory services and credit on easy terms. The assistance under this programme is given only to small-scale industries with a fixed capital of not more than M$ 100,000 and the loan is limited to a maximum of M$ 70,000 for each project.

The MARA Institute of Technology also conducts an Entrepreneurial Development Programme (EDP) for bumiputras over a period of three months. The training programme is designed to provide the necessary guidance, information, knowledge and encouragement to an entrepreneur to start his own business. The primary objective of the EDP is to raise the participants' motivational level, to encourage them to launch business enterprises and to enhance their capability to manage the enterprises profitably. The participants are also advised on the forms of assistance that are available to the potential small business entrepreneurs. The participants' performances are continually assessed even after the programme is over.

The National Productivity Centre which was established in 1962 as a joint project between the United Nations Special Fund and the Federal Government became an autonomous body in 1966. It organises a wide range of training courses and seminars, and is concerned essentially with management development.

In order to establish and maintain a high standard of skill to meet the requirements of industry, a National Industrial Training and Trade Certificate Board was set up by the Ministry of Labour and Manpower. The Ministry also set up an Industrial Training Institute and organises a National Apprenticeship Scheme to train skilled craftsmen in the engineering, electrical, building and printing trades, and a Preparatory Trade Course which provides training in basic trade skill.

There are other institutions which are also involved in providing training in Malaysia, such as the Malaysian Institute of Management and the Malaysia Institute of Public Relations.

Other Assistance. The Malaysian Industrial Estate Berhad (MIEL) designs and builds standard factories in industrial estates for small enterprises. Special terms and conditions are offered to bumiputra entrepreneurs, such as low interest rate, longer-term loans and easy repayment terms.

The Urban Development Authority (UDA) which was established in 1971 aims at increasing property ownership of bumiputras. The UDA provides bumiputra businessmen with shop premises and office space in urban areas on terms that are more favourable than those available in the prevailing market. It also provides financial, technical and management assistance to bumiputras to develop their own properties.

The Standards and Industrial Research Institute of Malaysia (SIRIM) which was established in 1975 as a result of the merger of two institutions, namely the Standard Institute of Malaysia (SIM) and the National Institute for Scientific and Industrial Research (NISIR), is involved in the promotion of quality improvement in production through standardisation, quality assurance, industrial research and consulting activities.

The Federal Industrial Development Authority (FIDA) is the agency delegated the task of evaluating applications for pioneer status and other incentives. It is also actively engaged in the publicity of entrepreneurial opportunities, provides help and guidance in the selection of products, prepares and evaluates likely projects, publishes literature useful to entrepreneurial development, and organises entrepreneurial forums. Its activities are directed towards encouraging small-scale industries as part of the overall strategy of industrial development.

As can be seen from the above discussion, there is an abundance of financial assistance, especially for the bumiputras. There are extension services to the farmers, although unfortunately an industrial extension service is still lacking. There is a need for more advisory and consulting assistance in the field by advisors with a practical orientation to small businesses. There is also a great shortage of qualified staff to provide advisory and consulting services.

Although the Coordinating Council was established to coordinate the different programmes offered by the various agencies, this has not been wholly successful. Of course, it has to be recalled that many of these agencies were not set up exclusively to assist the development of small enterprises, but rather with the general development of the manufacturing sector.

C. *The Philippines*

The government strategy for small industries development in the Philippines is to promote the organisation and establishment of new small and medium-scale industrial enterprises throughout the country with appropriate emphasis on small-scale industrial opportunities in urban industrial centres as well as rural developing areas. It also aims to provide the impetus and assistance for growth and expansion to large-scale operations, particularly for 'growth enterprises' which show satisfactory track records of successful management as a small-scale enterprise. In order to integrate and coordinate the activities of various government agencies in their assistance programmes to small enterprises, a Commisson on Small and Medium Industries (CSMI) was created in 1974 to develop and execute an effective and comprehensive national programme to accelerate the development of small and medium industries. The functions of the Commission are:

(1) To encourage and support existing and potential small and medium industries in the rural areas, to hasten the realisation of the national objective of regional industrial dispersal and thereby provide impetus to the all-round progress of the regions.

(2) To develop and implement a programme for the promotion, development and training of potential entrepreneurs in the rural sector by utilising the facilities of its member-agencies for this purpose.

(3) To promote an integrated form of assistance to existing entrepreneurs in project development, entrepreneurial training, consultancy and financing assistance.

(4) To encourage sub-contracting schemes between small/ medium industries and large industries whereby the small and medium industries shall supply the needs of the large industries, in as far as assembly parts requirements and processing can be produced and undertaken more economically by them.

(5) To formulate and recommend regulations and incentives supplementing and/or complementary to small and medium industries development.

The Commission comprises twelve national agencies. The agencies and their roles are as follows:

(1) Ministry of Local Government and Community Development – coordination with local governments.

(2) Ministry of Trade – establishment of marketing infrastructure for small and medium industries.

(3) University of Philippines Institute of Small Scale Industries – entrepreneurial and managerial training.

(4) National Manpower and Youth Council – technical and skill training.

(5) Development Bank of the Philippines – direct financing assistance.

(6) National Economic and Development Authority – credit and loan guarantee programme.

(7) Central Bank of the Philippines – credit and financing policies.

(8) Ministry of Agriculture – industrial project development.

(9) Ministry of Natural Resources – utilisation of natural resources in small and medium industries.

(10) National Science and Development Board – technology research and assistance.

(11) Bureau of Small and Medium Industries – identifying opportunities and assisting in setting up small and medium industries.

(12) Ministry of Industry – extension services.

Financial Assistance. The Development Bank of the Philippines (DBP) provides major financing assistance under its Countryside Development Programme for small and medium industrial projects in rural areas and in export-oriented activities. For small and medium industries the DBP offers loans on terms more favourable than those given to large-scale industries. DBP has a network of nearly 60 branches, sub-branches and agencies strategically located throughout the country. These branches and agencies are empowered to receive, process and grant loans not exceeding ₱ 150,000. Loans exceeding this amount are sent to the Industrial Project Development II (IPD II) at the DBP head-office for processing. The IPD II is the DBP unit exclusively dealing with the financing requirement of the small and medium industries sector.

The Industrial Guarantee and Loan Fund (IGLF), which is under the control and supervision of the National Economic Development Authority (NEDA), provides both direct lending and loan guarantees to small and medium industries. For collateral-deficient but deserving small and medium industry projects, the IGLF provides funds through a loan guarantee scheme. There are over one hundred institutions that have made available their facilities under this scheme. Most of the participating institutions are the rural banks. The other institutions include private development banks, non-bank financial intermediaries, commercial banks, savings and loan associations. IGLF offers a minimum loan of ₱ 50,000 to a maximum of ₱ 800,000 loan ceiling. In the case of rural banks, however, the loan ceiling is at ₱ 150,000 while DBP grants loans amounting from ₱ 100,000 to a maximum of ₱ 1 million to small industry borrowers and over ₱ 1 million to ₱ 3 million to medium-scale entrepreneurs.

Extension Services. The Ministry of Industry offers two extension programmes to the small and medium industries. The Medium and Small-scale Industries Coordinated Action Programme offers to assist small and medium industrial entrepreneurs in the preparation of projects and feasibility studies, and in complying with the documentation required for bank loans. The Small Business Advisory Centre offers management and technical consultancy services to small businesses. The scope of assistance covered includes setting up of book-keeping or accounting systems, cost analysis, plant layout improvement, quality control, inventory control and other marketing, technical, financial or organisational assistance and information services on different business needs. The services of both extension programmes are offered free of charge to clients. Limited consultancy services are also offered by the UP–ISSI and the Development Bank of the Philippines.

Training Assistance. The University of Philippines Institute of Small Scale Industries (UPISSI) is the major government institution whose primary function is to conduct managerial training and entrepreneurial development programmes for small and medium industries. The Institute conducts training courses throughout the year, with most being designed to upgrade the managerial competence of entrepreneurs, managers, engineers and technicians of small industries. The Institute also conducts an Entrepreneurship Development Programme (EDP) to stimulate entrepreneurial activities in the rural areas. The specific objectives of the programme are:

(1) to promote the development of small enterprises outside urban areas;

(2) to generate a self-employment scheme for potential entrepreneurs and provide employment to others;

(3) to encourage and develop the processing of local materials into finished or semi-finished goods for domestic consumption as well as for export;

(4) to promote the use of modern technology in small-scale manufacturing industries to generate higher productivity.

Other Assistance. The Ministry of Trade provides assistance in the commercial promotion of the products of small and medium industries with its Display and Distribution Centres. The Ministry also provides marketing consultancy services and free brokerage services for producers and potential buyers, and organises buying and selling missions, exhibitions and mini trade fairs. Technical information, advisory and consultancy assistance are also available from UPISSI, SBAC, NSDB (National Science and Development Board) and the Design Centre of Philippines.

As with Malaysia, the assistance programmes of the development institutions in the Philippines lack coordination among themselves in spite of the establishment of the Commisson on Small and Medium Industries. Inter-agency referrals were rarely made. Instead, those agencies in direct contact with regional entrepreneurs sometimes even give assistance in areas beyond their institutional competence.

The extension service is hindered by the fast turnover of the extension workers. There is also a lack of information on certain industries. However, according to one study, government assistance has contributed significantly to the economic performance of the firms during the period of study between 1975 to 1977.[6]

D. Thailand

The small industries in Thailand are not as fortunate as their counterparts in Malaysia and the Philippines. The history of small-enterprise development is much shorter and the government assistance available to small industries is less both in terms of the number of agencies and in the extent of assistance. The overall investment policy of the government has been heavily biased in favour of medium and large industries since the beginning of the

1960s. The Small Industries Services Institute which was established in 1966, for example, was renamed later the Industrial Services Division, so that assistance could be provided to all industries regardless of size. Hence, the small enterprises in Thailand have not been given as much attention and assistance as in other countries.

Financial Assistance. The Small Industry Finance Office (SIFO) was established in 1964 under the Department of Industrial Promotion with the objective of providing low interest loans of less than 500,000 baht to small industries. The Krung Thai Bank (KTB), a government-owned bank, provides 50% of the value of loans in a joint fund. SIFO screens the loan applicants, analyses and appraises loan applications, in terms of technical and economic feasibility, while KTB is responsible for financial assessment, collateral appraisal, disbursement of loan proceeds and collection of loan obligations. Since 1969, the KTB share in the joint fund has increased to three times the amount put in by SIFO.

Extension Services. The Small Industries Services Institute was established in 1966 by the government with the assistance of the United Nations Special Fund to provide technical assistance and services to small enterprises in the areas of modern production, technology, management and product design. Initially, its activities were confined to the metal working and textile industries. The institute was renamed the Industrial Services Division under the Department of Industrial Promotion in 1969 and now provides technical and advisory services to all sizes of industrial enterprises. However, about 90 per cent of the clients fall within the small-industries definition. The institute also organises technical training seminars and disseminates technical information and answers enquiries. In addition to the original institute in Bangkok, a second institute was set up at Chiengmai in 1972. Both institutes also undertake economic studies and market surveys on different industries.

Other Assistance. The Industrial Estate Authority of Thailand established in 1971 manages, builds and assists in building industrial estates. There is no special industrial estate exclusively built for small-scale industries. The Small Industry Association of Thailand (a private association) established in 1976 aims at promoting the sales of the members' products by actively participating in exhibitions, product displays and trade fairs. The Thailand Productivity Organisation conducts training programmes and provides consultancy services.

In general, most of the activities eligible for promotion by the Thailand Board of Investment require a minimum size of capital investment, ranging from 1 million to 50 million baht, and benefit mainly the larger industrial enterprises. The small industries are given very little absolute advantage over the larger industries. Finally, lack of coordination among agencies is also a problem in Thailand, particuarly between Industrial Services Division and SIFO.

E. Singapore

Small industries in Singapore are assisted for very different reasons from those of the other countries in the area. They are promoted in order that the large industries are able to obtain supporting services locally. Unlike the other countries, the development strategy of small industries in Singapore is focused on supporting industries and related services to attract more investments, and hence larger industries, into Singapore. Most of the assistance programmes however, are offered to all sizes of industries, with the exception of the Small Industries Finance Scheme. To discuss government incentives and assistance schemes in Singapore, an understanding of the background and functions of the Economic Development Board is necessary.

The Economic Development Board (EDB) was set up in 1961 as a statutory body to centralise the supervision and implementation of the industrialisation programme in Singapore. EDB offers a wide range of services to all industries irrespective of their sizes. Many units within the EDB subsequently expanded and became autonomous bodies. For example, the Industrial Research Unit of EDB became the Singapore Institute of Standards and Industrial Research (SISIR) which is also a statutory body. The Development Bank of Singapore was established to take over the financial function of the EDB. Some of the major investment incentives administered by the EDB include the following:

(1) Pioneer Status provides for zero tax on company profits for 5 to 10 years, depending on the merits of the project.
(2) The export incentive scheme provides for 4 per cent tax on

export profits instead of the normal 40 per cent on company profits. It is used to encourage export for cases where award of pioneer status is unjustified because of existing local manufacture.

(3) Investment Allowance provides for tax-exempt profits to a specified percentage (up to 50 per cent) of actual fixed investment on factory buildings and productive equipment for an approved project. The scheme is particularly beneficial to long-gestation projects which may not generate profits early enough to benefit much from a tax holiday scheme granted for a specified period commencing from the start of commercial production. In such instances, this is available as an alternative to pioneer status and export incentive scheme.

(4) International Consultancy Services incentive encourages 'brain' services in overseas projects involving plant and civil construction and related activities. The scheme provides five years company tax reduction from the normal rate of 40 per cent to 20 per cent on export profits.

(5) International Trade Incentives provide tax concessions to trading companies which export Singapore-manufactured products or domestic produce, or trade in non-traditional commodities, at 20 per cent on export profits for five years.

(6) The Capital Assistance Scheme (CAS) was established in 1975 to provide financial assistance to companies with specialised projects of unique economic and technological benefit to Singapore. Under the scheme, an industrial investor can obtain up to 50 per cent of the equity capital required with an option to buy back the shares subsequently. The scheme also provides long-term loans up to 70 per cent of the cost of fixed assets with favourable terms and a repayment period of up to ten years.

(7) The Product Development Assistance Scheme (PDAS) was set up to encourage local companies to develop new, or improve existing products or processes related to their manufacturing activities. The applicant must be a Singapore company with majority shareholding by Singapore citizens or permanent residents. The scheme provides a dollar-for dollar grant – the government and the company will bear equally the direct cost of the project. The maximum grant per project is S$ 100,000.

(8) For manufacturing enterprises conducting R & D and R & D institutions servicing them, tax incentives are provided including

double tax deduction of R & D expenditure, accelerated depreciation over three years for all plant and machinery for R & D, and investment allowances of up to 50 per cent of the capital investment in R & D.

All the above investment incentives schemes are available to all industries. Inevitably the majority of the beneficiaries are the medium and large industries rather than the small industries.

Financial Assistance. The only financial assistance provided exclusively for the small industries is the Small Industries Finance Scheme (SIFS). Established in 1976 by the EDB in collaboration with the Development Bank of Singapore, the scheme aims specifically at providing financial assistance for the expansion, modernisation and diversification of small firms, and in the starting up of viable small industries. Beside the Development Bank of Singapore, other local banks and a finance company also participate in the scheme. The CAS (Capital Assistance Scheme) Funds are provided to participating banks for on-lending to small viable enterprises. The EDB and the participating banks jointly administer the scheme and share the risks equally. Interest is charged at a fixed rate which is below the commercial rates. Only those industries with S\$ 2 million or less in fixed production assets are eligible to apply for the loan under the scheme. The loan amount applied for may not exceed S\$ 1 million for each application. The scheme is also being extended to medium-size companies with fixed assets of S\$ 2 million to S\$ 5 million. For these companies, the scheme is operated on more commercial terms.

In 1979, the Singapore Government abandoned its past practice of wage-control policy and introduced a corrective wage policy in order to achieve restructuring of the economy towards high technology and high value added industries. In the wake of increasing trade protectionism in the developed countries and labour shortage in Singapore, the high-wage policy encourages companies to use less labour by automation and mechanisation, and to upgrade the skill and technology of the workers and the production process. At the same time, the Skills Development Fund Levy Act was also introduced. Under the Act, employers will have to pay a 4 per cent levy on the salaries of all employees earning not more than S\$ 750 per month. The Fund will be used to promote the training of skills relevant to Singapore's economic restructuring efforts and for the retraining of redundant and retrenched workers arising out of this restructuring process. Only Singapore-based employers are eligible to apply for the Fund. There are three schemes under the Skills Development Fund:

(1) SDF Training Grant Scheme – Grants are provided on 30 per cent, 50 per cent or 70 per cent of allowable costs. The allowable costs include course fee, absentee payroll, return air fare, stipends or cost of living allowance, instructor's salary and equipment cost.

(2) SDF Interest Grant for Mechanisation Scheme – This scheme aims at encouraging and assisting firms in Singapore to invest or re-equip with new machinery and equipment capable of achieving significant increase in productivity. In the purchase of machinery and equipment approved by the SDF, the interest grant will pay 50 per cent of actual interest cost incurred or the full amount of interest computed at the rate of 7 per cent per annum whichever is the lower. However, the principal sum must not be less than S$ 30,000.

(3) SDF Development Consultancy Scheme – The purpose of the scheme is to encourage and assist local Singapore companies in seeking external expertise to help upgrade their business operations and training plans. Grants are based on 30 per cent, 50 per cent or 70 per cent of allowable costs. The allowable costs include the fees paid to external experts, return airfares and accommodation expenses in Singapore. Maximum amount of grant per company is S$ 250,000.

The Monetary Authority of Singapore provides pre-export and export financing under its rediscounting scheme. Under the pre-export financing scheme, the exporter is able to obtain funds to enable him to finance the cost of production of his goods, provided he has a firm purchase order. Under the export financing scheme, the exporter receives immediate payment as soon as his goods are shipped.

Other financial assistance under the EDB includes Overseas Training Scheme, Industrial Training grant Scheme and Industrial Development Scholarship Scheme.

Technical Assistance. The Singapore Institute of Standards and Industrial Research (SISIR) is a multi-disciplinary industrial research organisation, offering a host of services ranging from consultancy and industrial research to quality control, standardisation, technical information, product design and packaging. Recently, SISIR took over the functions of the Low Cost Automation unit of the National Productivity Board after the latter's reorganisation. The National Productivity Board (NPB) is another statutory body which is vested with the responsibility of promoting productivity consciousness and productivity improvement in Singapore. The Board was originally set up to concentrate on providing mainly industrial engineering consultancy services, supervisory and work-safety training to small-scale industries. After the recent reorganisation (which took place at the beginning of 1982), the Board will now focus its activities on personnel management and human relations training, supervisory development and development of workers for participation in small group activities. The Board is the leading institution in the promotion of the Quality Circle (QC) movement in Singapore.

Other Assistance. The Department of Trade was set up in 1973 to coordinate the export promotion activities of the government, and to assist manufacturers and exporters to locate new export markets and strengthen existing ones. It advises on tariff structures, quota restrictions, GSP (Generalised Systems of Preferences) Scheme, import and export regulations. The services of the Department are not exclusively directed towards small firms, but because large companies are more aware of these matters the Department is orientated towards the requirements of the small and medium industries. The Department gives preferences or considers favourably the very small companies in the allocation of quota for exports. The Department of Trade also organises seminars and talks to create awareness among manufacturers and exporters of international marketing requirements, the importance of participation in international fairs and other topics of interest.

The Local/Small Industries section within the EDB was set up in 1979 to help small manufacturers improve, upgrade and restructure their operations to meet changing market conditions. The section is directly involved in the processing of SIFS loan applications.

The Jurong Town Corporation (JTC) builds standard flatted factories in various industrial estates. Most are intended for light industries because of their proximity to residential areas. They have proved to be popular among the small industries because they are sited near the low-cost housing estates with easy access to a labour force and are available at reasonable rental.

Technical and vocational trainings are provided by the Vocational and Industrial Training Board (VITB). VITB also conducts commercial and trade skill training such as accounting, ladies' hairwaving and styling and men's tailoring courses. Supervisory training and management training are also provided by the Singapore Institute of Management, Singapore Chinese Chamber of Commerce and Industry, the University Extra-mural Studies Department, and other private institutions.

In general, assistance given exclusively to small industries is very limited. When it is given as in the Small Industries Finance Scheme, only approved manufacturing industries or projects are eligible. The other sectors such as the trade and services industries have been neglected in many of the incentives schemes. At the moment, the emphasis and priority is towards high technology. Hence, the traditional small industries and businesses may have to change their modus operandi or face the possible consequence of extinction in the future.

9.7. Prospects for Success and Future Development

The small firms in this region are at different stages in their development. At one extreme the role of small enterprises in Singapore is to support and service the large local and international corporations, whilst in Malaysia and Philippines, job creation and indigenous enterprise are the responsibility of the government. For industrial dispersal and regional development, small industries are in a better position to weather economic crises of inflation and recession than the large industries. The small industries are more flexible, can survive on smaller production runs and are more labour-intensive, hence they are not seriously affected by the energy crisis as much as the large industries. In any case, small-scale industries must be regarded as a complementary part of the whole industrial development programme. In some areas they must be content with servicing the large industries, while in other areas they must continue to be small because this is the only way they can exist, one example is the handicraft industry. For those industries with growth potential, it is a phase in their development towards larger-scale industries.

The Prime Minister of Malaysia, Dr Mahathir Bin Mohamad, in

his speech at a seminar in 1978 when he was then the Deputy Prime Minister and Minister of Trade and Industry succinctly put in a nutshell the role, prospect and future of small industries as follows:

> All industrial activities, big and small, are essential and complementary; they are a part of the whole, they should receive equal attention. The nature of each requires different kinds of support and policy. Small scale industries have their own advantages as much as big industries have theirs. The kind of support that is good for big industries may not be good for small industries and vice versa. Each should be considered as special and treated accordingly.[7]

Notes

1. P.L. Chee, M.C. Puthucheary and D. Lee, *A Study of Small Entrepreneurs and Entrepreneurial Development Programmes in Malaysia* (University of Malaya Press, 1979), p. 1.
2. ADIPA Research Project Report, *Development of Small and Medium Manufacturing Enterprises in Thailand* (1978), p. 3.
3. See H.D. Fong, *Small Industry in Singapore* (University Education Press, 1971), p. 9 and T.S. Tan, *Small Enterprises in Singapore* (Occasional Paper Series No. 1, Department of Business Administration, University of Singapore, 1977), p. 5.
4. UPISSI Report, *Entrepreneurship and Small Enterprises Development: The Philippine Experience* (1979), p. 143.
5. P.L. Chee *et al.*, *Small Entrepreneurs*, p. 122.
6. UPISSI Report, p. 150.
7. Speech by Dr Mahathir Bin Mohamad at a seminar on 'The Role of Small Industries in the Asean National Economies' held in Singapore in 1978.

Further Reading

ADIPA Research Report (1978), *Development of Small and Medium Manufacturing Enterprises in Thailand*.

Chee, P.L., M.C. Puthucheary and D. Lee (1979), *A Study of Small Enterpreneurs and Entrepreneurial Development Programmes in Malaysia*, University of Malaya Press, Kuala Lumpur.

Chua, J.E., S.C. Ling and C.H. Tan (1981), *Management of Business*, McGraw-Hill, Singapore.

Report on the Census of Industrial Production 1979, Department of Statistics, Singapore.

Second Five Year Development Plan, Republic of Indonesia.

Tan, T.S. (1977), *Small Enterprises in Singapore*, Occasional Paper Series No. 1, Department of Business Administration, University of Singapore.

UPISSI Report (1979), *Entrepreneurship and Small Enterprises Development: The Philippine Experience.*

Wong, J. (1979), *Asean Economies in Perspective*, Macmillan Press Ltd, London.

Yearbook of Labour Statistics 1980, Ministry of Labour, Singapore.

Annual Reports of the following organisations:

Singapore Chinese Chamber of Commerce & Industry (1981).
Singapore Economic Development Board (1980/1).
Singapore Institute of Management (1981).
Singapore Manufacturers' Association (1980/1).
Singapore Institute of Standards and Industrial Research (1980/1).
The Development Bank of Singapore (1981).
The National Productivity Board (1979/80).

Various papers presented at the conference on 'The Role of Small Industries in the Asean National Economies' held in Singapore in November 1978.

10 AFRICA*

10.1. Introduction

Africa, in keeping with the developing regions of Asia and Latin America and the Caribbean, faces the problem of high crude birth rates and natural rates of population growth. In Africa, the total population is expected to increase from 461 million in 1980 to more than 532 million in 1985 and 615 million in 1990.[1] The alarming features of this growth are two-fold. Firstly, the age distribution of the labour force shows that the young generation between the ages of 15 and 25 has been, and still is, increasing rapidly; secondly, as a result of improved education systems and general awareness, the female labour force is expanding steadily, thus contributing further to the general labour supply.

Faced with the fact that most government ministries and agencies do not have the necessary funds to increase their workforces, coupled with the fact that large-scale industries are turning more to improved technology rather than an increase in labour force to promote productivity, the problem of absorbing present and potential under-employment and unemployment has become critical. The obvious remedy lies in actively promoting small firms to assume this nationally important role.

Any critical review of small enterprise development in the African region needs to be viewed in the context of its particular setting, taking into account linguistic, cultural, prior colonial influences, political and social factors as well as the prevailing level of economic development.

The regional scenario encompassing the promotion of small firms appears to be one of marked hardship infrequently alleviated with opportunities and prospects for betterment. The short-term future does not look promising due to pressures and constraints imposed by the international recessionary trend, relatively high and unstable energy costs, weak consumer purchasing power, shortages in the supply of suitable equipment, spares and raw materials and the absence of a skilled workforce, weak infrastructure, less than perfect policy measures and the absence of clear strategic measures. Against this backdrop, the harsh realities of the region reveal that:

Africa has 16 of the world's 25 least-developed countries and 13 of the 18 land-locked, low income countries. Nine countries had a gross national product (GNP) per capita of only US$100, or less, in 1973; while seven countries (Equitorial Guinea, Chad, Niger, Senegal, Sudan, Upper Volta and Zambia) achieved an annual growth rate of only one per cent, or less, for the period 1965–73.

The Gross Domestic Product (GDP) for the whole region grew at only 4.6 per cent per year compared to the International Development Strategy target rate of 6 per cent. The GDP rate per capita also fell since the population grew by 2.6 per cent rather than the 2.5 per cent a year forecast for this period by the ECA.[2]

Given that GNP per capita may not necessarily indicate the true development level of a country, particularly where subsistence agriculture predominates, other measures can be used which also confirm the relatively low development profile of countries in the region. For instance, whereas life expectancy at birth exceeds 50 years for most North African countries, in West and Central Africa it barely reaches 40 years, with East African countries somewhere in between. Angola does not even reach one half of the life expectancy of most industrialised countries according to the United Nations data.[3]

Urban congestion is another problem in Africa. Commencing as the least urbanised region in the world (only 22 per cent in 1970), it has since experienced an urban growth rate of 5 per cent per year, the highest in the world. Migration from rural areas makes up more than one-half of this growth and contributes to the growing social and economic problems.

On the more positive side, considerable progress has been made in education. However, it can also be argued that most educational inputs have been directed towards the urban and modern sector minority groups. Furthermore, educational systems have generally expanded faster than the economic growth rate, particularly in the industrial sector, giving rise to problems of the educated unemployed, and initiating the rural to urban population shift.[4]

Workers migrating to foreign countries also feature on the African scene. Apart from workers moving from Northern Africa to Europe and the Middle East, and from the bordering and enclave countries into the South African Republic, other regional countries absorb part of the labour force. Libya took in more than 100,000 workers in 1975. In the Ivory Coast, immigrants from Upper Volta, Mali and Niger accounted for 21.3 per cent of the total resident African population, exceeding the national population in urban localities in the savannah region in 1970. Joshi, Lubell, and Mouly also found that only 25 per cent of small industrial enterprises were thought to be Ivorien.[5]

The slow growth of African economies is blamed largely on problems and failures in the agricultural sector. The disappointing results can be attributed, on the one hand, to natural causes such as droughts and land soil erosion, not the least of which is the Sahelian desertification phenomenon, and other unusual climatic conditions; and on the other hand, to ill-conceived agricultural programmes and the lack of such man-made contributions as appropriate infrastructure, technology, skills and economic incentives. Since more than 80 per cent of African populations live in rural areas, agricultural-based problems affect large proportions of the population.

The manufacturing sector has generally shown greater improvement than the agricultural sector. Eighteen countries exceeded their industrial Development Strategy targets for growth rate in manufacturing output between 1970 and 1973. (Examples are Algeria, Botswana, Gabon and Mauritius, growing at an average of 15 to 30 per cent annually.) However 21 countries did not reach the overall target growth rate of 8 per cent. For the period 1970–4 African manufacturing is estimated to have grown at an average annual rate of only 7 per cent compared with an 8.7 per cent rate during the 1960s decade.[2]

Decline in the manufacturing sector may be accounted for partly by the poor performance of the agricultural sector and consequent shortfall in supply of raw materials for agro-industrial production and partly by the decline in demand for industrial products. Nationalisation and Africanisation of industries, plus the rapid growth of the public sector, may have absorbed much of the entrepreneurial skills required by the manufacturing sector.

10.2. Definitions of the Small Firms

In Africa enterprises employing fewer than ten employees are not usually enumerated. Additionally, definitions and data are hard to find since small enterprise studies are confined mainly to productive industries. As a result, there is little quantitative economic and social data on small enterprises operating in trading, services, maintenance and repair, transport, construction and other sectors.

Studies of small industrial enterprises usually deal with firms employing fewer than 50 persons and omit artisan or craft enterprises considered to consist of a craftsman working alone or with only a few helpers or apprentices. Moreover, enumerative studies generally exclude part-time small-scale industrialists undertaking a mix of activities or seasonal work only. More recently, studies have included the so-called informal or unorganised sector and definitions have been drafted to take them into account.

As one example from the region, Chuta and Liedholm[6] quote the definition of 'small-scale industry' provided in the Sierra Leone Small Scale Industries Act, 1981, section 2:

'(a) An industry or enterprise whose fixed assets and annual output is not in excess of Le 100,000.00 (approx. $ US 118,000) and Le 200,000.00 (approx. $ US 236,000) respectively and employment is not less than 15 persons or not more than 50 persons;
(b) A cottage industry which is a well organised small scale production unit with limited capacity and output making use of manual mechanical or automated devices and producing items according to established production techniques.'

Although there does not appear to be a common definition of a small enterprise for the region, it seems that the 'owner-managed' enterprise is common. For example in Nigeria, Aluko[7] in 1973 reported that 99 per cent of small industrial enterprises were owned and managed by a sole proprietor, there being few partnerships, cooperatives and registered companies. However, for most purposes, it seems as though a definition based on the number of persons employed would be acceptable on the African scene.

A striking feature of small enterprises in Africa is that they are very numerous and very, very small. In a detailed study of Sierra Leone by Chuta and Liedholm,[8] the average employment in a small-scale industrial firm was found to be only 1.9 workers per unit rising to 3.5 workers per unit in the capital, Freetown. These figures are supported by Aluko[7] who shows that in rural Western Nigeria the average number of workers per industrial unit was three, which is consistent with ILO findings in the same area in 1970 of 2.5 workers per industrial enterprise. In Eastern Nigeria Kilby[9] reported an average of 2.7 workers while Callaway[10] estimated 2.8 workers per industrial enterprise. An ILO[11] report on Kenya also suggested that a typical rural small-scale industrial enterprise employed, on average, three workers. Studies in Senegal have shown that only 15 to 20 per cent of enterprises employed more than six persons and, in Ghana, 60 per cent of all enterprises were individual artisans accounting for 34 per cent of total employment.

10.3. Scope and Types of Small Enterprise

The Sierra Leone studies by Chuta and Liedholm indicated that small enterprises could be graded from purely traditional activities in rural areas to such advanced activities as motor vehicle repairs in urban areas. When moving from rural hamlets to cities there was an increase in size and sophistication of machines, accompanied by upward shifts in technology. Callaway also points out that enterprises using more advanced techniques were more likely to undertake multiple involvements. For example, 40 per cent of bakers also engaged in retail selling.

Few large-scale tracer studies have been carried out to provide a comprehensive coverage of African entrepreneurs in biographic or psychological terms. Most reports contain descriptions of 'cases' which may, or may not, be representative of this particular sector. It is generally thought that entrepreneurial development occurs on a non-formal basis, simply because few formal institutions exist to carry out entrepreneurial training and development. Yet entrepreneurs succeed in spite of the many problems. For instance, in Nigeria, Aluko reported that 44.2 per cent of rural small-scale industrial entrepreneurs were virtually illiterate, and 88.8 per cent had less than primary schooling. The lack of success suggests that a case can be made for developing entrepreneurs' numeracy and literacy skills. Studies from Kenya by Marris and Somerset[12] and from Nigeria by Nafziger[13] suggest a zero or a negative correlation between formal schooling and successful entrepreneurship in the footwear manufacturing business. Kilby found there was no correlation for bakers in this respect in Nigeria.[9] Harris, reported by de Wilde,[14] found there was a positive correlation between technical education inputs and success in technical-type enterprises such as printing; no correlation for those engaged in baking; and a negative correlation for rubber processors. The general picture is that the more complex and technological the enterprise, the more important education inputs become if entrepreneurs are to be successful.

At the enterprise level the lack of successful entrepreneurs is attributed to several possible factors. One explanation is that the financial and social attractions of paid employment in the public and large-scale private sector have attracted a large part of the available supply. Workers in recorded wage employment, who are the core of the labour force in the formal sector, are relatively well-off on the African scene. For instance, in Kenya, hourly wages in the unionised private and public sectors were between 16 and 30 per cent higher than the non-unionised sector, while the earnings of the self-employed in urban Kenya were reported to be 52 per cent less.[15]

In Africa there is a limited source from which entrepreneurs might emerge. They seem either to grow out of the informal sector or to emerge as the extra-curricula activities of established civil servants or salaried persons. Few entrepreneurs appear to develop directly from technical and vocational training institutions. Other explanations of the absence of entrepreneurship were suggested by Charlesworth,[16] who contends that role-strain problems affect the development of an entrepreneurial outlook. He argues the case for developing business attitudes to replace existing social value systems. The Partnership-for-Productivity project in Kakamega, Western Kenya reported positive results employing this approach, coupled with effective simple management practice improvements. In Ethiopia, De Missie[17] put this problem in a slightly different form; he claimed that the cultural attitudes to entrepreneurs which prevailed under the former pseudo-capitalistic type of government were regarded as degrading for 'proper' people. Finally, individuals, including many possessing entrepreneurial characteristics, emigrate annually, depriving their countries of origin of this special resource. Nationalisation and localisation programmes may even act to hasten this entrepreneurial demise.

10.4. Trends in the Small-Firm Sector

Recent reviews of the small firm sector by the World Bank,[18] indicate that there is relatively little information on this matter for developing countries in general and a paucity of data on Africa in particular. Moreover, the most significant gaps in knowledge relate to growth aspects of small-scale activities. Indeed, by design or necessity, most studies refer to a single point in time, so that issues such as growth and trends are treated from an extremely limited viewpoint.

This situation is regrettable since trend information is vital for building a basis on which to launch small enterprise development policies and programmes. However, a comparative study by Chuta and Liedholm of small-scale industries surveys in Sierra Leone in 1974 and 1980 throws some light on aggregate enterprise and employment growth, changes in sectoral employment patterns, start-up and mortality rates and upon the patterns of innovations and reinvestment. This cameo of a study provides at least some indicators of the growth patterns operating in the region:

> Larger urban localities showed an annual rate of increase in employment approximately double that of smaller localities and significantly greater than small villages.
> Growth in the number of manufacturing establishments did not keep pace with employment growth.
> The average size of small-scale manufacturing enterprises increased in localities of all size while the percentage of one-person enterprises declined.[6]

Sectoral employment growth patterns indicated important variations. In all localities food industries, maintenance and repair services increased most rapidly. Urban areas experiencing housing and construction booms not unexpectedly spawned high growth rates in trades such as metalwork. As in other regions of the world, data on birth and death rates of small firms in Africa are desperately scarce. One noted observation was the marked degree of instability among small firms, particularly within the first two to three years of life, which reflects findings from other regions. In urban localities, on an annual basis, the mortality rate was 9.5 per cent while in other smaller areas the rate was higher than 11 per cent. Approximately 10 per cent change their activity or location with better financial gain being the main reason given for the change. An interesting finding relates to age patterns, in that approximately one-third of the sampled firms were less than three years old, while the number of firms in older age brackets progressively declined to the point that less than five per cent were more than 15 years old.

Patterns of innovation suggest nearly one-half of small-scale entrepreneurs initiated at least one kind of change over a five-year period with product changes being the most common form of change.

Table 10.1 provides some insights into the situation in Sierra Leone.

Table 10.1: Innovations Introduced by Small-scale Enterprises of at Least Five Years Standing in Sierra Leone, 1975–80

Type of innovation	% of respondents
1. Restyled goods and services	47.6
2. Started making entirely new products	38.5
3. Transformed the workshop	34.5
4. Bought new machines	22.5

Note: The sum of the percentages exceeds 100 because each of the respondents had the opportunity to give more than one positive response.
Source: Chuta and Liedholm (1982).

A noteworthy point is that high energy costs had (in the case of bakeries) rendered the use of modern equipment unprofitable and the trend has been towards using improved traditional methods in place of new investment in modern equipment.

While studies of the propensity of small firms to save from profits generally indicate the approximate proportion of total profits which they are willing or able to save could be of the order of one-half to two-thirds,[19] the Sierra Leone situation shows this savings figure is only around 10 to 12 per cent (in real terms). Nearly one-half of the reinvested money went towards the purchase of tools and equipment, and the bulk of the balance was allocated for raw materials or other forms of the enterprise's economically related activities. It can be supposed that most profits were channelled into private consumption, educating family members, meeting demands of extended family networks or other ventures.

10.5. The Role of Small Firms

The African region virtually mirrors the world with regard to the economic and social role that small firms play in the development process. Economically speaking, small firms in segments of the Republic of South Africa can be said to match those found in several industrialised countries in terms of efficiency and quality. Small firms in Egypt, Ethiopia and Nigeria could well be placed at a middle-order level of ranking on any world scale. Countries in transition from agricultural to industrial activity include Kenya, Zimbabwe, Ivory Coast and Ghana. The first steps in the orderly development of the small enterprise sector have been taken in Cameroon, Malawi, Morroco, Mauritania, Botswana, the enclave countries of Southern Africa, Senegal, Zambia, Upper Volta, Mauritius, Niger, Zaire, Togo and Tanzania. The centrally planned approaches adopted in Congo-Brazzaville, Madagascar, Algeria, Libya and Benin present a different profile in the small enterprise sector.

Political instability or government by military rule has hampered the sector's progress in such countries as Uganda, Liberia, Chad, the Gambia, Tunisia, Namibia, Central African Republic, Angola, Somalia and Sudan. The very special problems of being landlocked or deficient in natural resources and lacking a skilled workforce severely hamper efforts to promote the small enterprise sector in Rwanda-Burundi, Guinea-Bissau, Mali and Equatorial Guinea.

It would be pleasing to be able to report that deliberate efforts were made to incorporate the small enterprise sector as an integral part of the development process. Unfortunately, this is not the case usually, and the quite substantial contribution made by the sector to economic and social development generally appears to have arisen by default rather than as part of any grand design.

The modern, organised or formal small enterprise sector represents a relatively small part of the gainfully employed workforce; whereas, at the same time, the informal sector (over and above the contribution of agricultural and seasonal workers) in Africa can be seen to contribute as much as 20 per cent to GNP and employment.[11]

Apart from the fact that such a relatively large percentage of the economically active population find employment in the informal sector this alone does not do justice to its real importance. In economies where paid employment scarcely matches demand this sector is important by itself. Moreover, even if it does not generate incomes comparable to the modern sector it certainly provides incomes which otherwise would not exist. The informal sector creates jobs using funds from mostly family savings outside traditional financial channels which leaves funds intact to be invested in the formal sector. Additionally, the capital required for job creation compares more than favourably with that required by the formal sector. This is a major bonus for countries characterised by shortages of capital.

From a human resources development point of view, the modern informal sector contributes to forming a pool of skilled labour – perhaps less theoretically equipped than those from the formal training institutions – but certainly no less practical, with the added advantage of introducing a more positive and economically healthy regard for manual work as a means of earning a livelihood. It should also be mentioned that such training usually occurs at no expense to the government.

The informal sector produces goods and services specifically targetted towards the low-income strata of society, while also introducing a measure of equity into income distribution, since other income categories are included as part of its total market segment. When compared with the output of the modern formal sector, the informal sector requires fewer imports with consequent less drain upon the balance of payments. It can be further argued that the informal sector has a propensity to consume more locally produced rather than imported goods, giving a genuine cutting-edge to the notion of self-sufficiency proposed in so many of the development plans found in the region. By and large, whether formal or informal, the small enterprise sector has a rightful place in promoting the economic and social well-being of all countries in the region.

10.6. Difficulties Facing Small Firms

Covering a wide spectrum of economic activity it is to be expected that small firms in Africa experience different sets of difficulties depending, amongst other things, on whether or not they are in the formal or informal sector and on the stage of economic development in the country.

In the organised or formal sector, demand aspects or marketing issues, apart from exports, are not usually considered problems. However, supply aspects present real handicaps. Raw materials are either in short supply, low quality, or both; a skilled workforce is difficult to develop and maintain; licensing and quotas are restrictive; adequate and continuous power supplies are hampered by shutdowns and loadshedding; communications are unreliable; transport is expensive and irregular; and harassment by officialdom and corruption are often considered to be part of daily life.

Most governments continue to offer substantial monetary and fiscal subsidies and tax concessions to large-scale enterprises, which effectively penalises smaller firms by reducing their competitiveness. Physical premises of sorts are generally available, but the zoning of industrial estates frequently raises problems of proximity to markets and labour force. While it is recognised that industrial estate projects in Africa are at best questionable from a strict cost-benefit viewpoint, it also has to be realised that they serve a necessary purpose by providing a demonstration effect of possibilities of industrialisation to a population moving from a subsistence to a cash economy and, to a large extent, moving from rural to urban settings.[20]

Unquestionably, the most commonly stated major problem confronting small firms is knowledge of, and access to, financial and technical assistance. Novel ways have been introduced to overcome these difficulties such as the use of village story tellers in West Africa to spread news about the workings of co-operative savings groups as a medium for financing projects. As far as the informal sector is concerned the problems are similar in kind but different in degree to those facing the formal sector. Their major limitation is the lack of managerial knowledge illustrated by the fact that they operate with a highly restricted time-horizon so that medium and long-term planning is virtually non-existent. This limitation impedes the possible transformation of informal-sector entrepreneurs into a body of modern formal-sector operators. Indirect problems such as those beyond the entrepreneur's control are covered in the next section dealing with government initiatives.

10.7. Government Initiatives to Assist Small Firms

Problems facing small firms in Africa are usually the same as those in other countries – only worse. The common backdrop for nearly all countries in the region is a colonial heritage. As a consequence of gaining independence, these countries simultaneously lost the economic thrust normally provided by the private sector since incoming independent governments found they had to assume the dual roles of public administration and the promotion of economic development. Because experienced, qualified personnel are in such short supply, available talent is often concentrated on such designated priority areas as government and political matters. This is at the expense of the industrial and economic sectors where, in colonial times, expertise was provided by the expatriate private sector. After independence a good deal of thrust, effort, initiative and entrepreneurship therefore disappeared.

Moreover, those appointed to government departments with responsibilities for promoting the small enterprise sector are, in the main, first-generation management types lacking commercial-industrial experience. The net result is a lack of appropriate and effective development policies and programmes despite widespread expressions of goodwill and sound intentions.

A. Policy Measures The medium and long-term development plans for nearly all African countries set the order of priority as (1) agriculture, (2) infrastructure and (3) industrialisation, emphasising self-sufficiency and self-development. Consequently, small enterprises in Africa mostly revolve around, or become a downstream product of, agro-industry. This places the sector in straitened circumstances should the agricultural sector fail for whatever reason.

Initially, policies of self-dependence were often interpreted to mean import-substitution. However, some countries, realising they did not know what and how much was imported, turned to encouraging selective exports instead. This switch often hindered small enterprises which did not appreciate what was going on. Long-lasting and effective small enterprise development also depends on sound infrastructure. An example is provided by the United States where small enterprise development followed the wagon-trains, was expanded with the introduction of railway networks and, more recently, changed its shape and nature when highway construction and high-rise dwellings appeared. In Africa, similar developments to this form of sector growth can be seen in Nigeria and Egypt, which are embarking on infrastructural development programmes.

For most African countries integrated development is a post-independence phenomenon. Without representative statistical and other supportive data, it is unfair to expect well-integrated, all-encompassing developmental policies at this early stage, particularly when the more industrialised countries also lack clearly expressed, well-conceived policies for small enterprise development. Because industrialisation influences other sectors of the community by binding them together in certain proportions, policies for small enterprise development must take into account the leverage exercised by the industrial sector.

Although development strategies for the small enterprise sector may not obviously be seen in many African countries, people responsible for developing related sub-sector activities like handicrafts and cottage industries, rehabilitation of handicapped workers and industrial estates projects, have not remained idle. Many worthwhile projects exist. However, this sometimes means duplication of institutions and overlapping efforts because there is no integrated overall approach to sectoral development.

In countries like Kenya and Tanzania, amongst others, this problem has been realised for some time and proposals to set up Small Enterprise Development Organisations or Corporations have been made, but are only starting to be put into effective practice. On the other hand, institutions like OPEI in Ivory Coast, Centre d'Assistance aux Petites et Moyennes Entreprises in Cameroon, the Ghanian Business Bureau and OPEV in Upper Volta whilst having a longer history show quite mixed results. Some writers recommend selective specialisation rather than global efforts when promoting small enterprise development. How this might be done without fragmenting the total development effort is not clear but it requires careful consideration in the light of the none too successful efforts made to date.

One disturbing feature about policies for the sector has been the lack of awareness amongst those people they were designed to help. In the Sudan policies for the sector were found to be widely unknown by entrepreneurs.[21] This finding is also reported in similar studies from other regions.

B. Institutions to Promote Small Enterprise Development An encouraging feature of the African scene is the wide range of financial, technological, managerial, developmental and membership institutions with the capacity, potential, or both for assisting small-enterprise development. Although most structures are not specifically geared to assist the smaller enterprise, they can be expanded or strengthened to do so.

C. Financial Institutions Whereas governmental and non-governmental financial institutions exist in most countries, the major hindrances to development by small enterprises appear to be lack of experienced personnel and access to domestic and foreign funds.

Staffing problems emerge in many forms. One obvious area is the lack of qualified project officers capable of preparing, or assisting entrepreneurs to prepare, feasible proposals. Officials able to appraise proposals are also scarce. Major personnel short-comings are inexperience and lack of knowledge about such production processes as machinery utilisation and equipment requirements. Other deficiencies include loan officers able to assess a proposal on its developmental potential rather than approve a loan based on collateral security. It is fair to say that ultra-conservative funding practices are the norm throughout the region. The abnormally large numbers of delinquent accounts in the small-enterprise sector, in some cases close to 100 per cent, are due to a mix of causes. These include lack of adequate supervision, providing loans for reasons other than the proposal under alleged consideration, the absence of appropriate extension services, and poor management. The common finding is that many of these problems could have been avoided if qualified supervisory finance staff were available. Further cause for concern is the shortage of foreign exchange. Not only is its scarcity a problem in itself, but it also leads to time-consuming struggles between rival promoters for these same hard-to-come-by funds. When allocations are not made quickly enough inflation can force project costs to escalate beyond realistic breakeven levels for the projects concerned.

Other complaints include high borrowing rates, short repayment periods and similar issues. These problems, however, appear only minor compared to the problems of having no funds at all. A general conclusion for the African region is that, in spite of the many and varied developmental financial institutions which exist, most adopt conservative philosophies and commercial practices. They seldom exhibit the developmental outlook and behaviour necessary for growth and promotion of small enterprises in the region. The World Bank's interest in promoting small enterprise development for the region may provide some of the necessary stimulus to move things in the right direction.

D. Technological Development Institutions

Institutions enchancing development and transfer of appropriate technology are probably the weakest of all structures which should assist small enterprise development in the African region. Because there are such large managerial and technological gaps to be overcome, it seems logical that an 'only the best will do' approach should be adopted. However, findings suggest that technological development is either poorly served or ignored altogether. Perhaps the one exception is the Technology Consultancy Centre, University of Science and Technology, Kumasi, Ghana.

There are many problems but a frequent handicap is the absence of such basic industries as iron and steel, and cheap energy. Most observers conclude that viable basic industries require regional, or sub-regional, participation. Unfortunately such proposals often clash with the feelings of nationalism generally associated with newly-found political independence.

It is also difficult for developing countries to find the right technical partners. Kalomo[22] says the Tanzanians complained about difficulties in negotiating with principals to obtain favourable terms of agreement. They suggest standardising agreements to soften the hard ride so often sustained when dealing with experienced industrialised partners. They also complain that technical partners can be unwilling to train local people as expeditiously as they might, but mention exceptions when dealing with friendly countries.

On the domestic scene it may also be difficult to overcome consumer preferences for foreign-made goods. Additionally, there are often production problems in developing or acquiring the technology necessary to convert local produce into acceptable consumer goods. Attempts to acquire or develop technological capacity in Africa are handicapped by underqualified technical personnel, outmoded and broken-down equipment, lack of access to new equipment, spare-parts and materials. Few institutions in the region can deliver adequate technical extension services.

E. Management Development Institutions

That management development problems exist is clear, but it is more difficult to know where to begin tackling them. Tandon and

Tome[23] argue convincingly that we should commence with techno-economic and manpower-planning surveys to assess the potentialities and requirements necessary to frame policies and programmes. Management development is a long-term exercise requiring suitable planning, programmes and evaluation. In the absence of follow-up and review exercises, it is difficult to assess whether 'crash' programmes in the region succeed or, indeed, crash! Most people agree that foreign-based training, except in special circumstances, is expensive, often inappropriate, and may produce undesirable long-term effects such as 'brain-drain'. However, local management development programmes also have problems because facilities are generally limited, institutions employ inexperienced or under-qualified instructors, teaching equipment is difficult to obtain and repair, and teaching materials and approaches become out of date.

Most African countries have experimented, with mixed results, in using expert-counterpart type training schemes as part of technical assistance programmes to develop or upgrade management trainers. Commonly reported successes of such projects include: creating and developing viable institutions such as productivity and management development centres; conducting courses in management development, particularly in functional areas; fellowship training; developing management training materials applicable to the local scene and surveys and needs analysis for sectoral development. However, these programmes also have had problems such as advisers unable to adjust to the particular demands of their assignments, shortage of counterpart staff, and attempts to implement project designs that were altogether too ambitious. Another relevant feature is the need to accommodate industrialised managerial practices within the ideological and philosophical framework of religious and cultural groups in the region. Training for the small enterprise sector suffers from a mismatch in demand and supply and from lack of harmonisation. Those responsible for training do not always react to signals put out by the labour market, but seem to react to communicational and other social values. For instance, following independence in the Cameroons, a large boost to vocational training resulted in a new skilled labour force with no jobs available. One considered solution was to promote self-employment which, in turn, led to demands for managerial training. However, such training was unavailable at that time.

Today, the absence of appropriate curricula and training methods for the small enterprise sector is still obvious.

F. *Industrial Development Institutions*

In reviewing small enterprise development in the African region, the size of the problem comes into focus when sectoral development aspects are examined. Africa, being the youngest continent and the most recent to start the development process, has had a slower start than other regions. Unlike many industrialised countries and developing regions such as Asia, with a well-established private sector, recent political independence has thrown greater responsibility for development on to governments. Consequently, African countries are faced with the task of managing a newly-formed civil service enmeshed with industrial sector management and its accompanying responsibilities. On top of this, emergent nationalism almost precludes opportunities for promoting regional growth during the formative stages of nation building.

Although small enterprise development structures for co-operation may exist, they do not appear either to accept the responsibilty or to command the authority required to do the job expected of them. These structures should not be expected to undertake all development activities, but they should see that they are carried out and appropriate assistance provided.

10.8. Initiative for Development

A. *Legislation and resource allocation*

Obtaining resources for sectoral development requires some form of legislation. Human resources need to be allocated as either management or labour; financial resources need to be provided as appropriate equity and loans; and material resources such as access to equipment, supplies and the necessary raw materials should be made available. Something like a small enterprise development corporation supported by membership association could conduct the necessary research, initiate legislation, provide the impetus to obtain government consent, and organise beneficiaries to exert proper pressure to ensure they receive fair treatment.

B. *Markets and marketing*

Almost universally, the market system serving small enterprise development in Africa is severely restricted because adequate

·communication and distribution networks are not available. The few available studies show marketing channels to be outmoded in the extreme and may, qualitatively at least, be assessed as the single biggest hindrance to progress.[24] An unusual feature of this particular problem is that distribution systems can often be improved at a relatively low capital cost. But such issues call for departures from traditional ways and introducing innovative practices; for instance, in some areas, it could mean enhancing the role of, rather than abolishing, the often misunderstood 'middleman'.

A further problem arises from the lack of impact in foreign markets of small-scale industrial goods. Poor quality control seems to be the ubiquitous bugbear, although the sophisticated merchandising techniques used by large-scale enterprises may have something to do with the difficulties experienced by the smaller producers. These marketing and related problems might possibly be looked after by a developmental structure set up to protect the interests of small enterprises.

C. *Infrastructures*

The lack of 'hardware' infrastructure, such as roads, handicaps small enterprises engaged, for example, in mining and agriculture. Because such projects do not obviously demonstrate an immediate and direct impact on economic development, obtaining central government approval for allocating funds for such infrastructural necessities is often difficult. Additionally, high illiteracy rates such as the reported 95 per cent of the workforce in Ethiopia[17] can deplete the 'software' component of developmental infrastructure. Again, it is usually difficult to obtain the funds to overcome these types of problems.

Developmental 'packages' can be expensive, inappropriate, or both, if designed in a donor country only. It may not necesssarily be a question of open bias by the designers, but local preferences may subconsciously come into play when, for example, choosing equipment. This happens simply because project designers usually understand and prefer familiar equipment.

In Africa, there is relatively little backward-integration incorporating industrial production functions within foreign-owned companies. Most foreign-based parent companies are more concerned with the primary production or the end-marketing aspects, than in promoting industrialisation within developing countries. Consequently, opportunities for sub-contracting work, with small enterprises providing speciality services, such as repair and maintenance, do not readily emerge.

Many reasons, real and imaginary, are offered to explain why foreign companies are reluctant to set up production units in Africa. These include fears of nationalisation and loss by takeover, with or without compensation; difficulties in obtaining special materials such as sheet metal and spare parts; lack of a skilled and disciplined labour force; and political turbulence and unpredictability. The small-enterprise sector in Africa will, most likely, continue to suffer until these developmental inputs are put in order, and are seen to be put in order. This could mean that well-conducted public relations campaigns are needed to highlight genuine investment opportunities when these problems no longer exist.

10.9. Prospects for Success

The immediate and medium-term prospects for promoting small-enterprise development in Africa are not encouraging. Few, if any, countries in the region possess a clear, workable strategy for orderly development of the small enterprise sector. Until definite policy issues are developed, the sector will continue to shudder along, as it has in the past, operating mainly in an ad hoc opportunistic manner.

Policy deliberations on which strategies might be based usually emerge from political actions which, in turn, are initiated by representatives from organised groups. The diversity of entrepreneurs does not easily permit them to form tightly knit groups (such as farmers) capable of presenting a united front to defend their interests. Consequently, the sector can expect to continue to receive low priority when it comes to allocating government resources for development.

On the other hand, in the absence of governmental support, there is increasing evidence of the efficacy of non-government organisations (NGO) in promoting the sector's interests. Successes of NGOs in Zambia in developing rural artisans have been reported with this being confirmed from other quarters.[5]

With a view to expanding their membership base, employers organisations are also taking an active interest in promoting small enterprises in Africa, with these being the front line of organised NGOs in this field. Other groups are also quite active including the

Pan-African Institute for Development, and international groups such as the YMCA. Amongst the international agencies the World Bank, ILO and UNIDO have substantial assistance programmes under way. Bilateral agencies from countries like the UK, USA, Sweden, Canada, Norway, Denmark, France, Switzerland and Italy have also made significant contributions.

The small enterprise development scenario within the present economic and social environment in Africa is a mixture of challenges and problems. Challenges emerge because, although the continent has had a relatively late start in development there is an expressed enthusiasm by all concerned to accelerate the process. Little information is readily available about the sector which ranges from informal artisans to formal modern enterprises. African entrepreneurs tend to be self-developed rather than products of organised development schemes. Little literature is readily available about small enterprise development schemes based on indigenous socio-cultural systems.

Policies for the sector are often unclear, fragmented or absent. Where policies do exist, entrepreneurs may be unaware of them, or do not know how to make best use of them. Because political independence is relatively recent, most African governments are expected to provide the development initiatives for small enterprises traditionally left to the private sector.

Well-established financial, managerial and developmental structures exist to serve the sector. In many cases, they need reorienting, or strengthening, or both. Technological, development and membership associations are generally weak. Wide-ranging assistance programmes are available but appear to need integration to promote more effective growth. A major common problem faced at policy level is that of co-ordination at two levels: the sectoral level and the geographical or regional level. Owing to their relatively recent accession to economic independence, the accelerated development of many African countries has tended to favour the choice of large units and projects. Whenever this is the case, there should be a policy of sub-contracting complementary products and services to smaller enterprises.

Existing legislation in a good many African countries is not particularly favourable to the survival and growth of small undertakings. A revision of the legal framework is a not inconsiderable ingredient of policies aimed at stimulating smaller enterprises. While certain African countries lack policies specifically directed to the small enterprise sector, other countries have set up a varying range of strategies whereby, for example:

(i) nationals are encouraged to become entrepreneurs by providing a sufficiently motivating infrastructure of training, financial and extension services (e.g. Kenya and Togo);
(ii) the government itself takes a primary initiative in setting up small and medium undertakings (e.g. Algeria);
(iii) potential national entrepreneurs are encouraged to buy viable small enterprises from expatriates (e.g. Ivory Coast).

Implementary policies to promote small enterprises might be furthered by establishing a network of institutions providing the necessary support and the drawing up of specific sector programmes. Such institutions would cover training and extension, financial questions, development needs and developing membership associations. As far as financing is concerned, only a fraction of loans to development banks for this purpose actually reaches the small enterprise since these banks tend to consider loans to small undertakings to be risky and costly. New financial intermediaries and channels are needed to reach the sector, while development bank and loan officers need training in project assessment and evalution.

At the country level, some countries (e.g. Sudan) report that entrepreneurs' only external source of finance is the commercial banks but they provide only up to 10 per cent of the cost of the venture and require extensive collaterals and guarantees. Other countries (e.g. Ivory Coast) have set up special guarantee funds with state participation to finance as much as 80 per cent of the cost of forming or expanding a small undertaking. The availability of necessary credit at the right time seems to be the most crucial financial factor for the entrepreneur, rather than the interest rate charged.

Development institutions providing support include industrial estates subsidising essential services to small enterprises as well as institutes conducting technical and economical feasibility studies and exploring market potential for local goods and services. In cases like Swaziland such services are grouped in one institution, which also provides training services. There is everywhere a pressing need in African countries for a service to provide small entrepreneurs with help in choosing and adapting technology.

Some countries (e.g. Nigeria, Kenya and Ivory Coast) are experimenting with establishing small entrepreneurs' associations to play a useful role in pressing for reform of existing small enterprise development schemes. Such reform could touch on policy issues, or deal with simplifying the procedures to be followed in establishing and strengthening small enterprises. One unfortunate observation is that such associations may be perceived as latent or potential political entities.

In most African countries it is necessary to allocate sufficient resources to building and strengthening support institutions. It is estimated that the training and extension services institutes of many countries could provide facilities for no more than one per cent of the small enterprises in the country – a ratio not uncommon in many other regions. A related issue is the cost of technical assistance provided by such institutions. In certain countries (Togo and Zaire) it is provided free of charge, while in others such as Kenya a nominal fee is charged. No institutions appear to be financially self-supporting.

Contrary to experience in countries such as India there are only limited cases where the selection of eligible potential entrepreneurs for training or financial assistance is based on tests aimed at assessing the individual's entrepreneurial outlook and his ability to rationalise operations entailing risk. Some benefit might be drawn from the experience of others in this respect.

With regard to training, the lack of managerial competence is considered to be the single most important factor contributing to the failure of small enterprises. Training efforts should aim at imparting knowledge, developing skills and changing attitudes, the last of which is often neglected. Some countries are experimenting to introduce modules of entrepreneurial skills in vocational training courses. Similar experiments have been designed to find short-cuts to skill formation by selecting potential entrepreneurs among persons already possessing technical or commercial skills. The need to develop occupational, entrepreneurial and managerial skills is very acute.

In many cases African countries often restrict development schemes for small enterprises to manufacturing concerns. Such schemes should also cover activities such as trading, transport, construction and service undertakings. Similarly, policies in this field should at times consider regional and community needs, irrespective of whether or not the proposed ventures are financially attractive. The conditions of work in small enterprises in many African countries leave much to be desired.

There is also the need to introduce into government circles persons equipped with the right sort of experience and interest to foster and promote development of small enterprises, especially in those sensitive units where development funds are allocated and approved. Some countries attempt to undertake too many projects at any one time, when it might be better to adopt a selective rather than an all-fronts growth strategy. A responsible developmental structure or institution is usually required to look after these pertinent environmental and infrastructural problems if the sector is to receive its fair share of attention and assistance.

By and large there is no doubt that the African region has need of tremendous inputs in the field of small-enterprise development. The task is formidable but challenging, the prospects exciting but frightening for, if development efforts fail, social and economic development will be seriously affected.

Notes

1. International Labour Organisation (1977), *Labour Force Estimates and Projections, 1950–2000*, ILO, Geneva, 2nd edition, volume V.
2. Economic Commission for Africa (1974), *Survey of Economic and Social Conditions in Africa*, ECA, Part 1.
3. United Nations (1974), *Demographic Yearbook*.
4. Bairock, P. (1973), *Urban Unemployment in Developing Countries*, ILO, Geneva, pp. 37–9.
5. Joshi, H. Lubell, H. and Mouly, J. (1976) *Abidjan, Urban Development and Employment in the Ivory Coast*, ILO, Geneva.
6. Chuta, E. and Liedholm, C. (1982), 'Employment Growth and Change in Sierra Leone Small-scale Industry 1974–80', *International Labour Review*, vol. 121, no. 1 January–February 1982, pp. 101–13.
7. Aluko, S.A. (1973), 'Industry in the Rural Setting in Rural Development in Nigeria', *Proceedings 1972 Conference of Nigerian Economic Society*, Ibadan University Press.
8. Chuta, E. and Liedholm, C. (1975), 'The Role of Small-scale Industry in Employment Generation and Rural Development: Initial Research Results from Sierra Leone', *African Rural Employment Research Network*, Department of Agricultural Economics, Michigan State University, East Lansing, Michigan, USA.
9. Kilby, P. (1962), *The Development of Small Industry in Eastern Nigeria*, USAID/Ministry of Commerce, Lagos.
10. Callaway, A. (1977), *Education for Self-Employment: Africa's indigenous apprenticeship training and its modern adaptations*, ILO unpublished manuscript, Geneva.
11. International Labour Organisation (1972), *Employment Income and*

Equality – a Strategy for Increasing Productive Employment in Kenya, ILO, Geneva.

12. Marris, P. and Somerset, A. (1971), *African Businessmen – a Study of Entrepreneurship and Development*, Routledge and Kegan Paul, London.

13. Nafziger, E.W. (1970), 'The Relationship between Education and Entrepreneurship in Nigeria', *The Journal of Developing Areas*, vol. 4, no. 3, April.

14. De Wilde, J.C. (1971), *The Development of African Private Enterprise*, Report AW–31, International Bank for Reconstruction and Development IDA, Washington.

15. Johnson, G.E. (1971), *The Determination of Individual Hourly Earnings in Urban Kenya*, Institute for Development Studies, University of Nairobi Discussion Paper No. 115 pp. 23–4.

16. Charlesworth, H.K. (1975), 'Role Strain and the Development of Entrepreneurship among Countries and Regions of the Emergent World', *Entrepreneurship and Enterprise Development: a worldwide perspective*, Proceedings of project ISEED Centre for Venture Management, Milwaukee, pp. 141–6.

17. De Missie, S. (1975), 'Cross-Cultural Entrepreneurship: African and Middle Eastern Countries', *Entrepreneurship and Enterprise Development: a world-wide perspective*. Proceedings of Project ISEED, Centre for Venture Management, Milwaukee, p. 132.

18. World Bank (1978), *Employment and Development of Small Enterprises*, Washington.

19. Ranis, G. (1961), *Industrial Efficiency and Economic Growth: a Case Study of Karachi*, Institute of Development Economics, Karachi.

20. United Nations Industrial Development Organisation (1976), *Report on the Industrial Estate Programme in Six Countries*, UNIDO and SIDA, UNIDO/16, Vienna.

21. Fitzpatrick, D. (1976) *Small Enterprise Development in Sudan*, Joint Study Series, Irish Government/ILO, Geneva 1976.

22. Kalomo, H.M. (1976), *Problems Concerned with Industrialization in the Least Developed Countries and Their Possible Solution*, paper presented at UNIDO Intergovernmental Expert Group Meeting 15–24 November, Vienna, Austria.

23. Tandon, N. and Tome, B. (1976), *Special Problems Facing Least Developed Countries in Promoting Industrial Development: Actions and Special Measures Required to Meet the Needs for Accelerating Their Industrialization*, UNIDO Intergovernmental Expert Group Meeting on the Industrialization of LDCs, Vienna, Austria.

24. Meissner, F. (1974), 'Marketing as a Tool of Development', *Development Digest* vol. XII, no. 4, October.

25. Quednau, H.W. (1981), 'Study for GTZ for German Bilateral Technical Co-operation Programme' German Agency for Technical Co-operation (GTZ), Eschborn/Taunus (Frankfurt–Main).

* The views expressed in this chapter are the author's and do not necessarily reflect the views of the ILO.

INDEX

administrative guidance 69, 70, 72
alternative economy *see* informal
    economy
Annual Census of Employment 92
apprenticeships 164
Association for the Promotion of
    Subcontracting Firms 72
Australian Academy of Technological
    Sciences 134

bank loan 73, 208
Bank of Japan 73
Bank Pembangunan Malaysia BPM
    221
bankruptcy 22, 58, 64, 131, 132–3,
    161–2, 187, 209
Barclays Bank 113
barriers to entry 100, 133, 222
basic law relating to small and medium
    sized firms 1963 47, 48
Bolton Committee 84, 87, 112, 133,
    136
British Steel Corporation 93
Bureau of Industry Economics 142
Bureau of the Census' *Enterprise
    Statistics* 10, 11, 12, 21
business cycle 132, 145, 164
business failures 22, 27, 94–7, 131, 160

cash flow 27, 108, 145
Census of Production 91, 93
Central Bank for Commercial &
    Financial Co-operatives 75, 76
closures *see* bankruptcy, business
    failures
Committee of Inquiry into the
    Australian Financial System
    144
Commonwealth Development Bank
    144
Community Development Company
    Loans 34, 35 ·
Company Registrations 94, 97
compensatory deposits 74
competition from large firms 25, 33,
    145
competition, potential and actual 133,
    136–8, 145, 169, 172, 192

co-operatives 5, 78–9, 114, 190–2, 210
Co-ordinating Council for the
    Development of Small-Scale
    Industries (CCDSI) 230
Corporate Income Tax 29
Corps of Active Executives (ACE) 36
credit guarantee scheme *see* loan
    guarantee

deaths of firms *see* business failures
definitions of small firm 7, 46–50, 88–
    90, 120–1, 153–4, 181, 250–2
Development Bank of Singapore 242
displaced business loans 35
dual industrial structure 62
Dun & Bradstreet 10, 12

economic and legal bonds 196
economic opportunity loans 34, 35
economies of production *see* scale
    economies
employment 4, 8, 10, 13–19, 20–1, 48–
    62, 101, 120–9, 155–60, 163–4
Employment Retirement Income
    Security Act 32
energy efficiency 74, 86
energy extension service 9
energy problems 33, 61, 64
enterprise zones 113
Environmental Improvement Finance
    Corporation 75
Equal Employment Opportunity 32
ERP Special Fund 6, 169, 170
European Recovery Programme in
    Germany 169
Expenditure Committee of the House
    of Commons 99

factories *see* premises
Fair Trade Commission 70
Federal Reserve Bank 25–7
finance 5, 25–7, 34–5, 40, 72–8, 107,
    143–5
Foreign Takeovers Act 135
franchising 115, 126, 145–6

gearing 19, 22, 188, 221

For Product Safety Concerns and Information please contact our
EU representative GPSR@taylorandfrancis.com Taylor & Francis
Verlag GmbH, Kaufingerstraße 24, 80331 München, Germany